DETOX DOODLES

Replacing Scrolling with Sketching

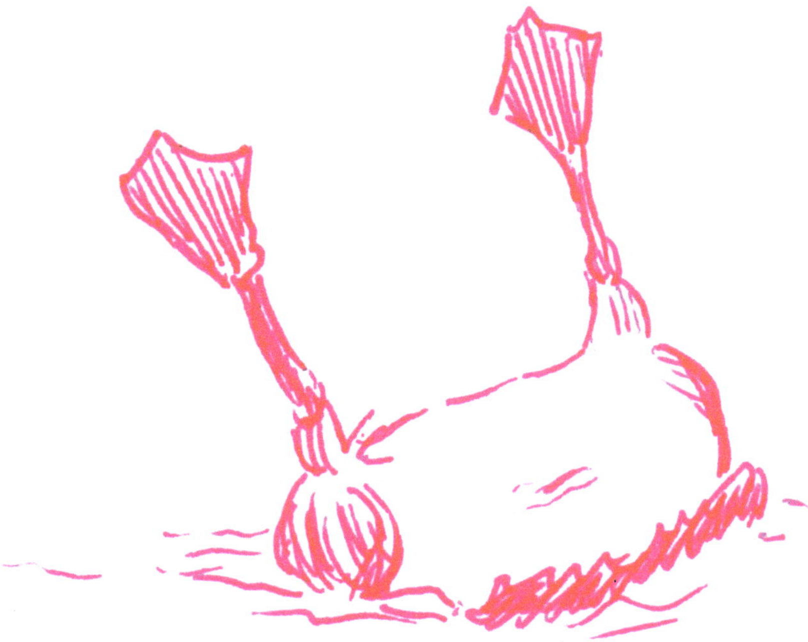

Written and Illusrated by Joy Chew

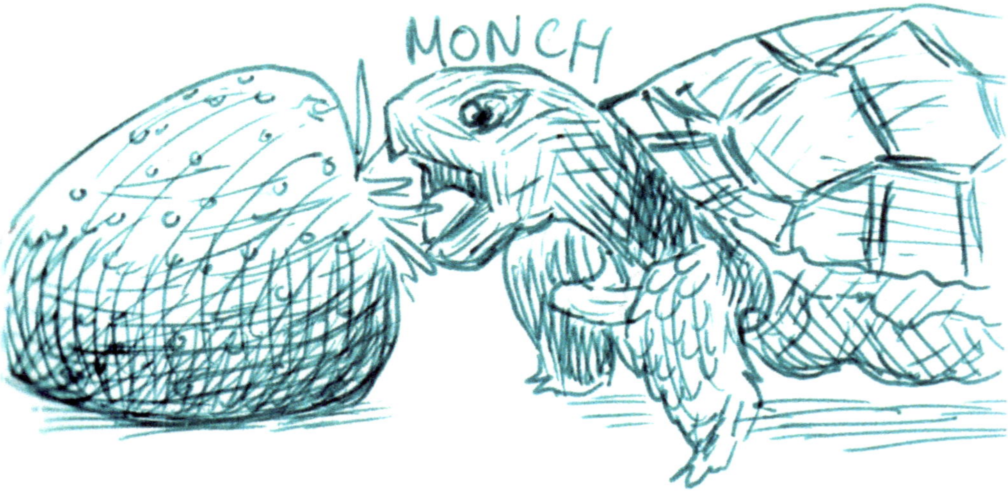

10 9 8 7 6 5 4 3 2 1

Published by Joy Chew.
Book Cover by Joy Chew.
Illustrations by Joy Chew.
Written and Edited by Joy Chew.

ISBN: 979-8-9931253-0-5

www.joyousjoyness.com
Instagram and Bluesky: @joyousjoyfuljoyness

This Book is dedicated to
my amazing husband Gregory and
my two wonderful boys, Victor and Brandon.

INTRODUCTION

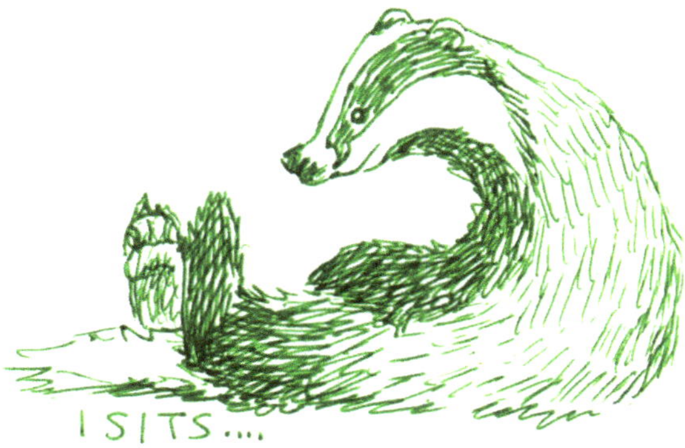

You know the feeling, because you've probably done it too.

The automatic reach for your phone, scrolling through noise before your feet even hit the floor. I was stuck in that loop, desperate for a way out.

On May 5, 2025, I made one small choice: I picked up a pen and my sketchbook instead of my phone.

What started as simple doodles quickly evolved into a 100-day project of drawing an animal every single day. This simple, intentional act became my daily meditation, replacing the empty feeling of wasted time with the rich satisfaction of simply being present.

The pages in *Detox Doodles* are the hilarious and adorable visual record of those 100 days. They are the paper trail that led me back to myself. Every page of sketches, complete with its silly expressions and funny comments, transformed empty time into a source of peace and delight.

This book is the spark that ignites your journey back to mindfulness.

I hope these animal sketches inspire you to find your own quiet rebellion: put down your screen, pick up a pen (or whatever calls to you), and discover the genuine peace that waits for you when you choose to be truly present.

5/5/25

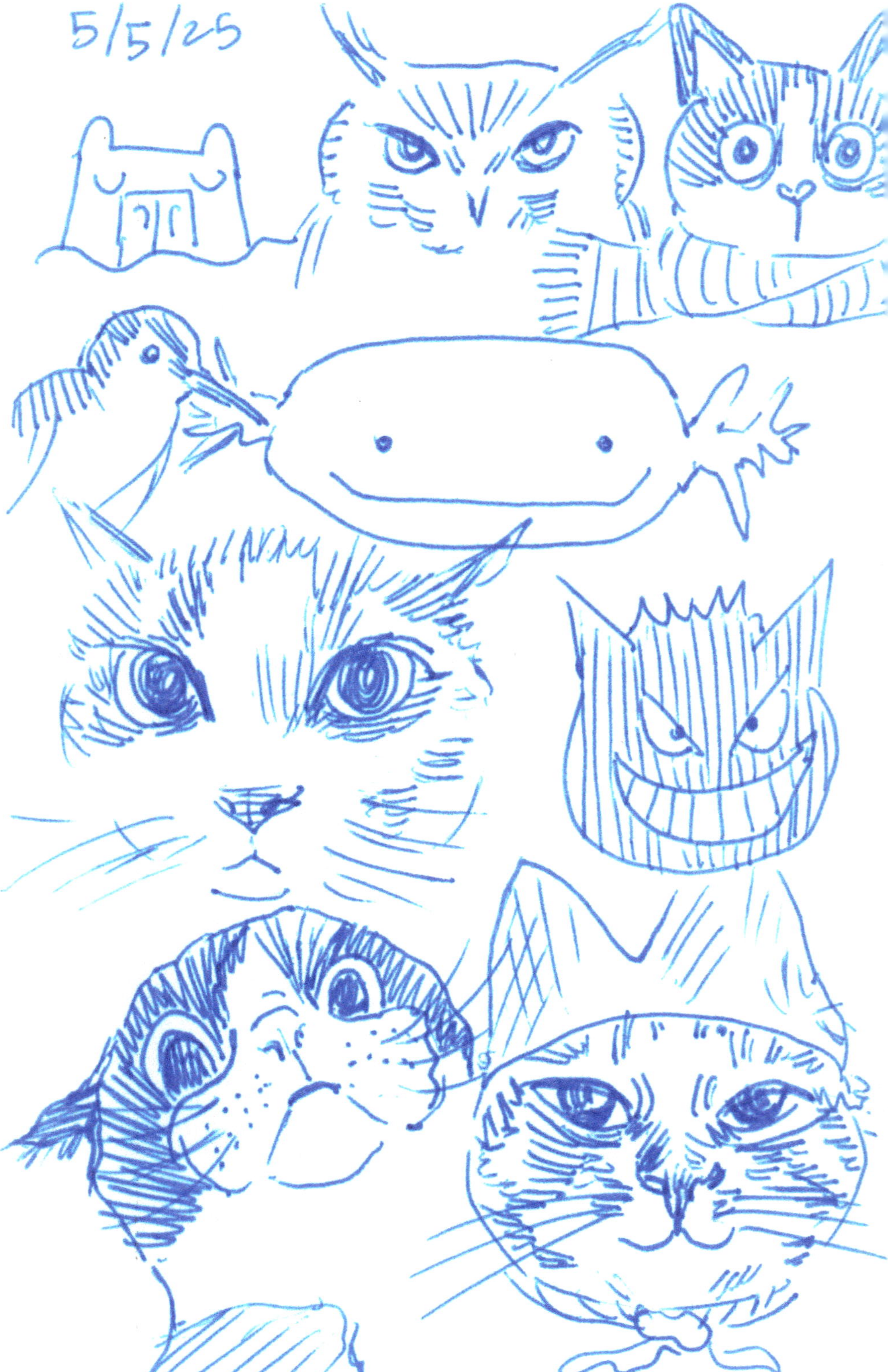

5/6/25

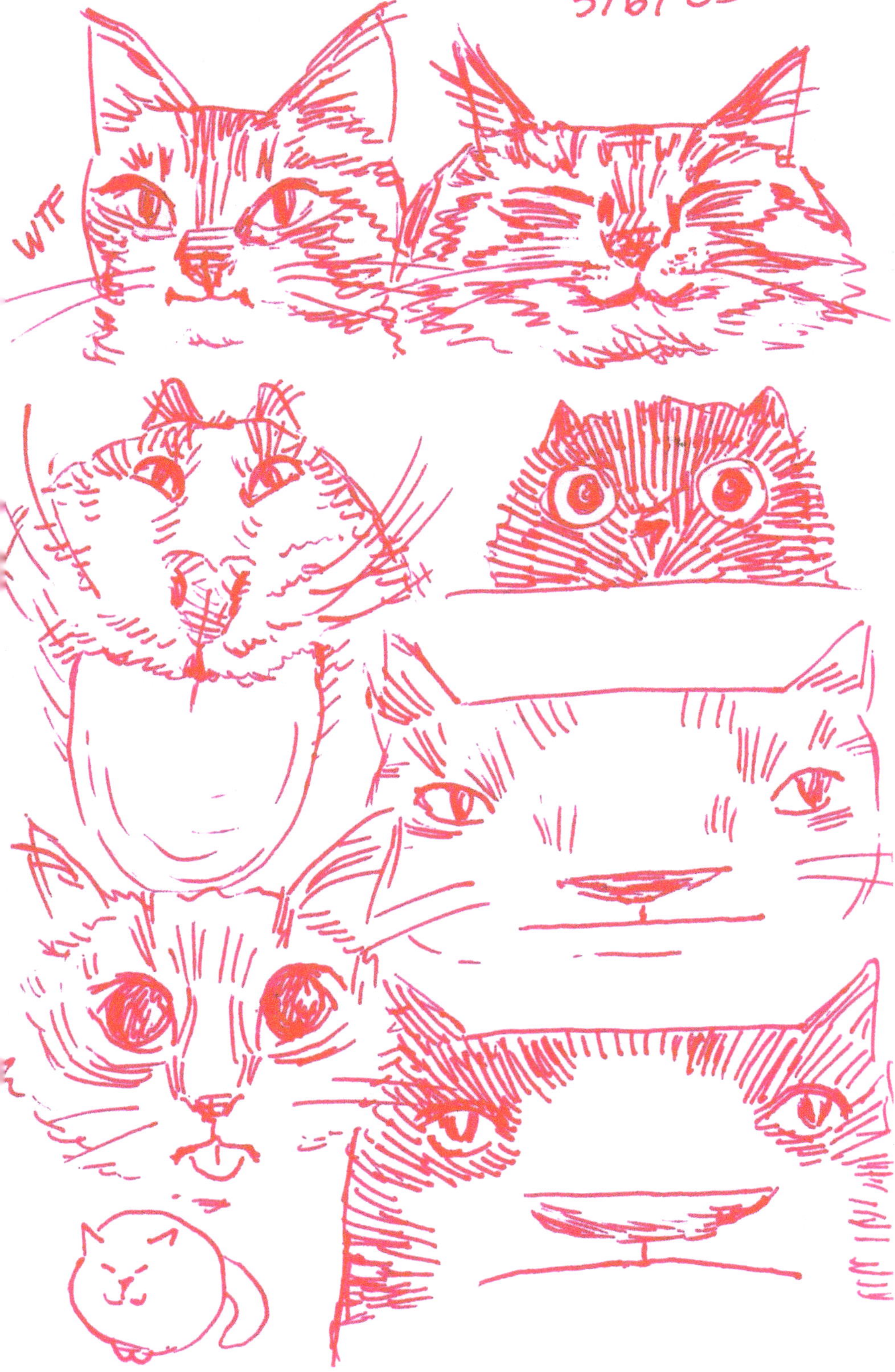

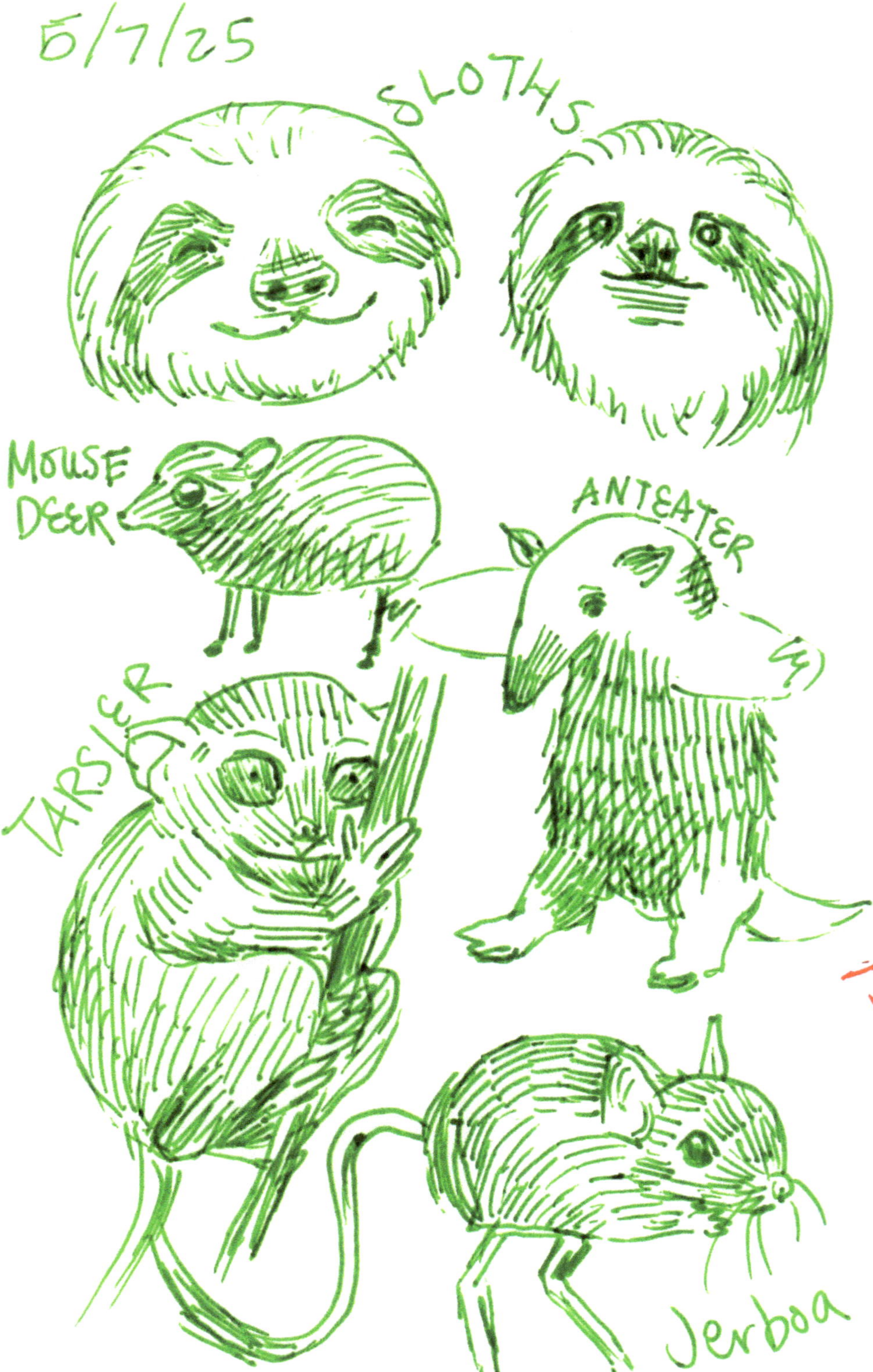
5/7/25
SLOTHS
MOUSE DEER
ANTEATER
TARSIER
Jerboa

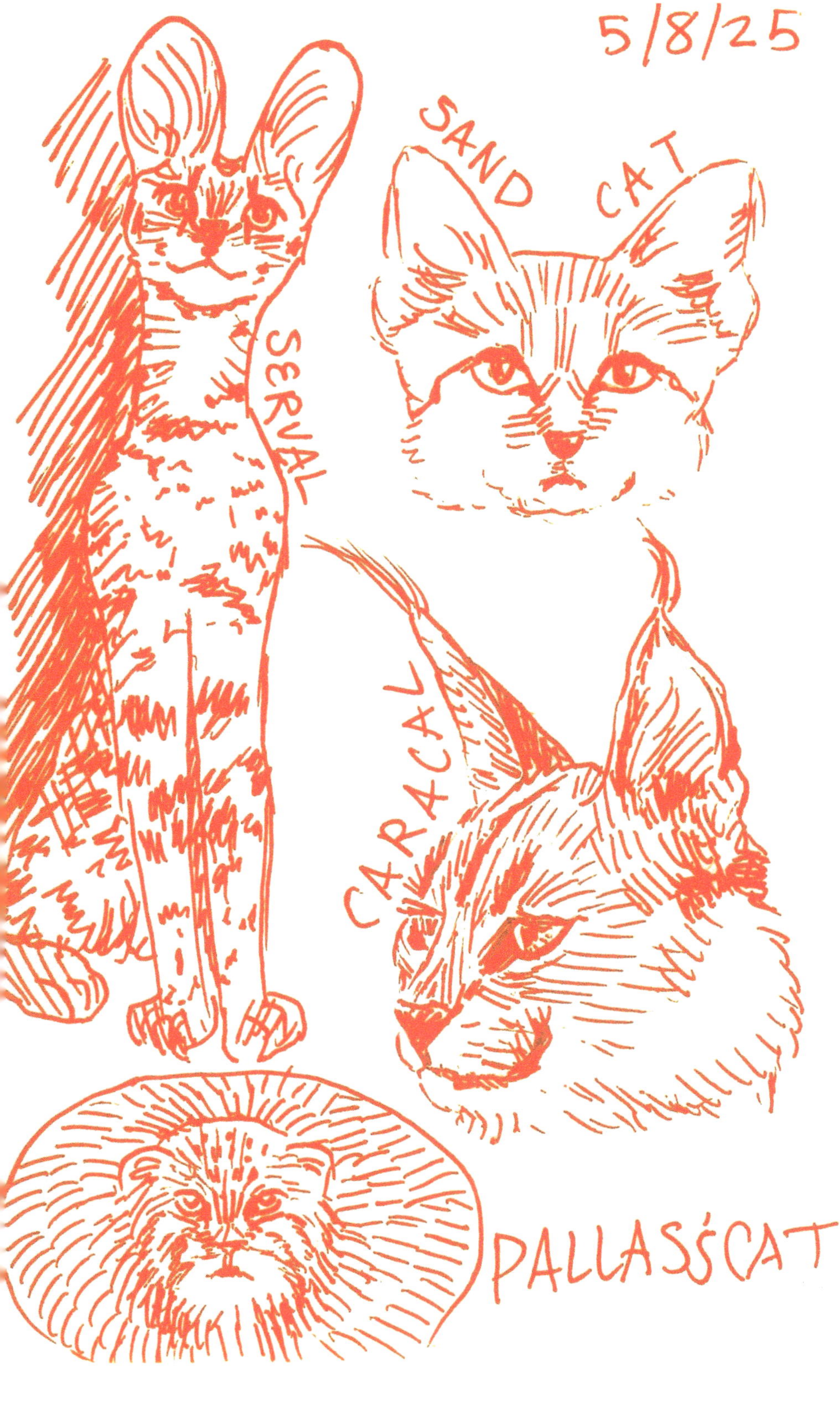
5/8/25
SAND CAT
SERVAL
CARACAL
PALLAS'S CAT

5/9/25

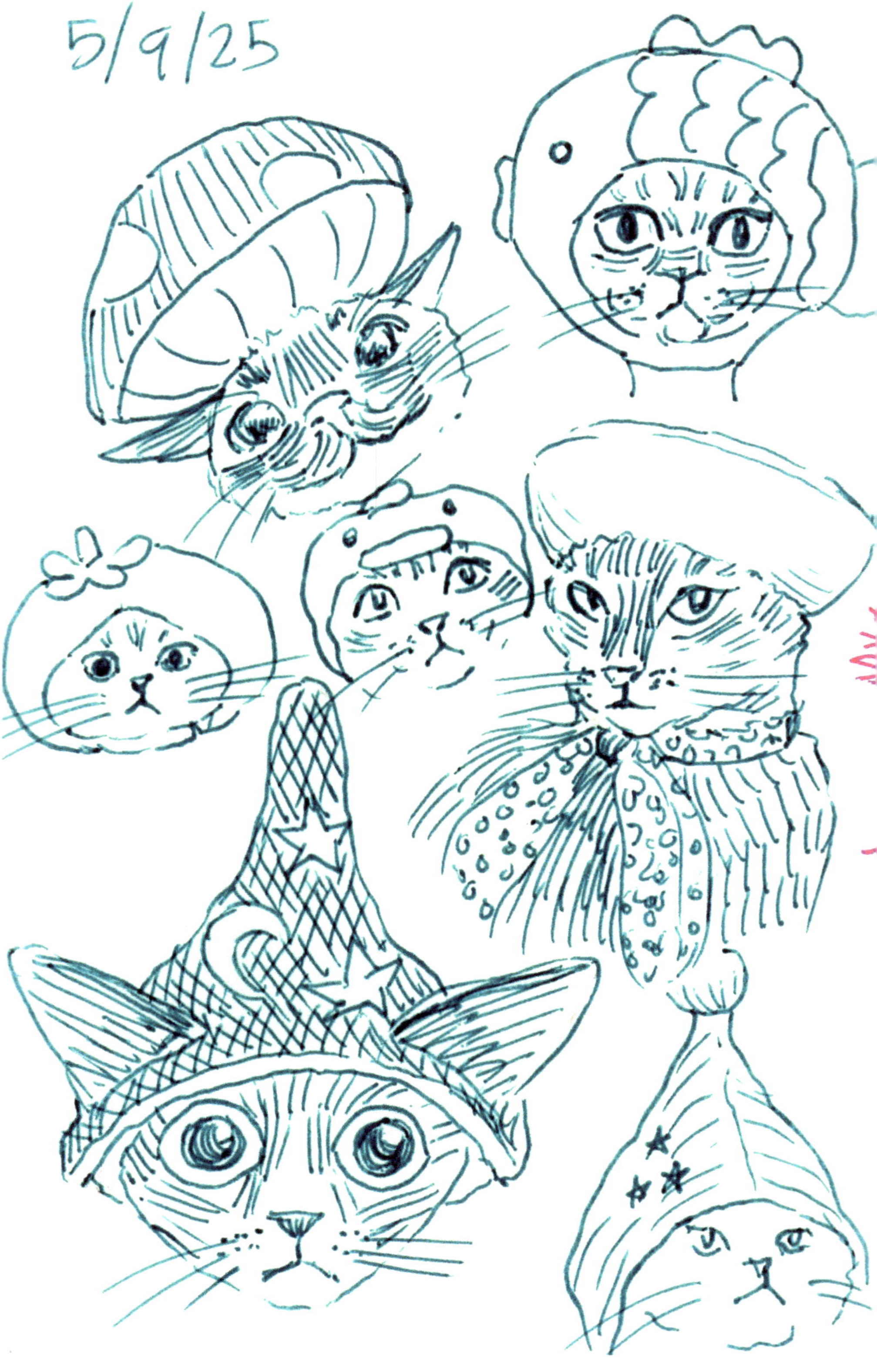

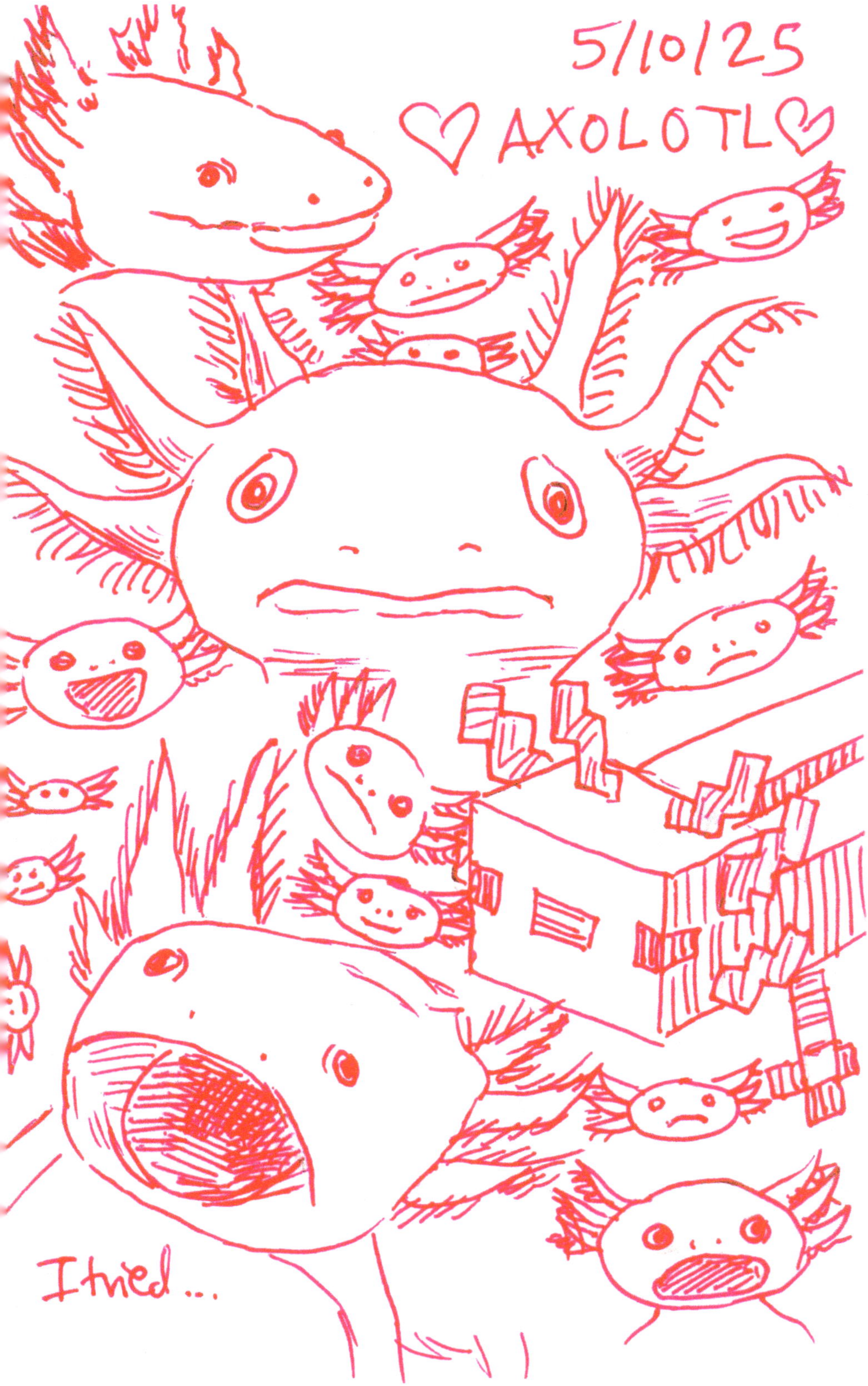
5/10/25
♡ AXOLOTL ♡
I tried ...

5/11/25 POTOO + TAWNY F

(They're basically Muppets)

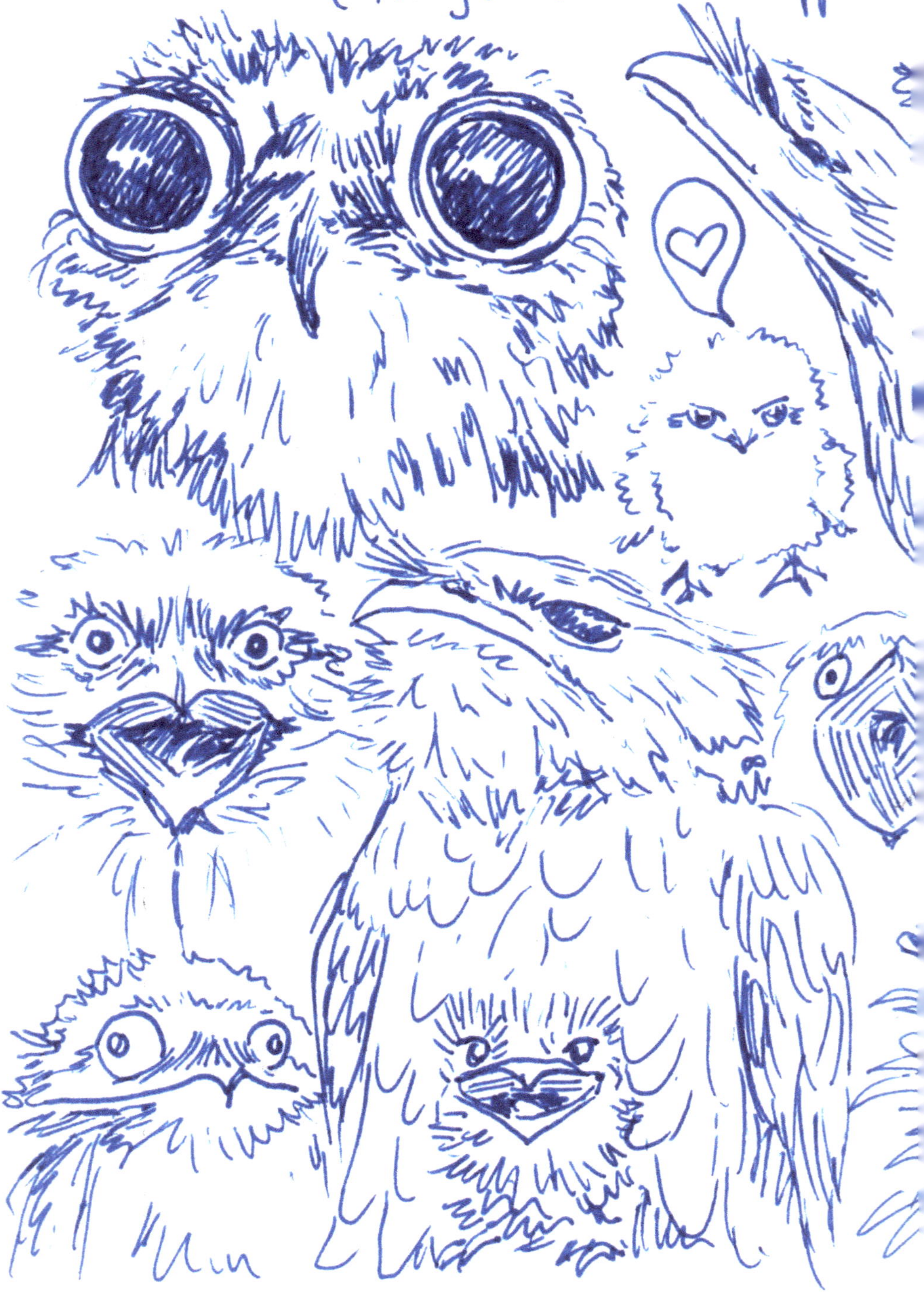

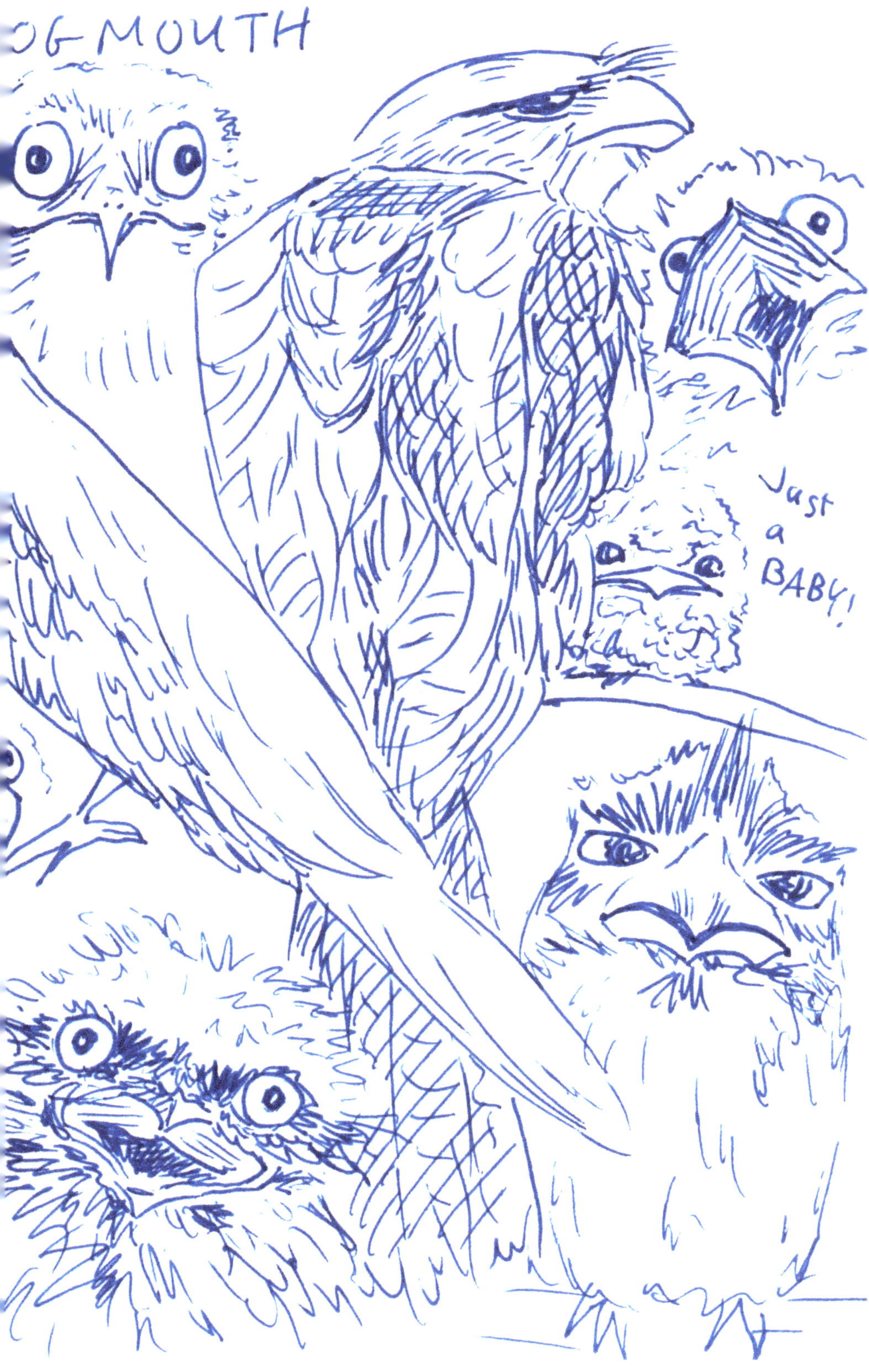
OGMOUTH
Just a BABY!

HIGHLAND COWS 5/12/25

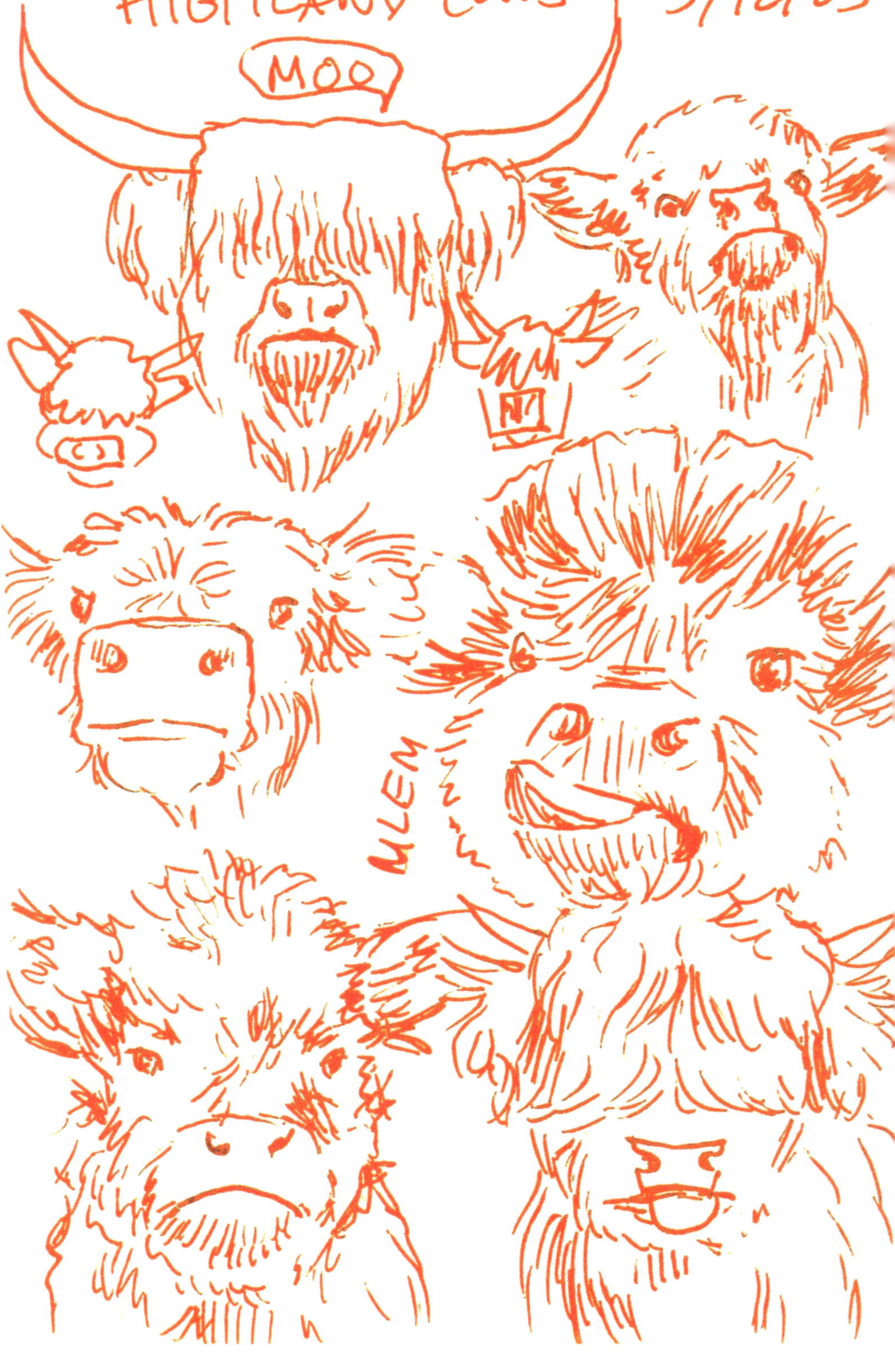

OPPOSUMS 5/13/25

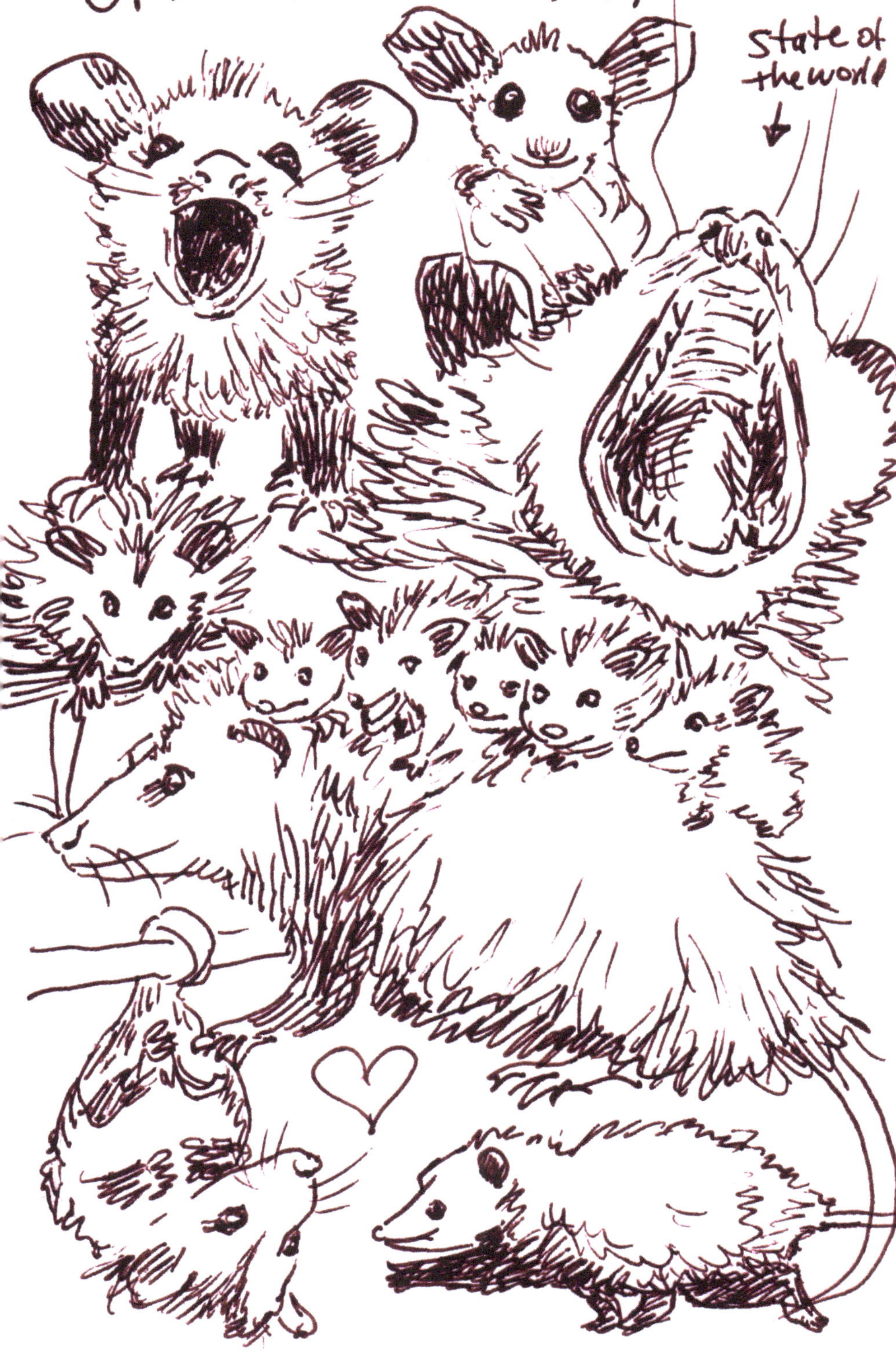

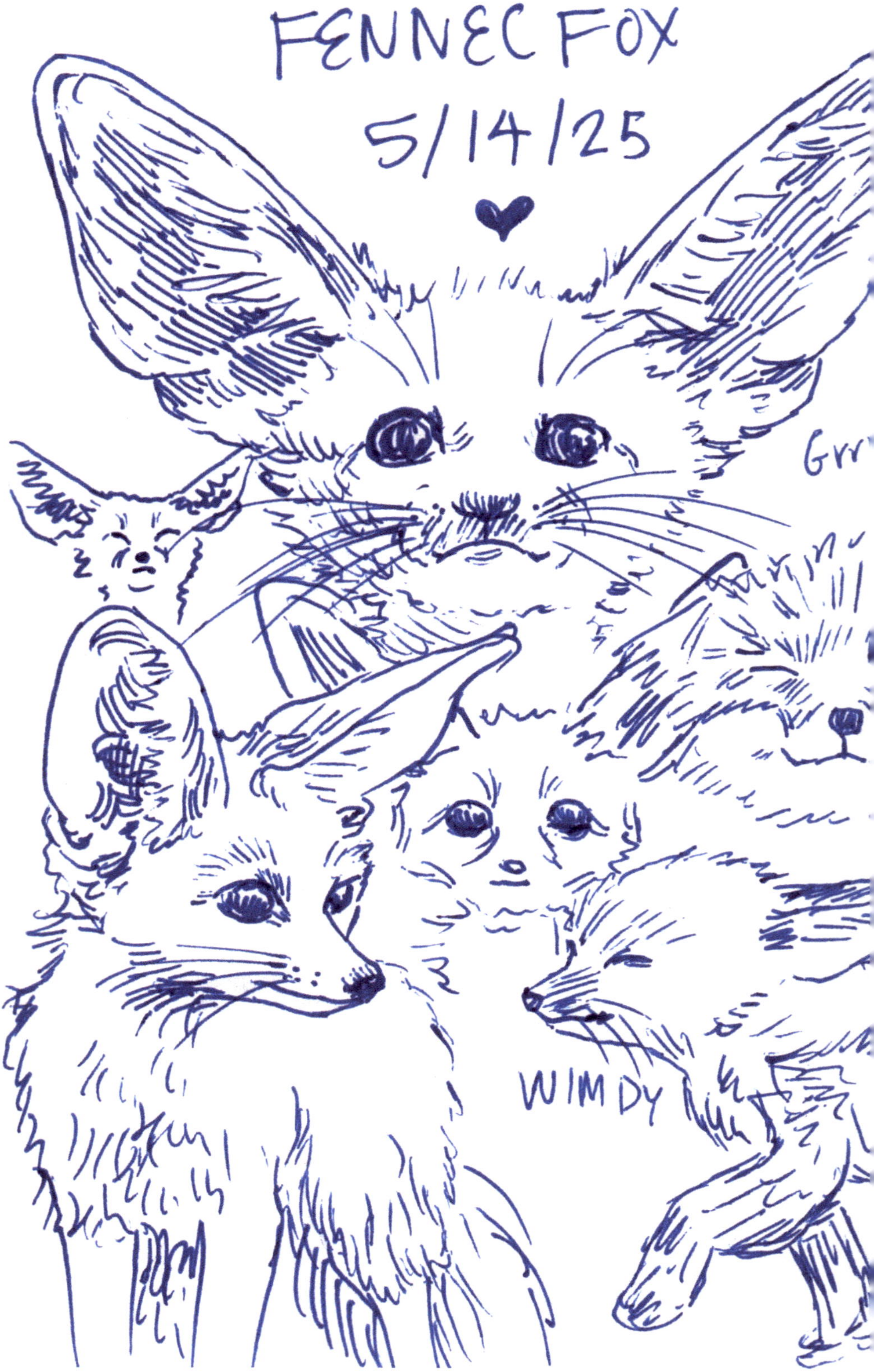
FENNEC FOX
5/14/25
Grr
WIMDY

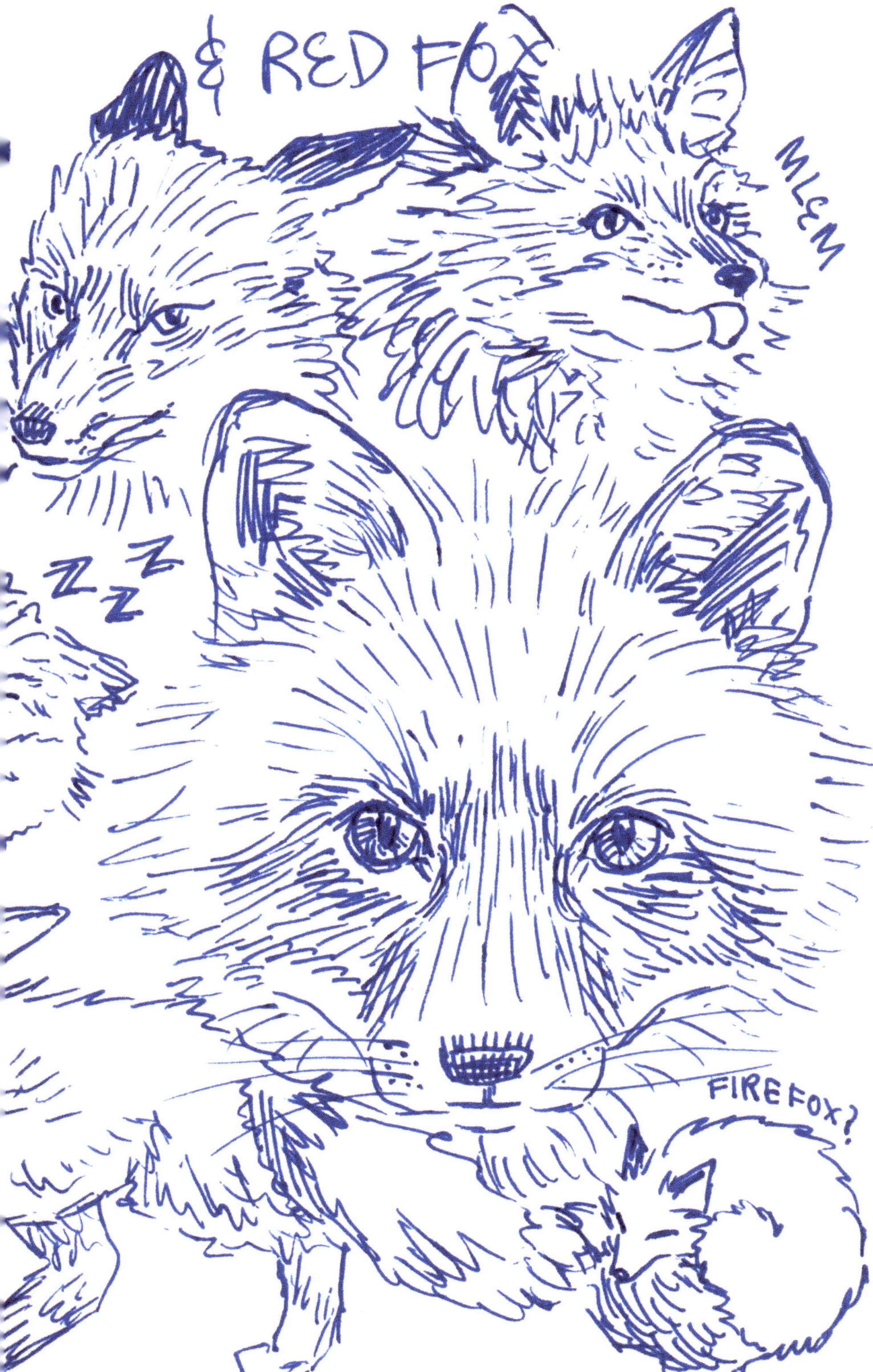
& RED FOX
MLEM
Z Z Z
FIREFOX?

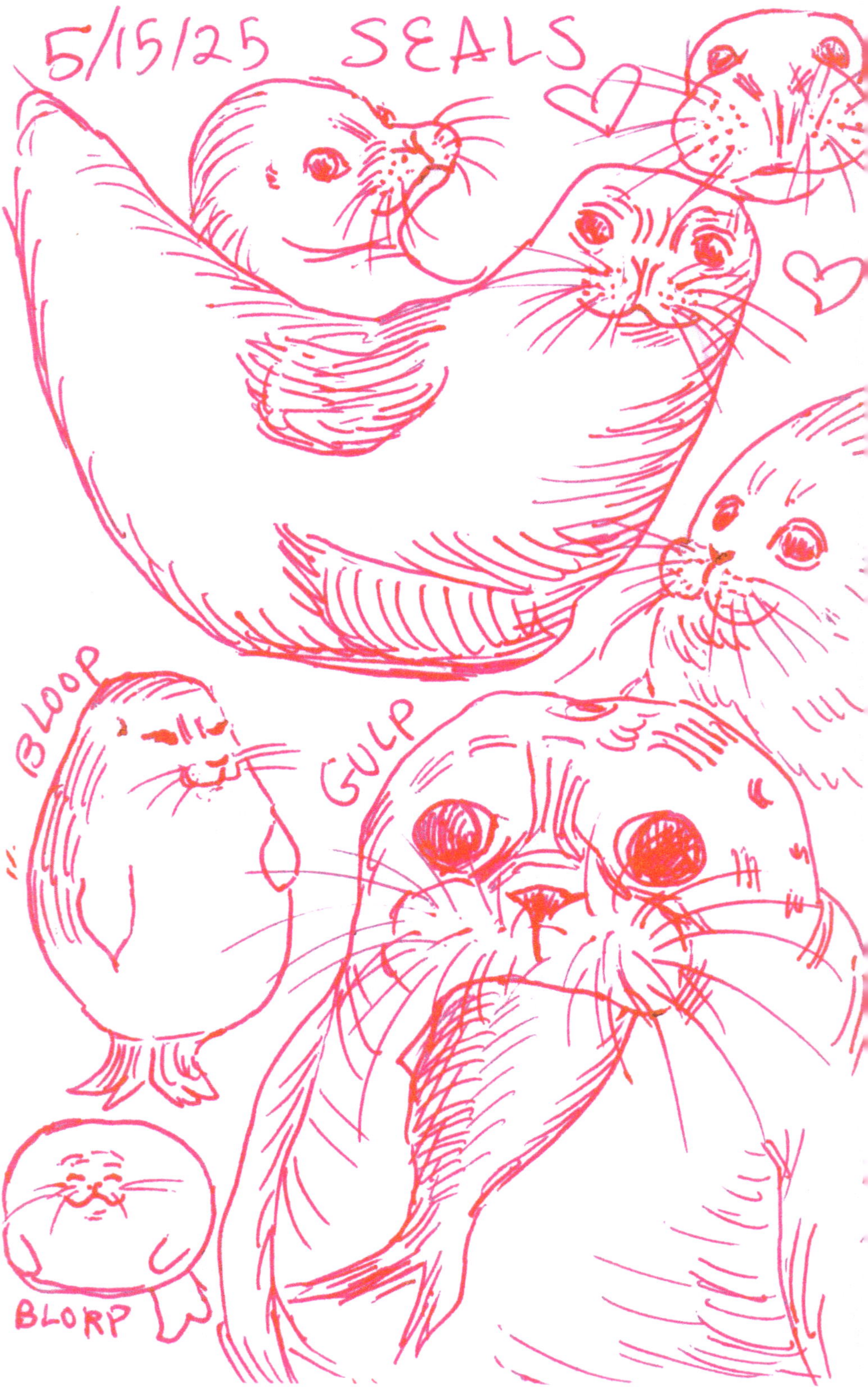
5/15/25 SEALS
BLOOP
GULP
BLORP

OWLS 5/16/25

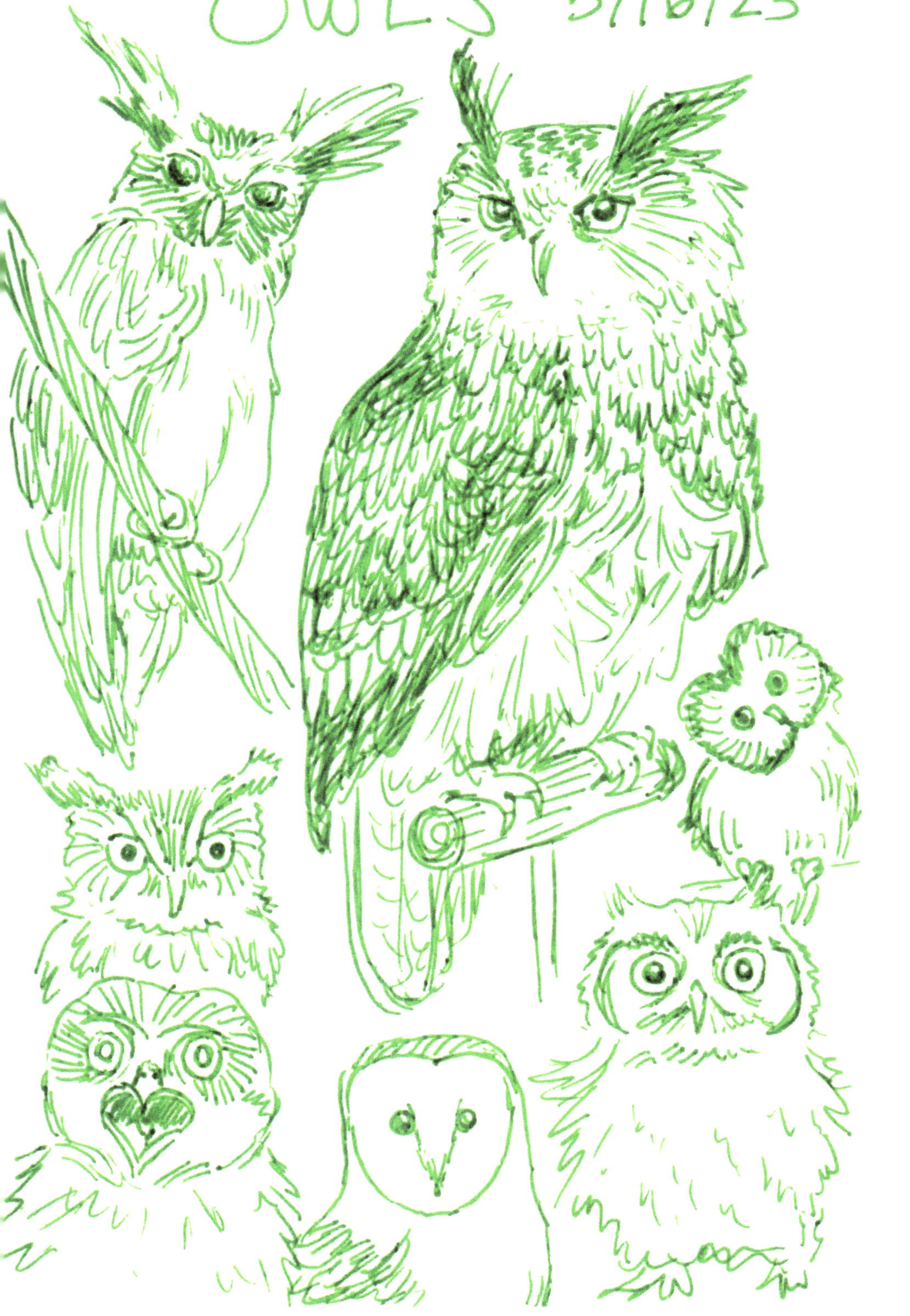

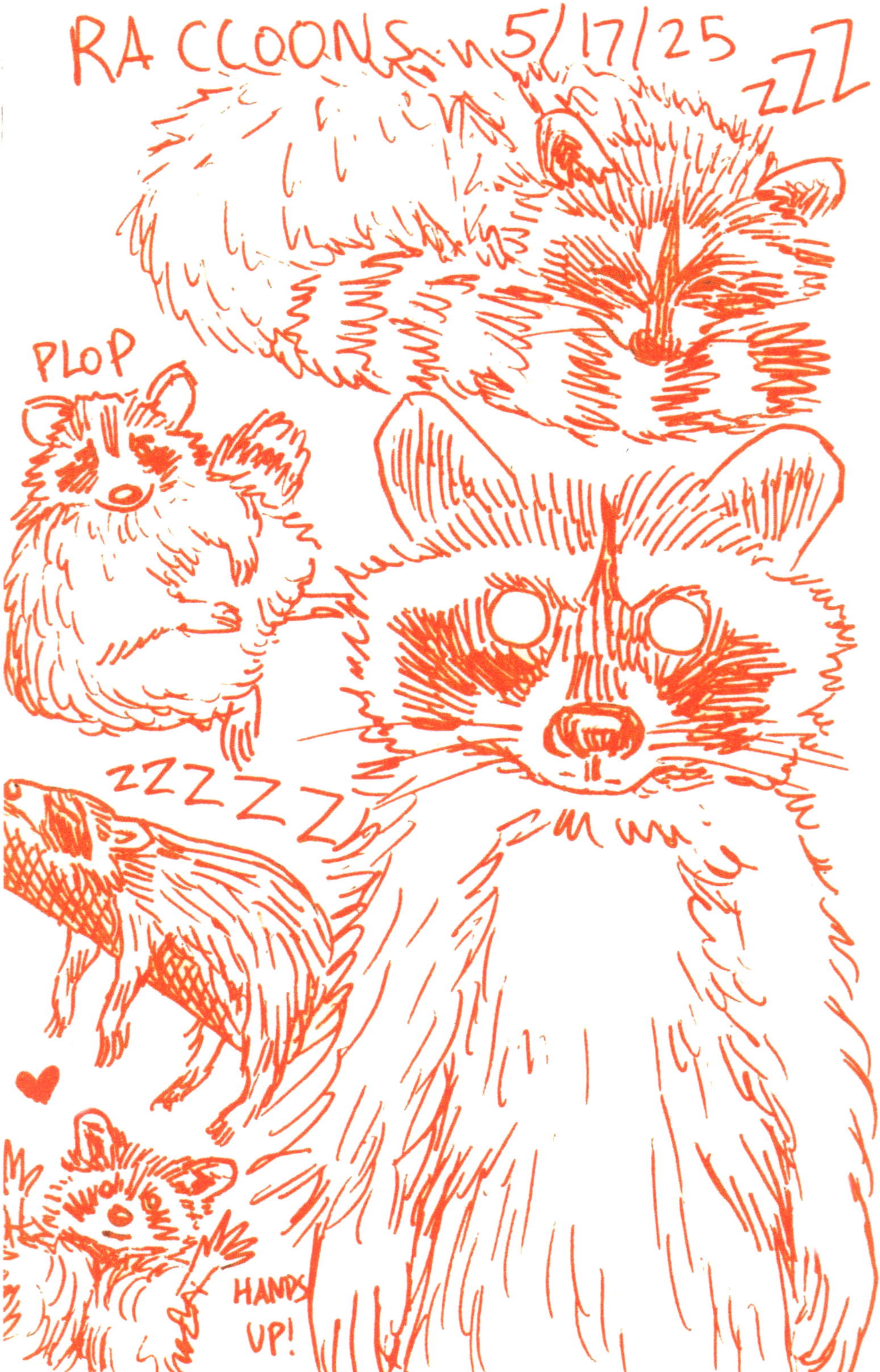
RACCOONS 5/17/25
ZZZ
PLOP
ZZZZZ
HANDS UP!

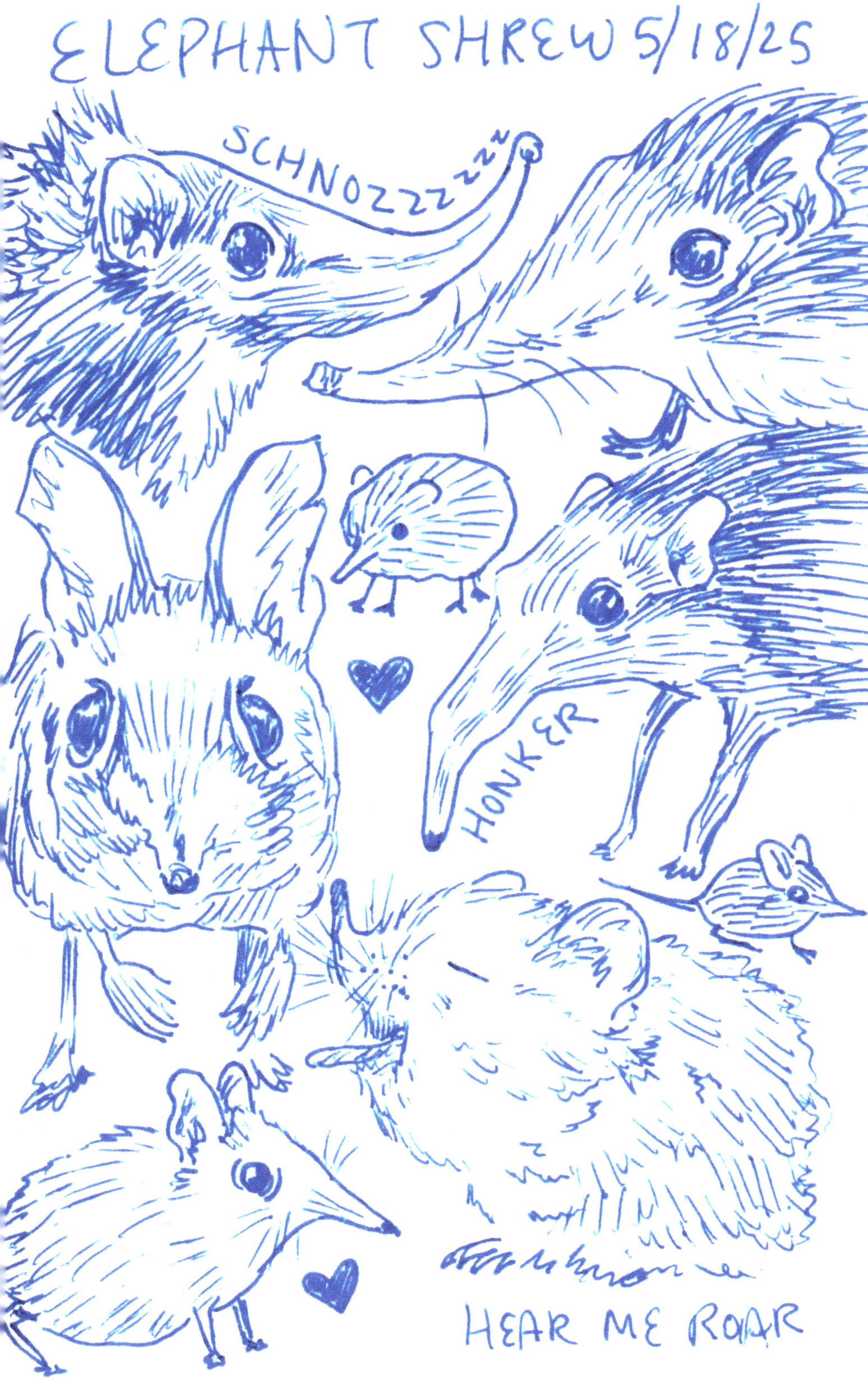
ELEPHANT SHREW 5/18/25
SCHNOZZZZZZZ
HONKER
HEAR ME ROAR

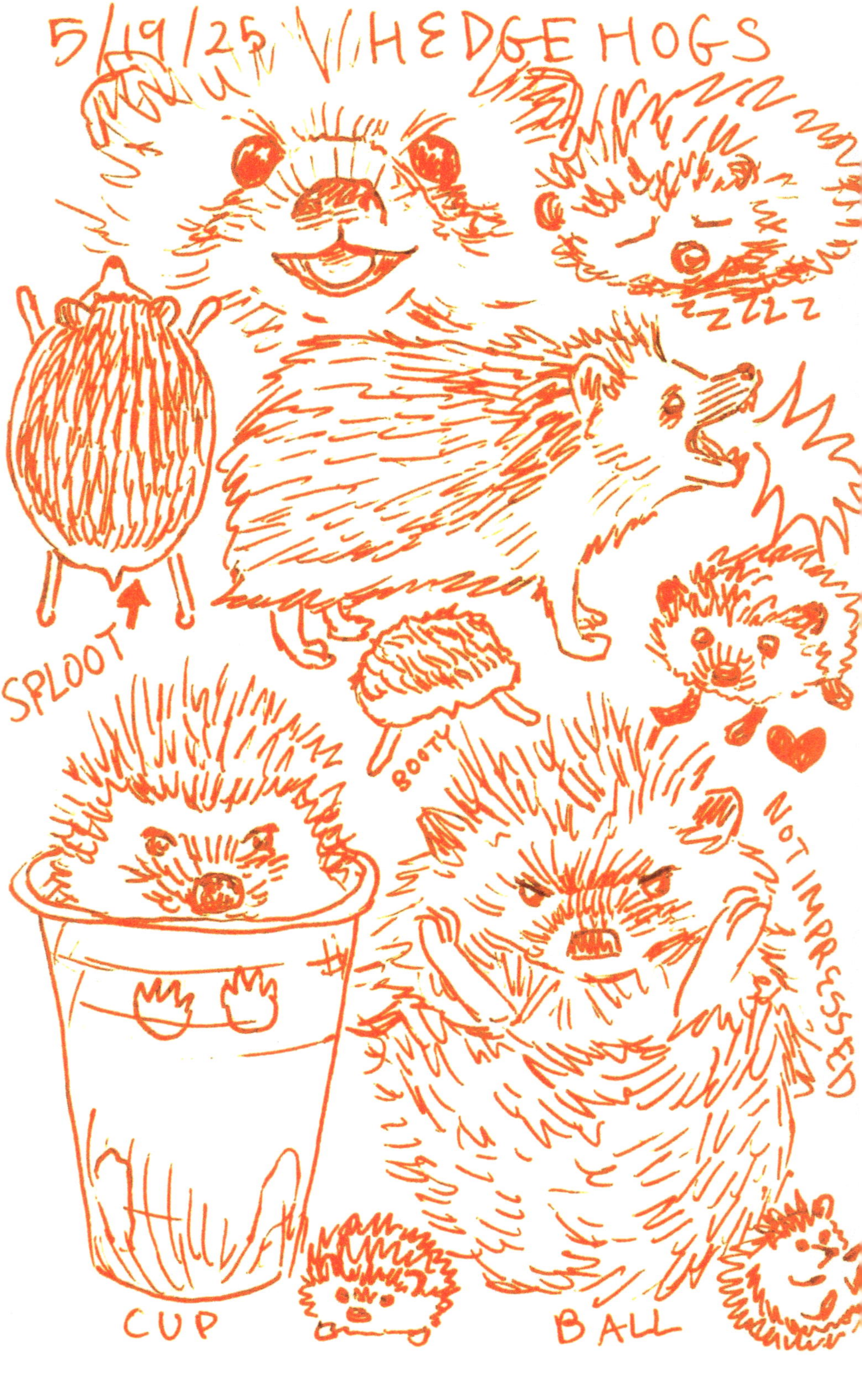
5/19/25
HEDGEHOGS
ZZZZ
SPLOOT
BOOTY
NOT IMPRESSED
CUP
BALL

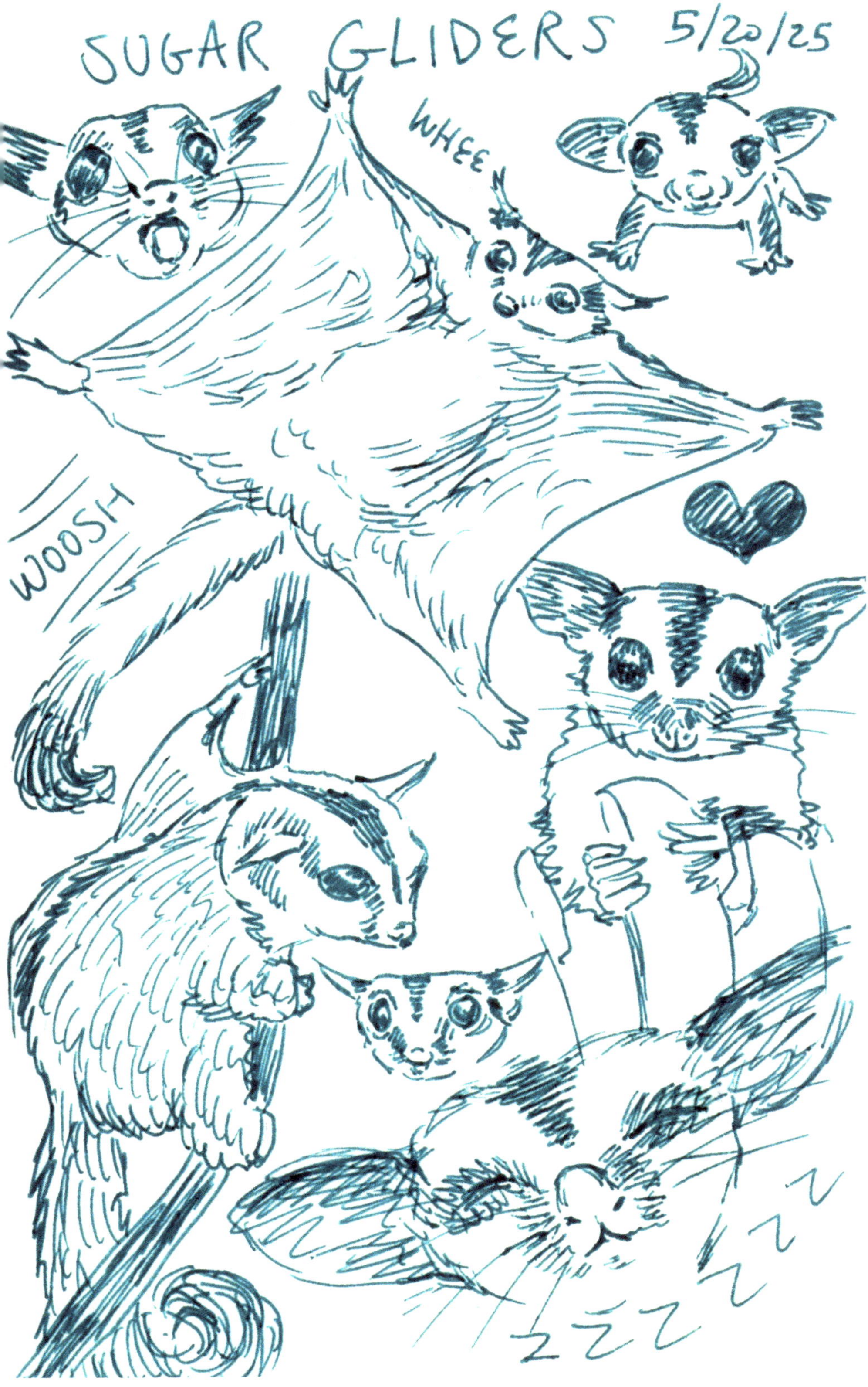
SUGAR GLIDERS
5/20/25
WHEE
WOOSH

5/21/25 RED PANDAS

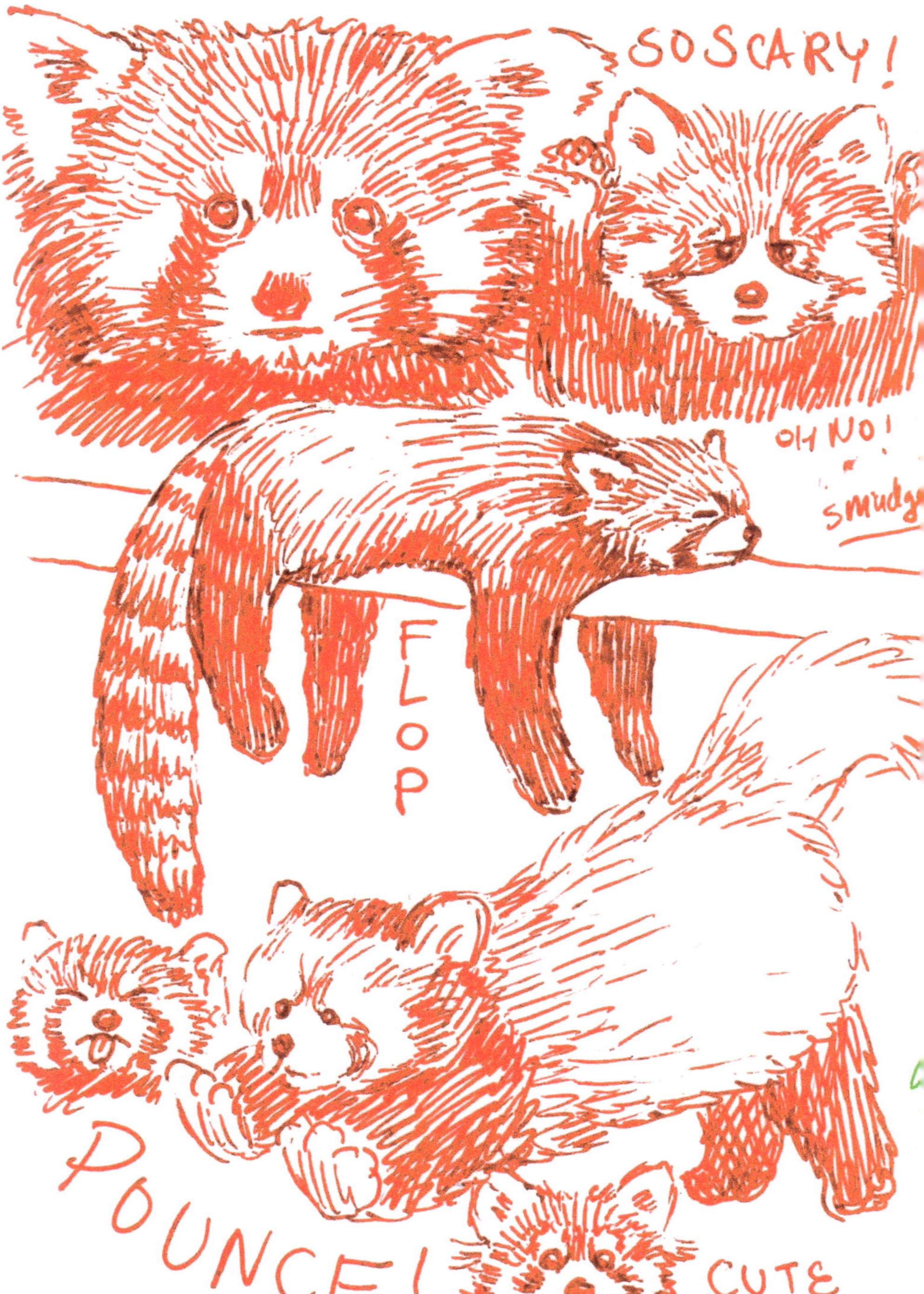

BURROWING OWL 5/22/25

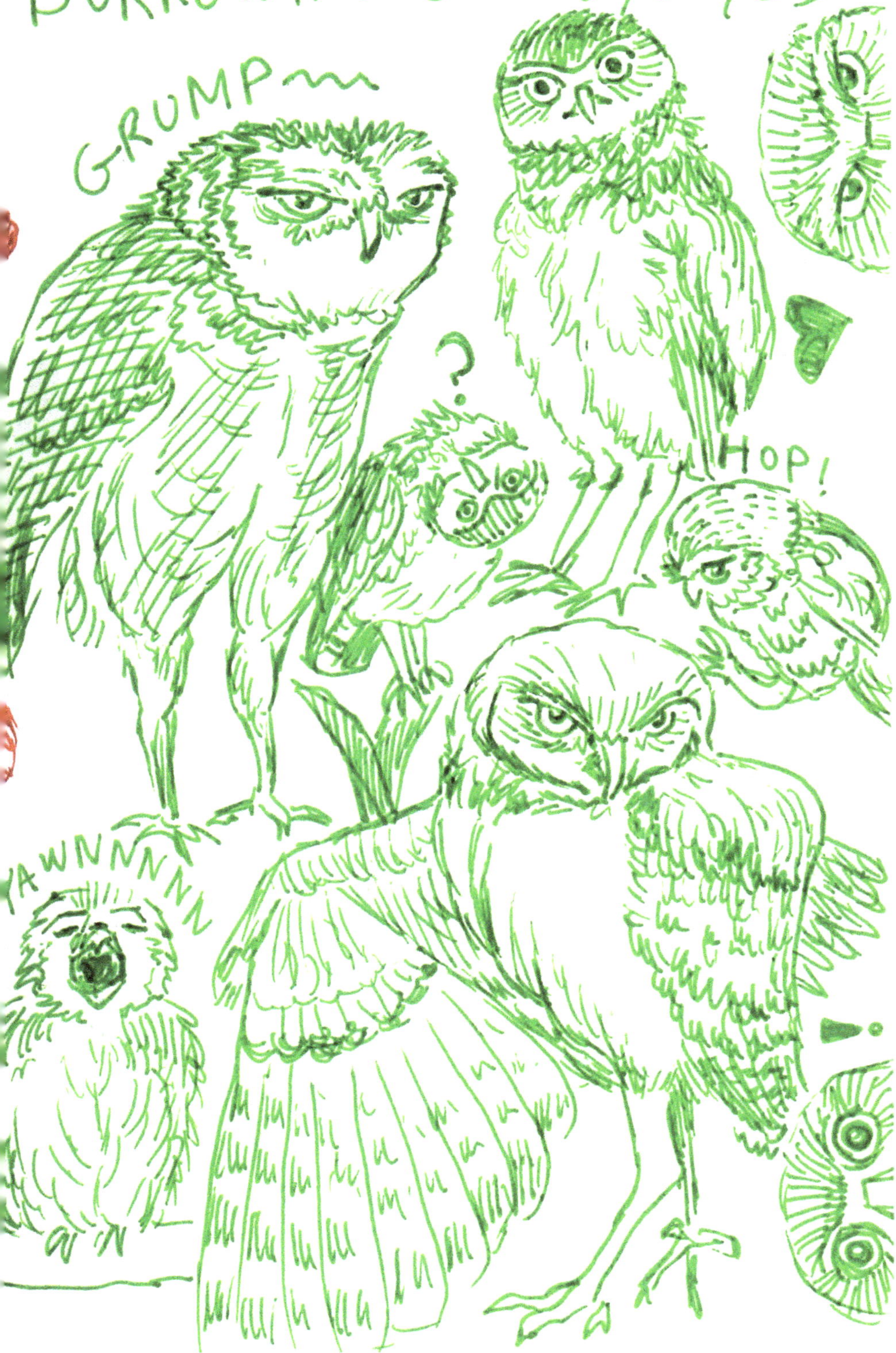

5/23/25 WOMBATS

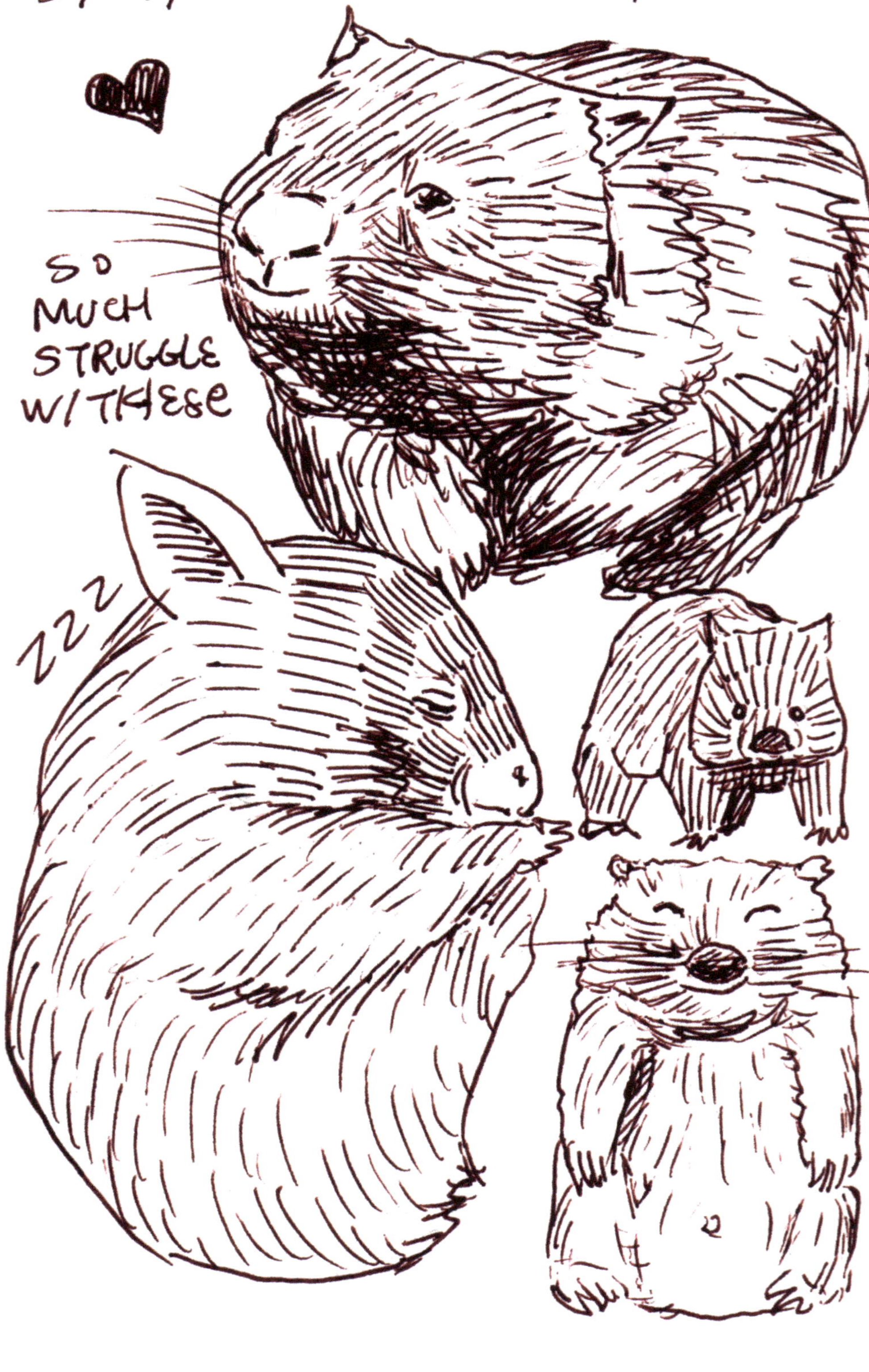

LET'S TRY AGAIN!

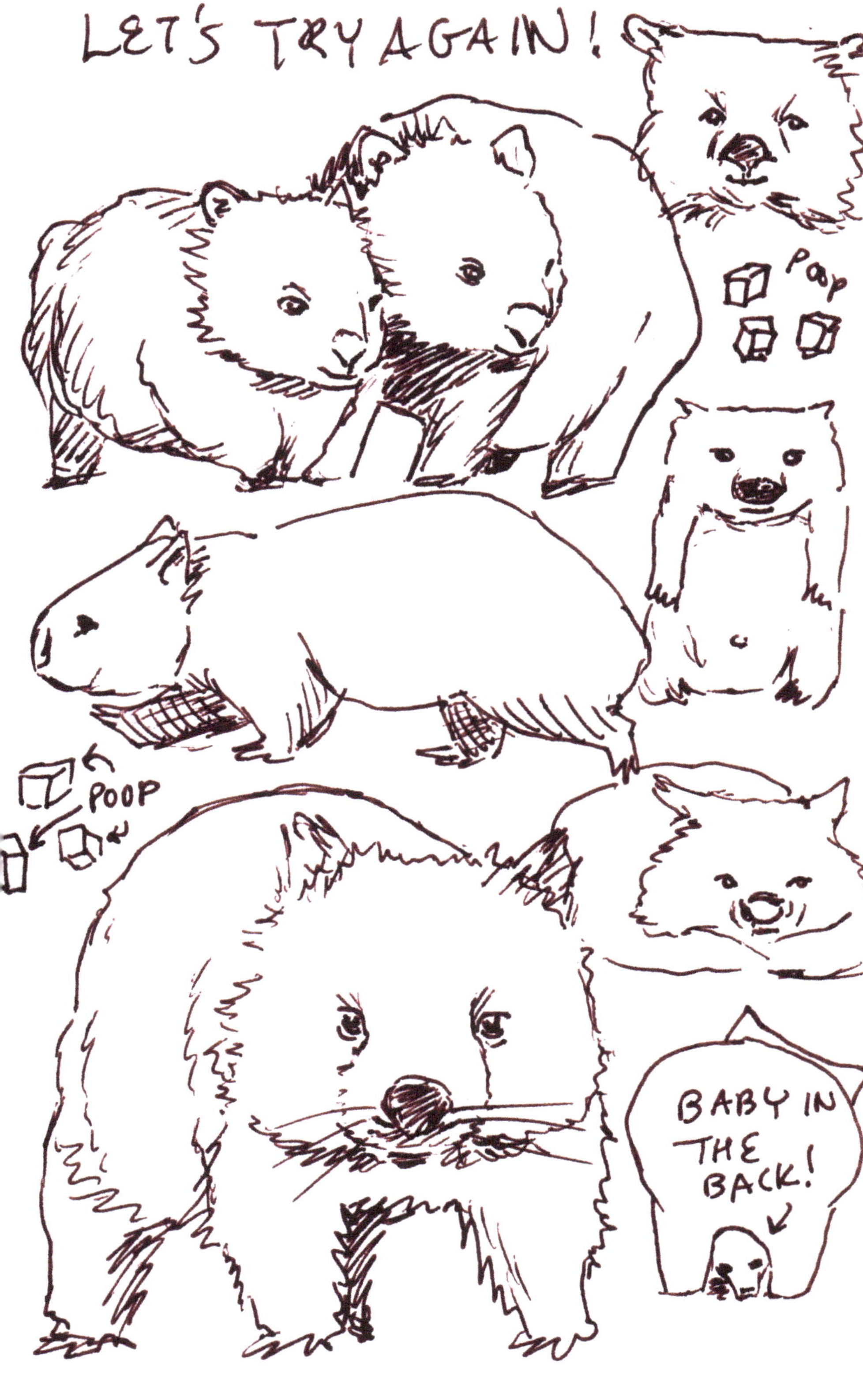

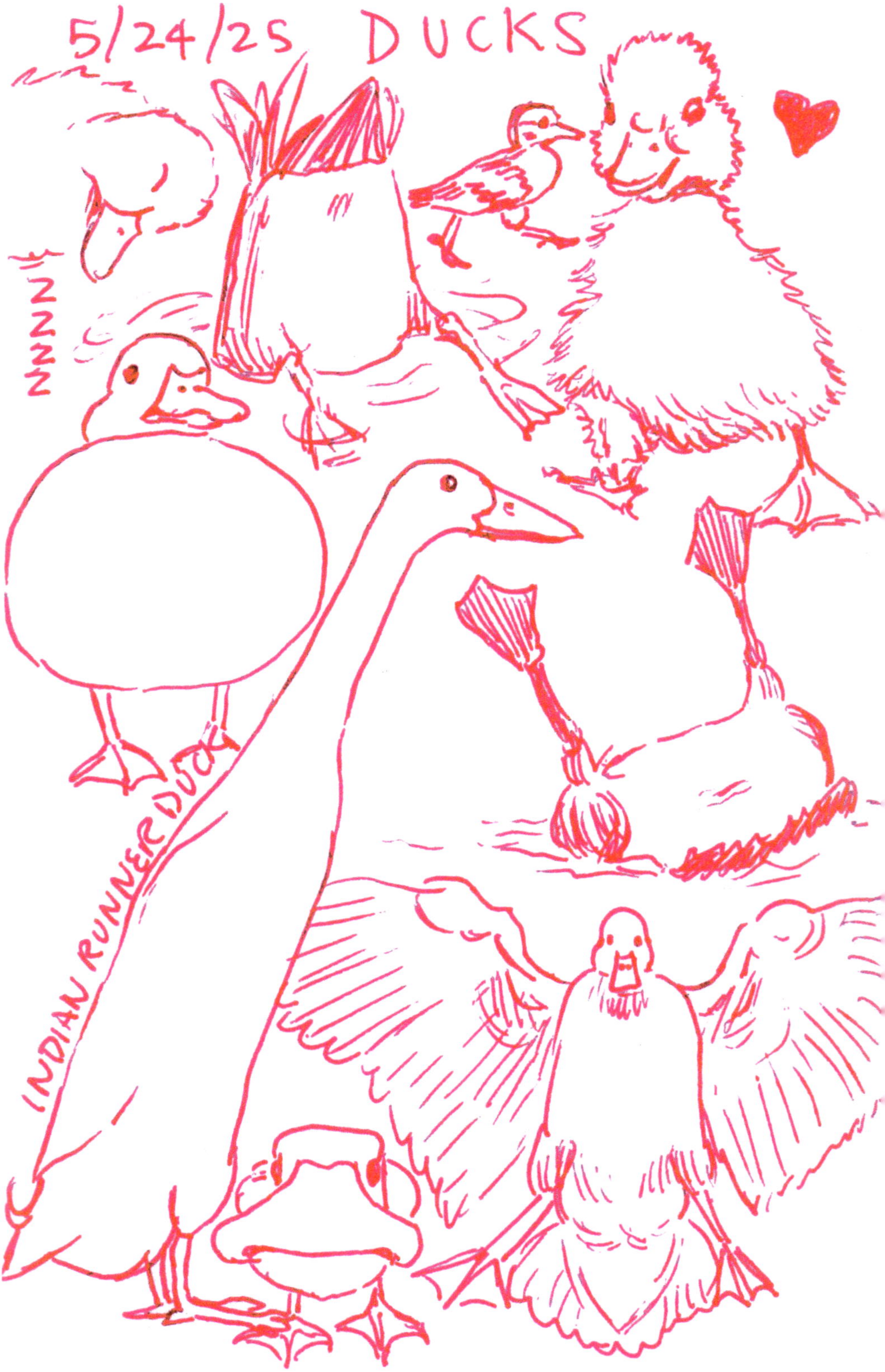

5/24/25 DUCKS
NNNNN!
INDIAN RUNNER DUCK

ARMADILLOS 5/25/25

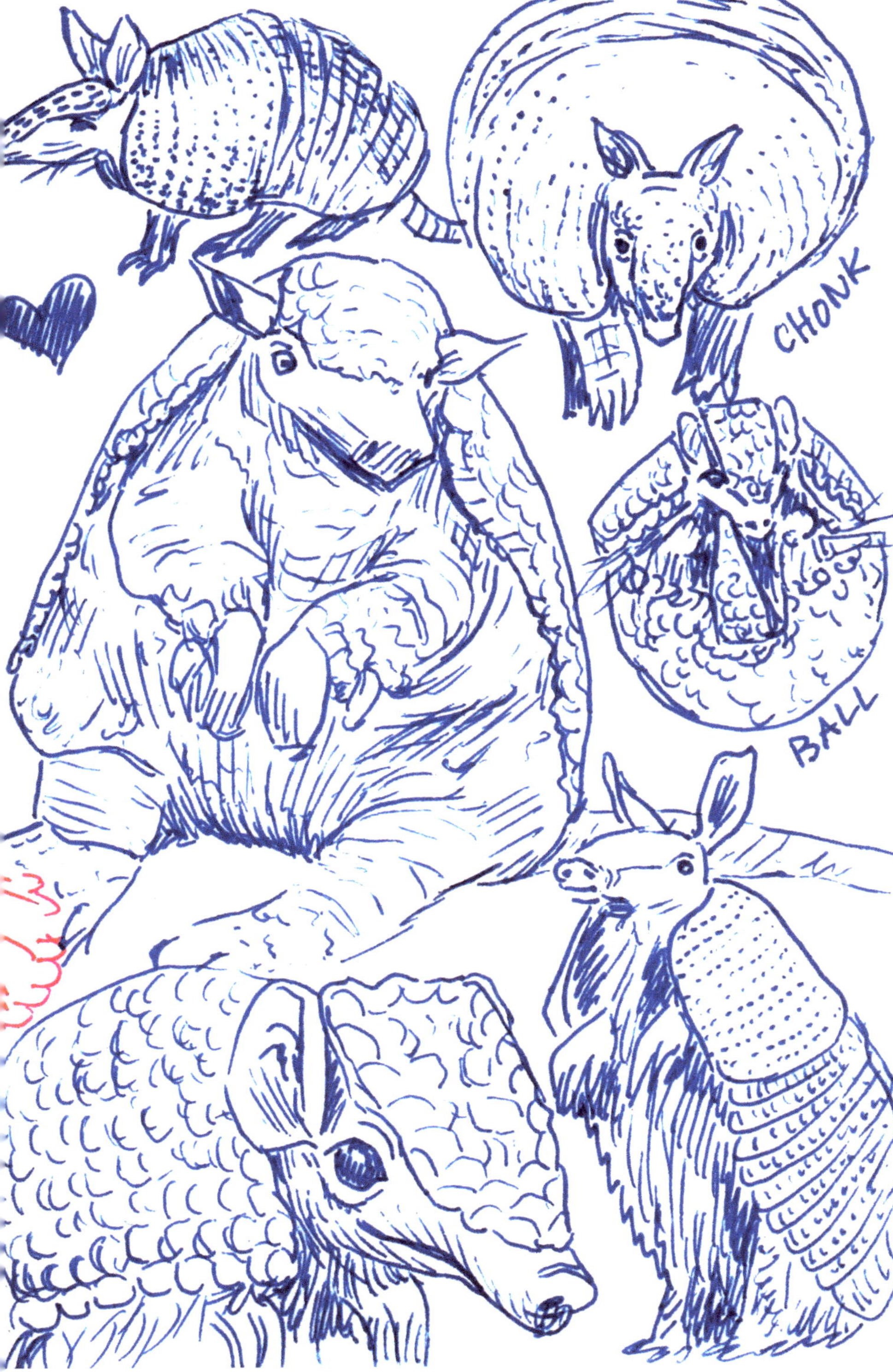

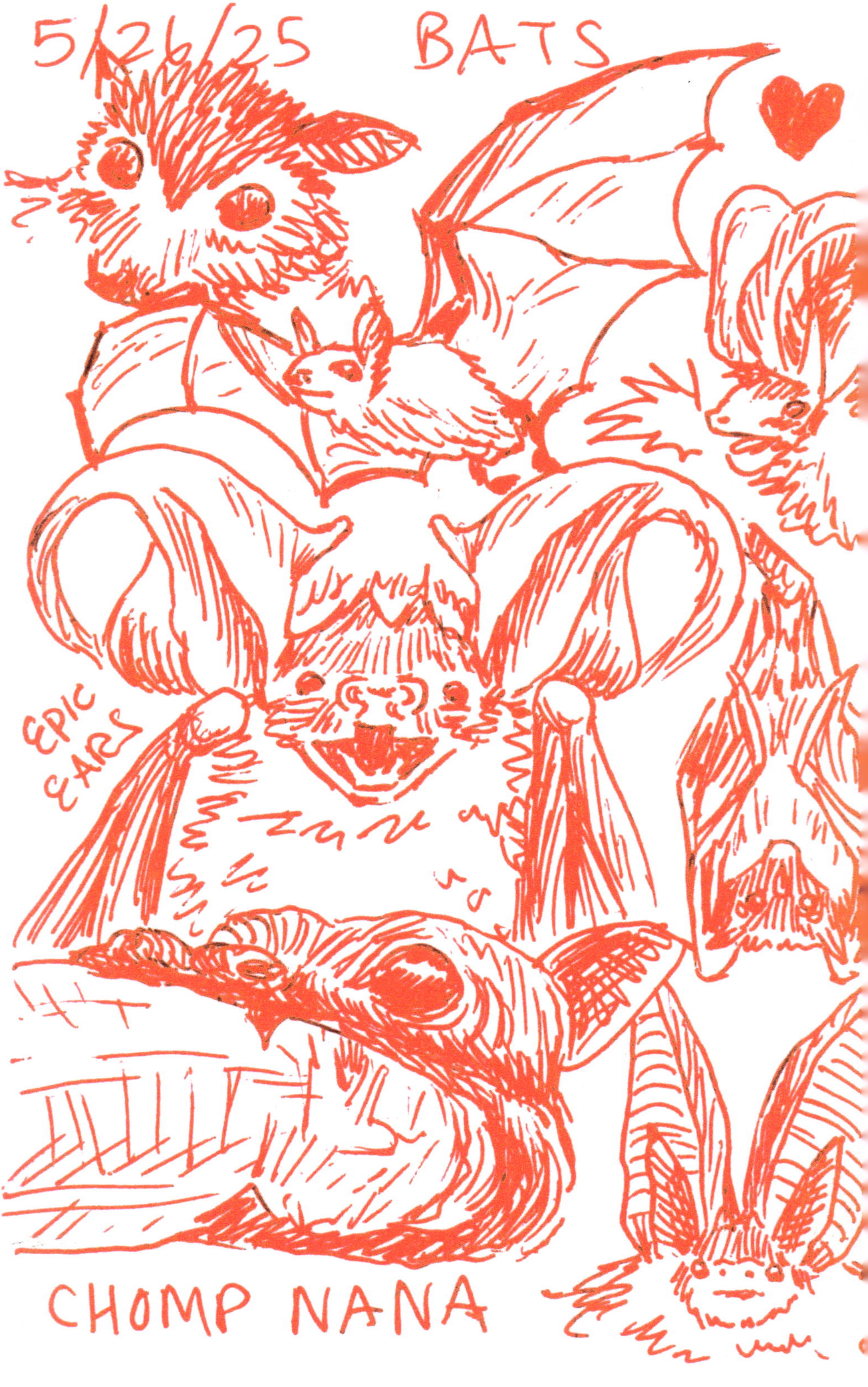

5/26/25 BATS
EPIC EARS
CHOMP NANA

ANTEATERS 5/27/25

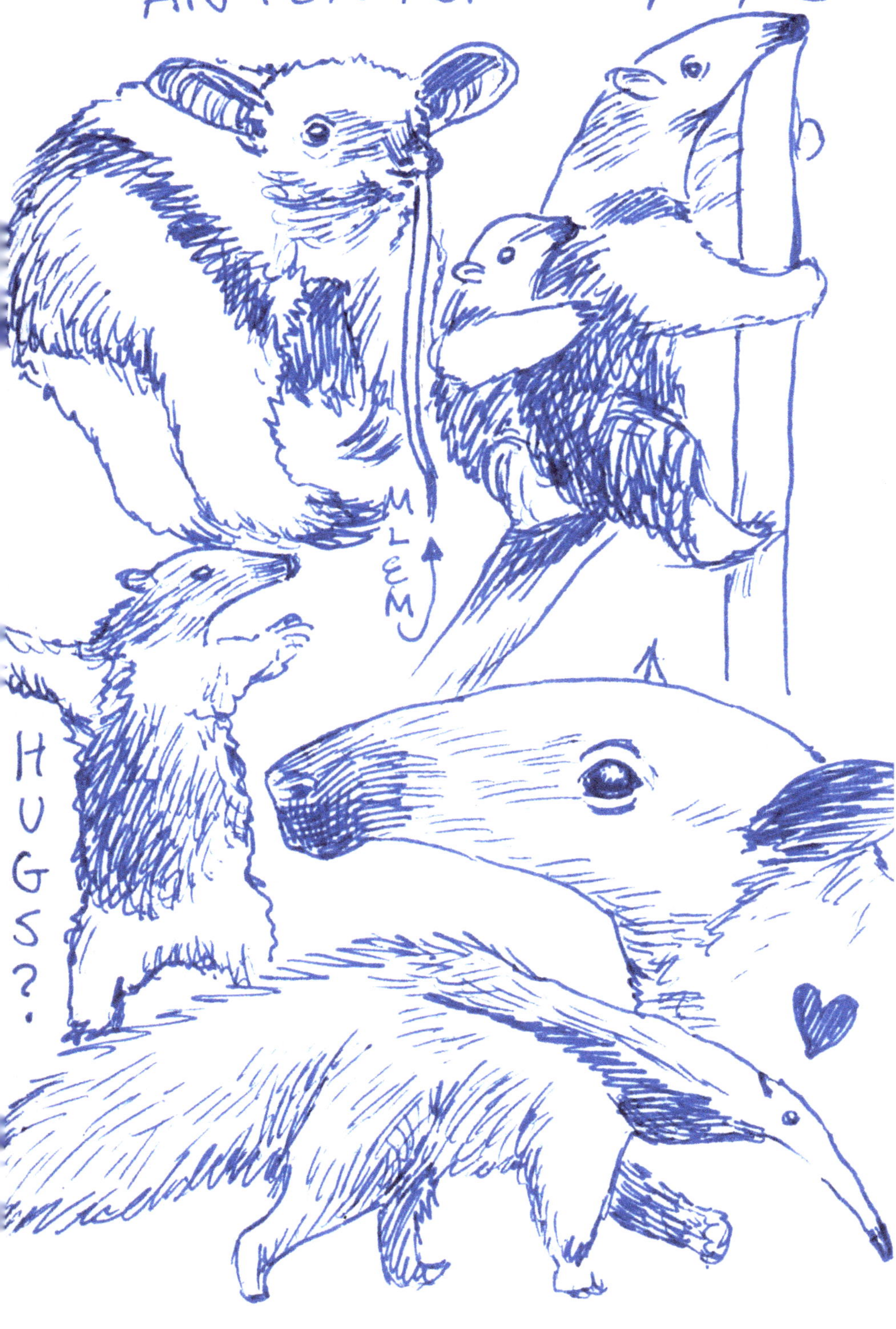

5/28/25 EGRETS

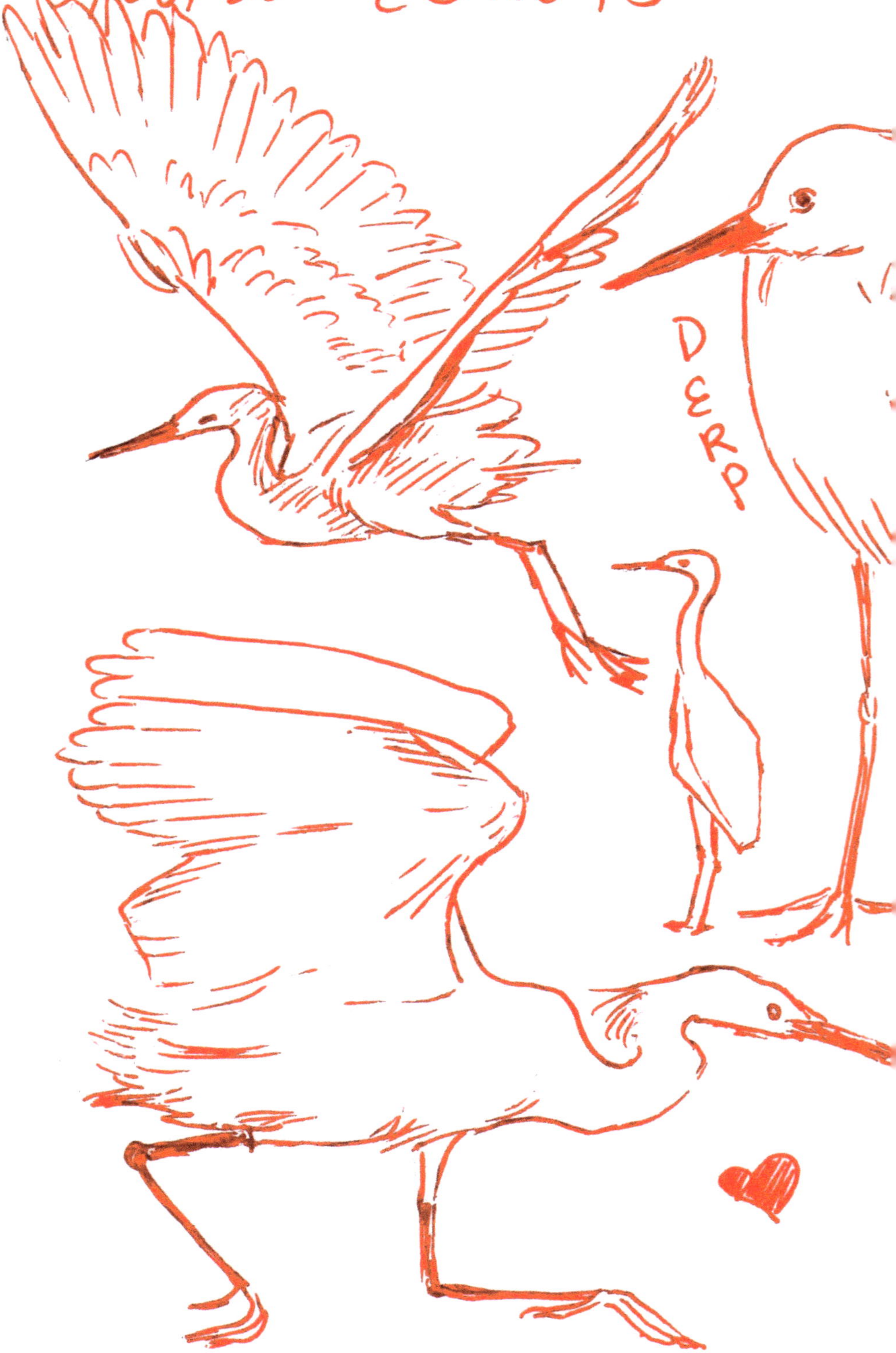

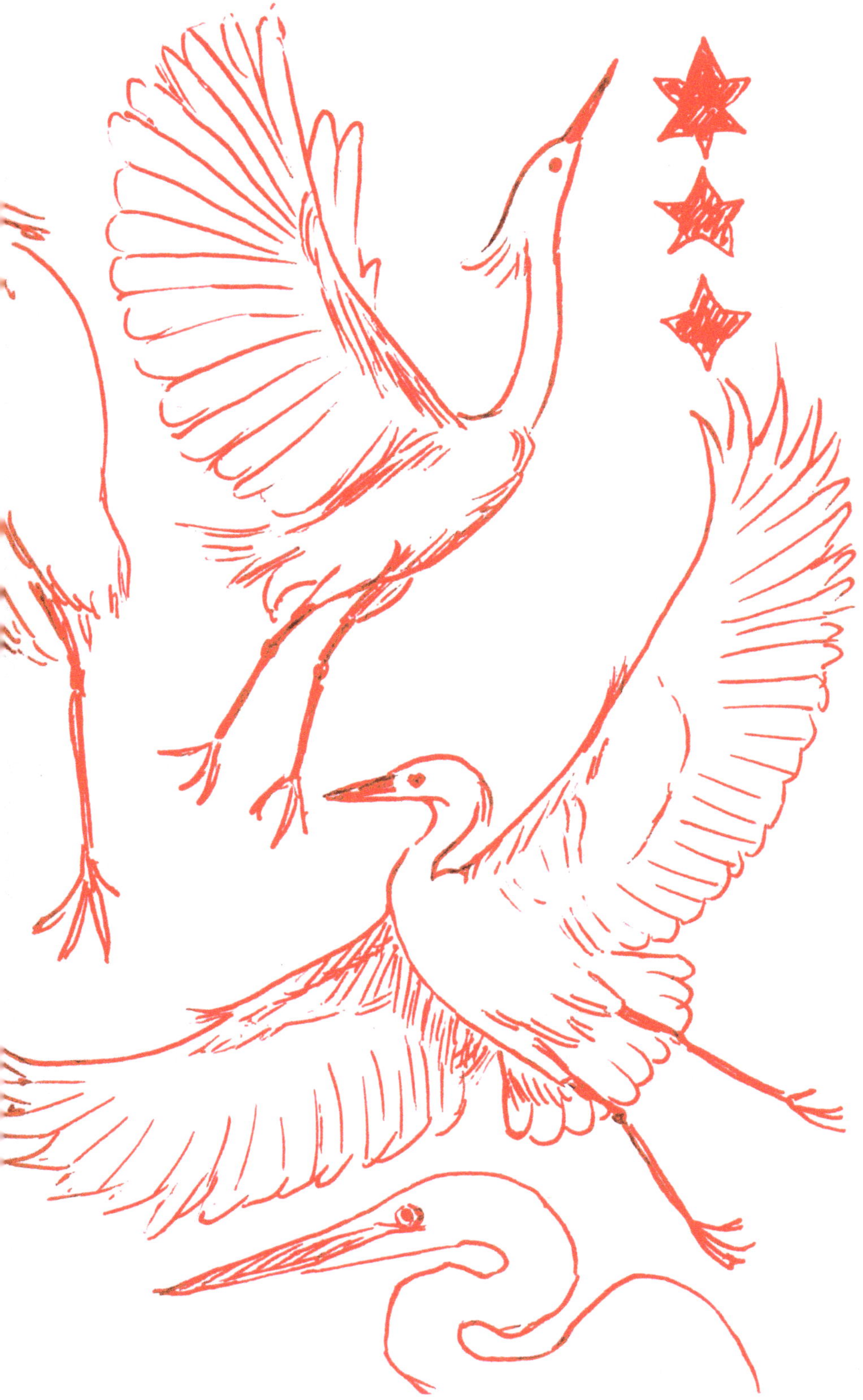

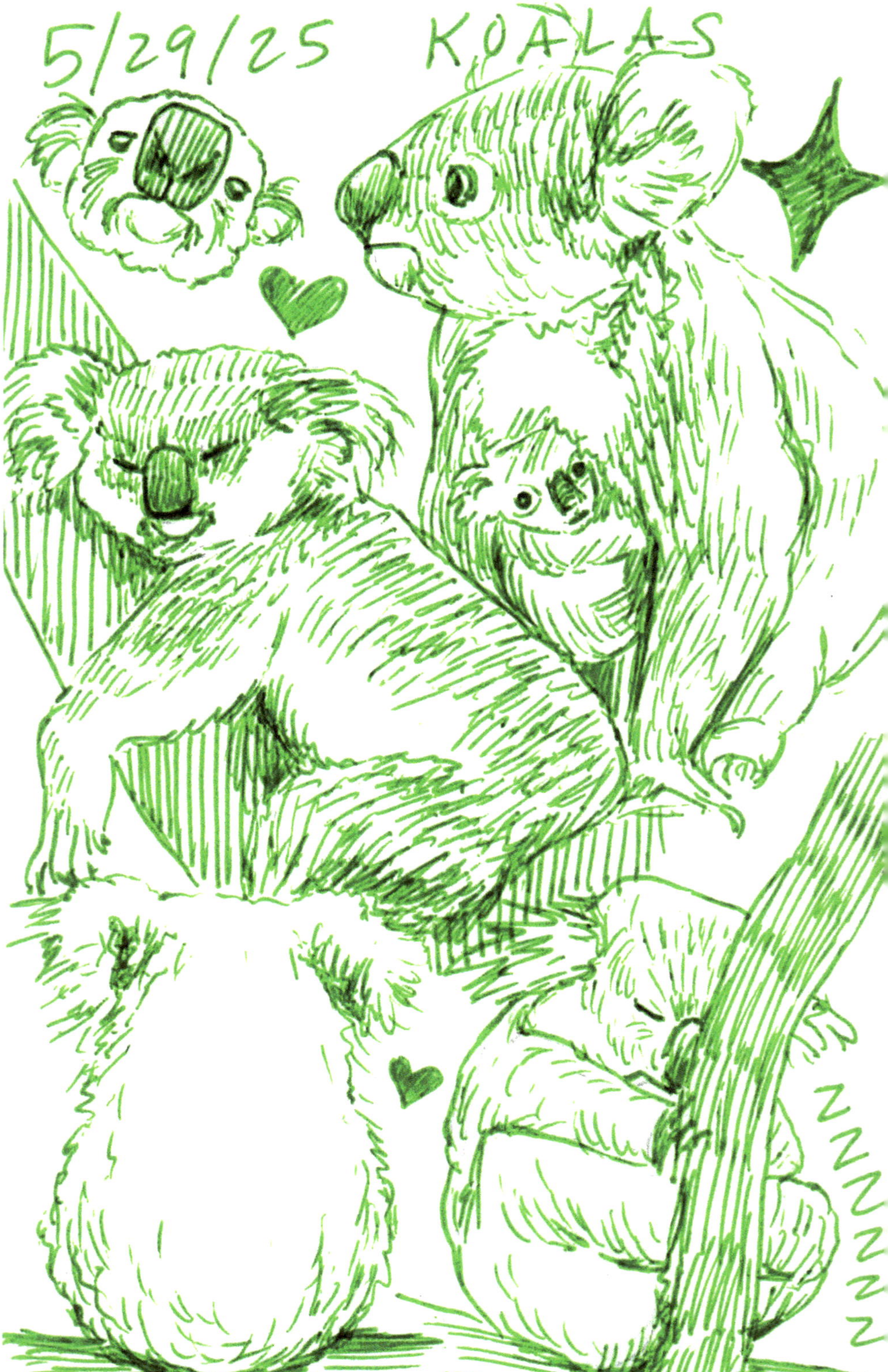
5/29/25 KOALAS

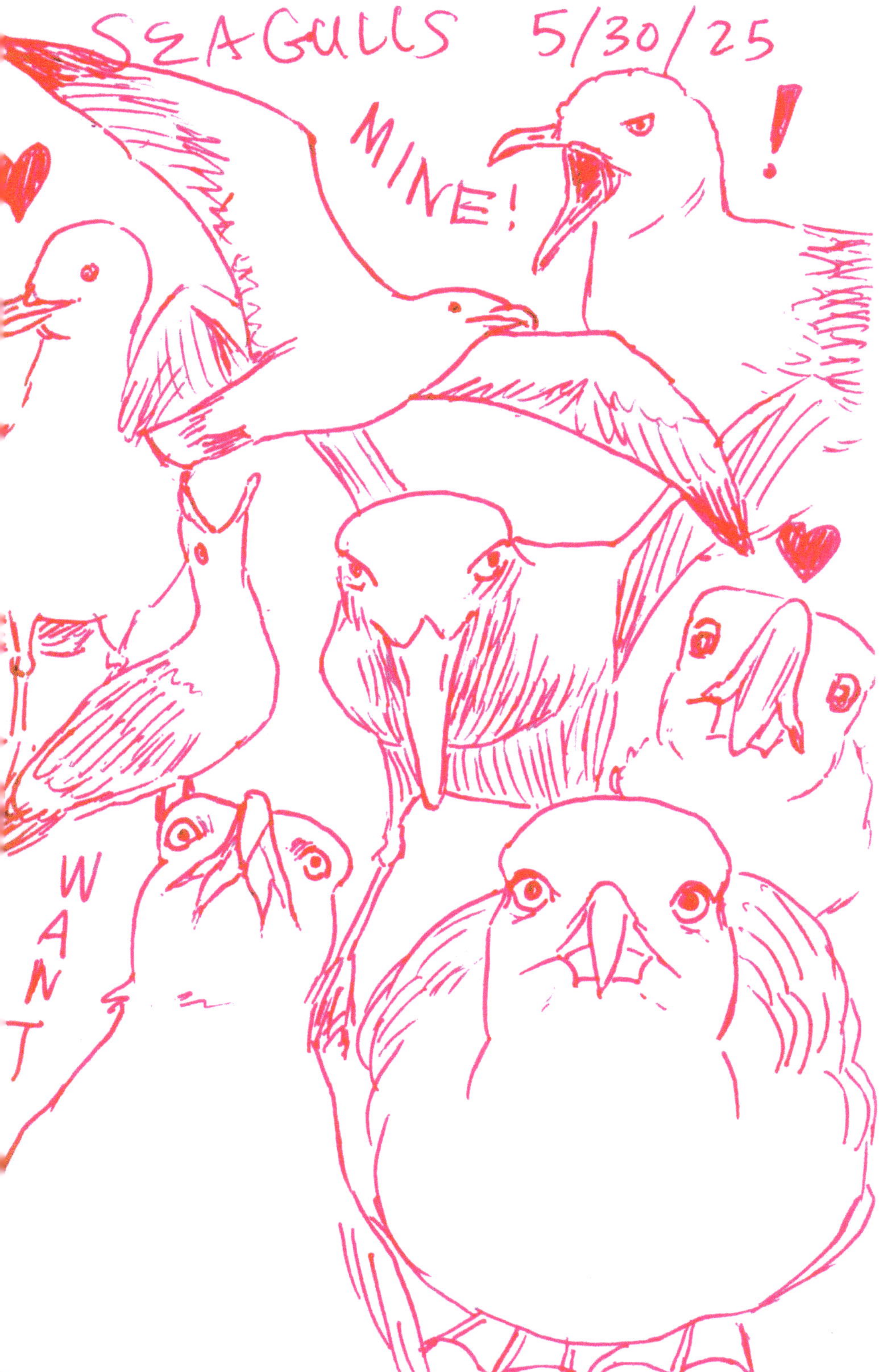
SEAGULLS 5/30/25
MINE!
!
WANT

5/31/25 BEAVERS

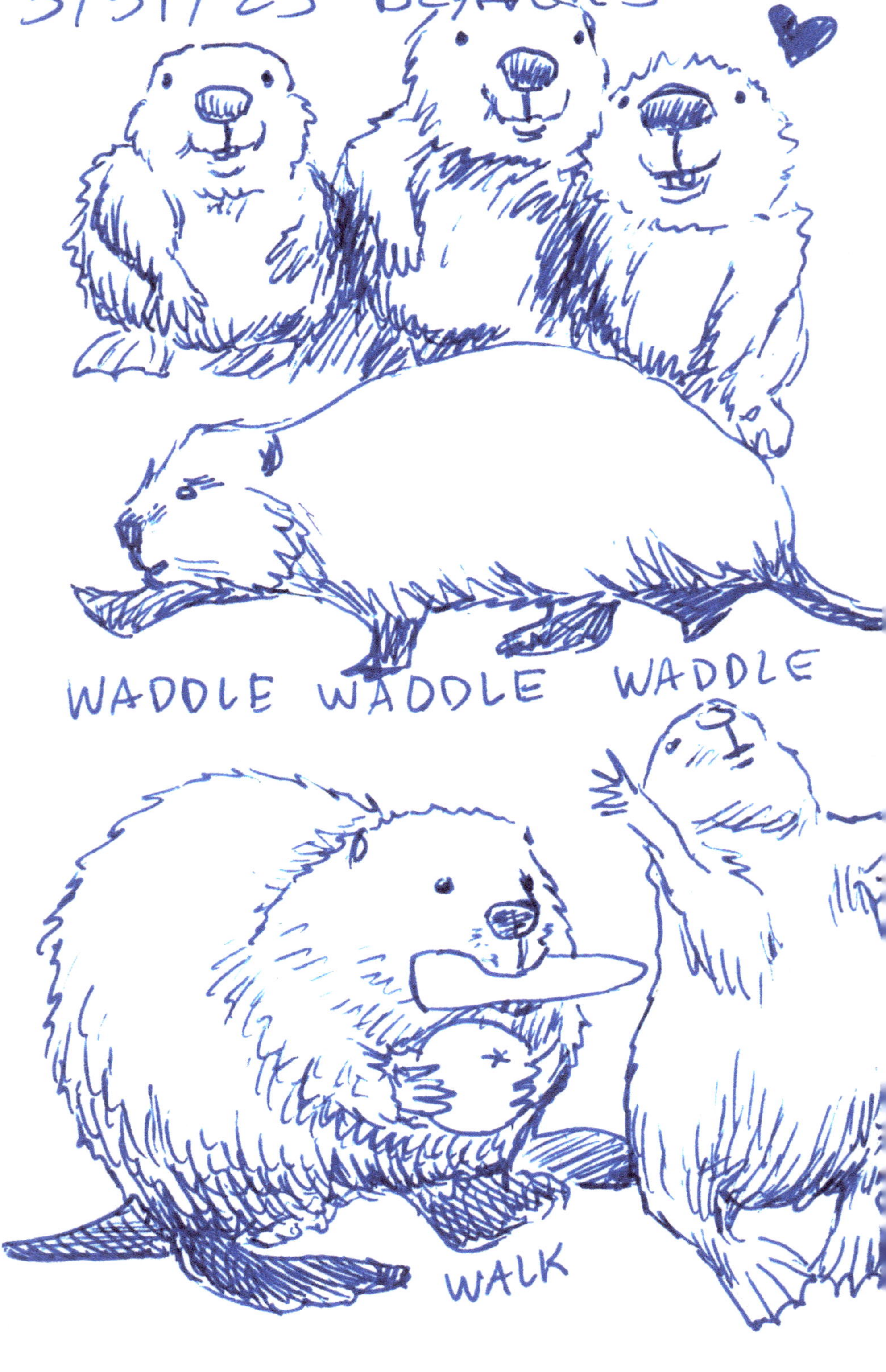

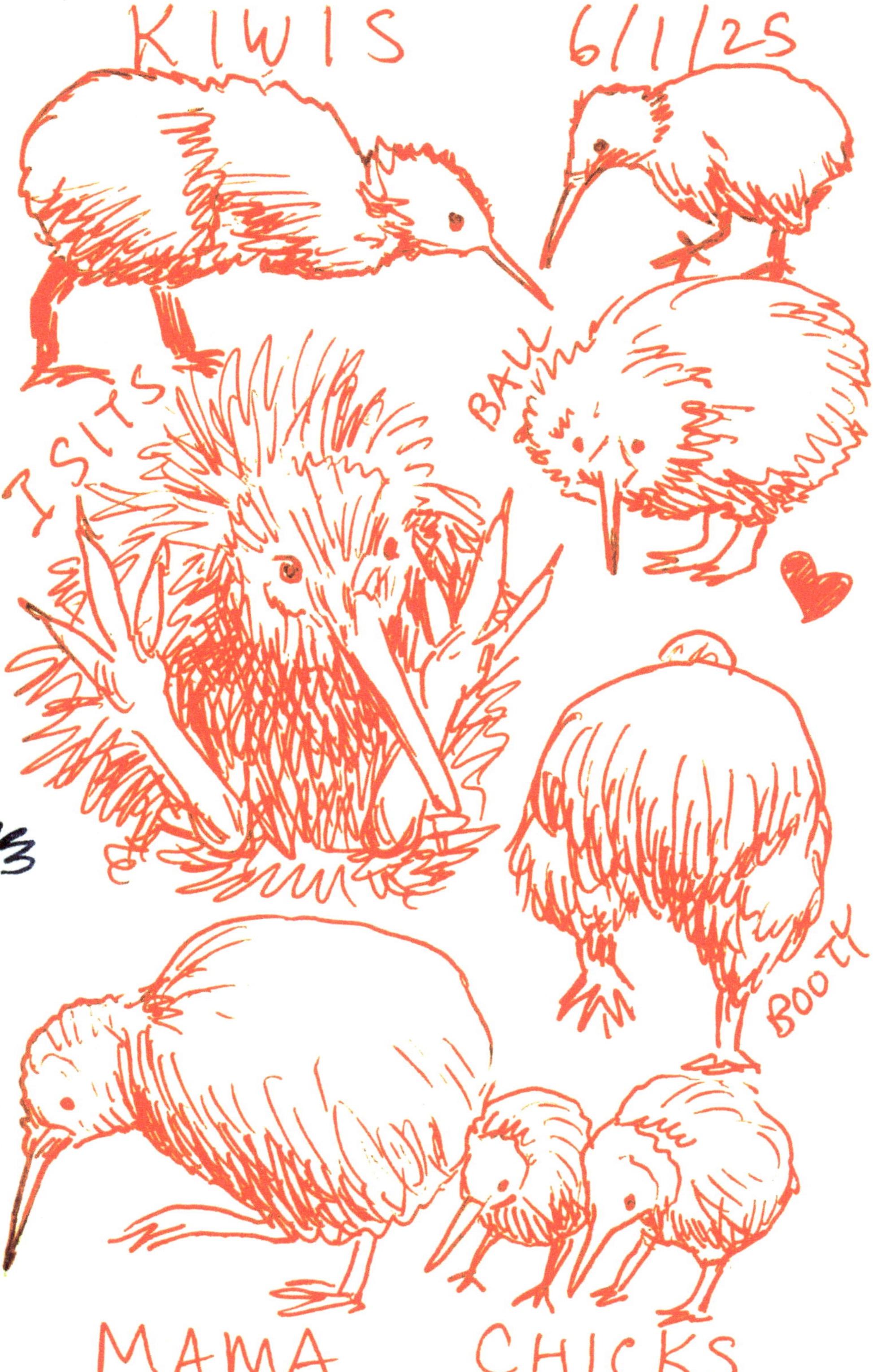
KIWIS
6/1/25
SITS
BALL
BOOTY
MAMA
CHICKS

6/2/25 EUROPEAN BADGERS

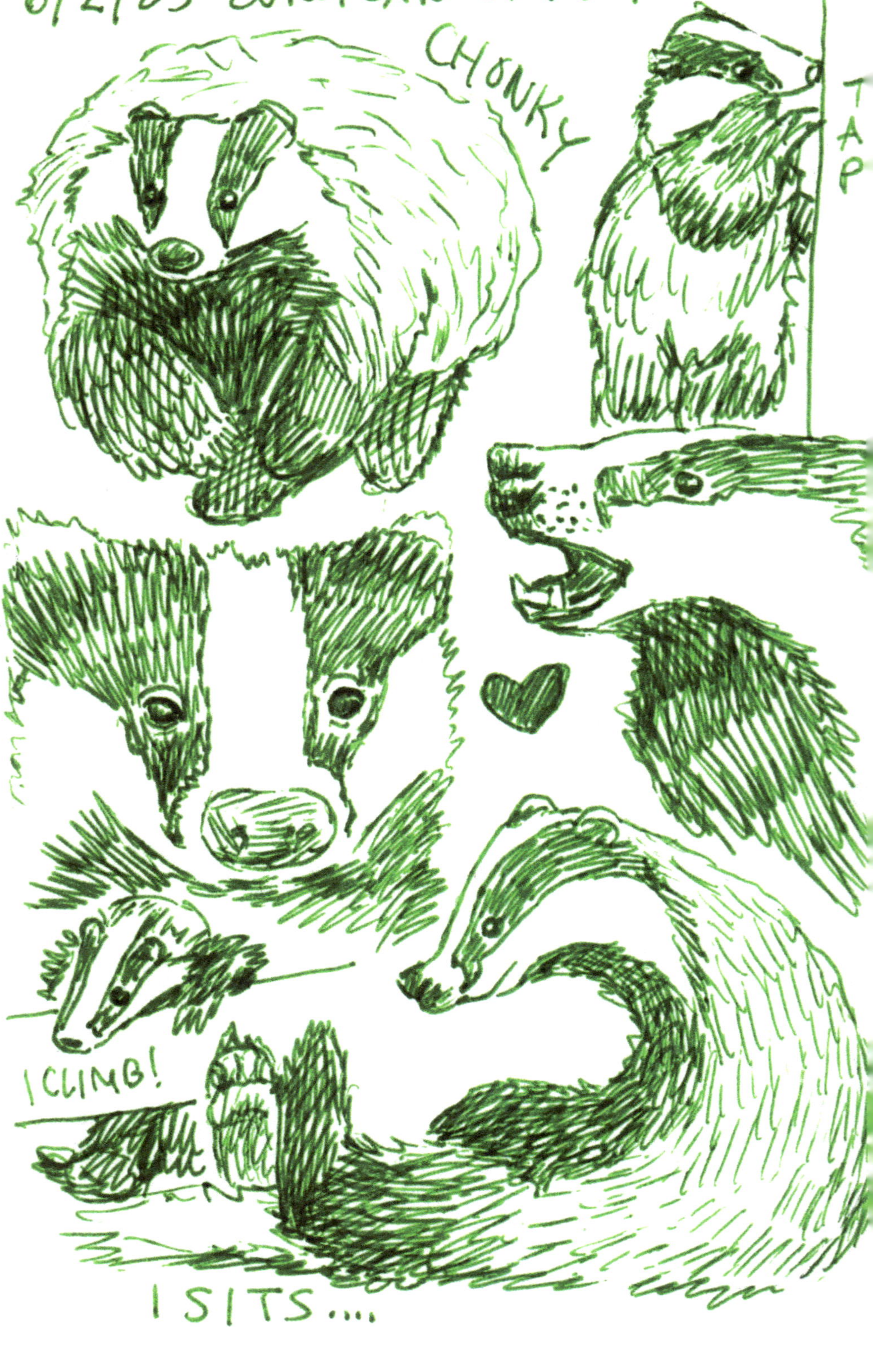

CHAMELEONS 6/3/25

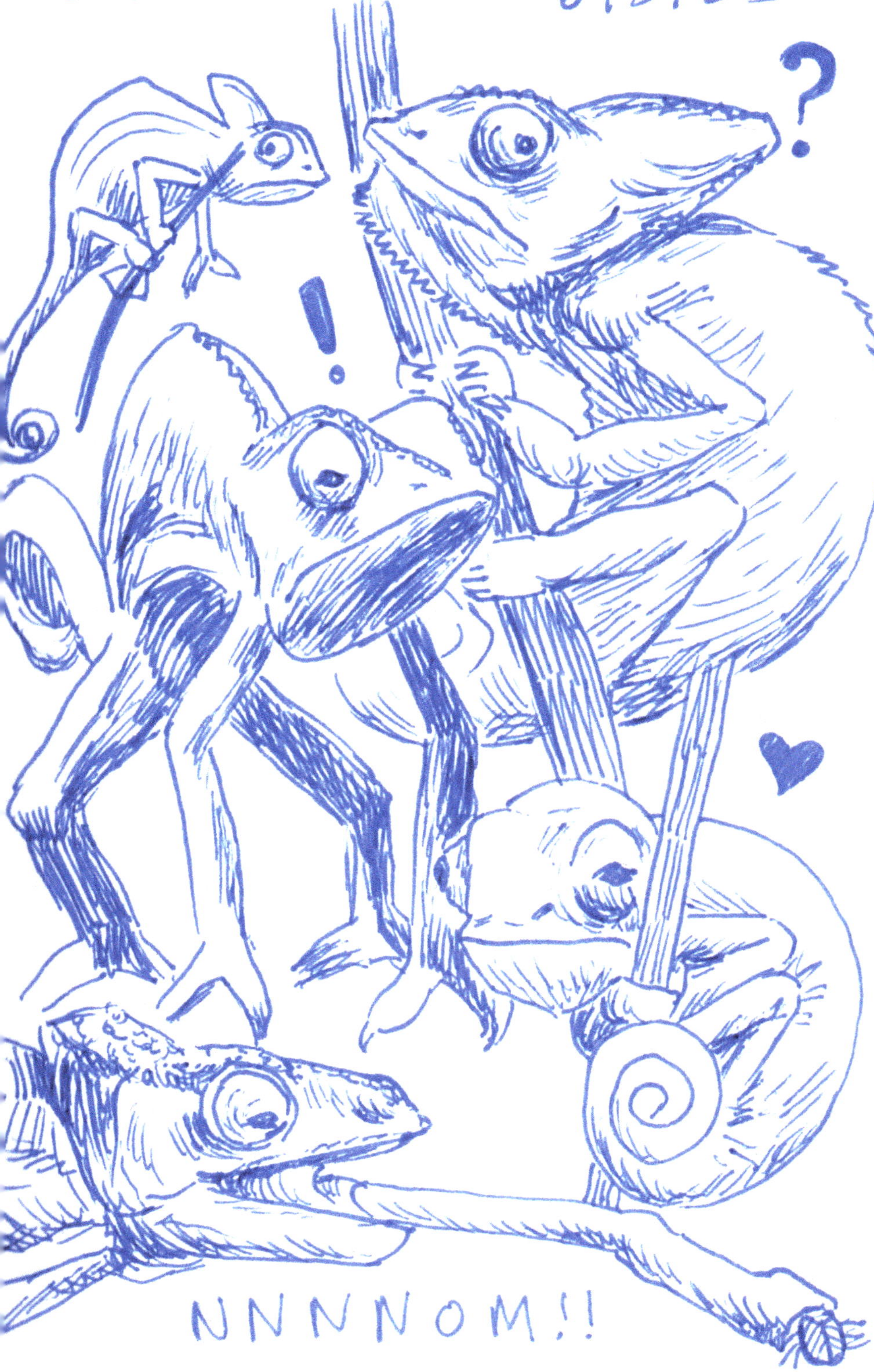

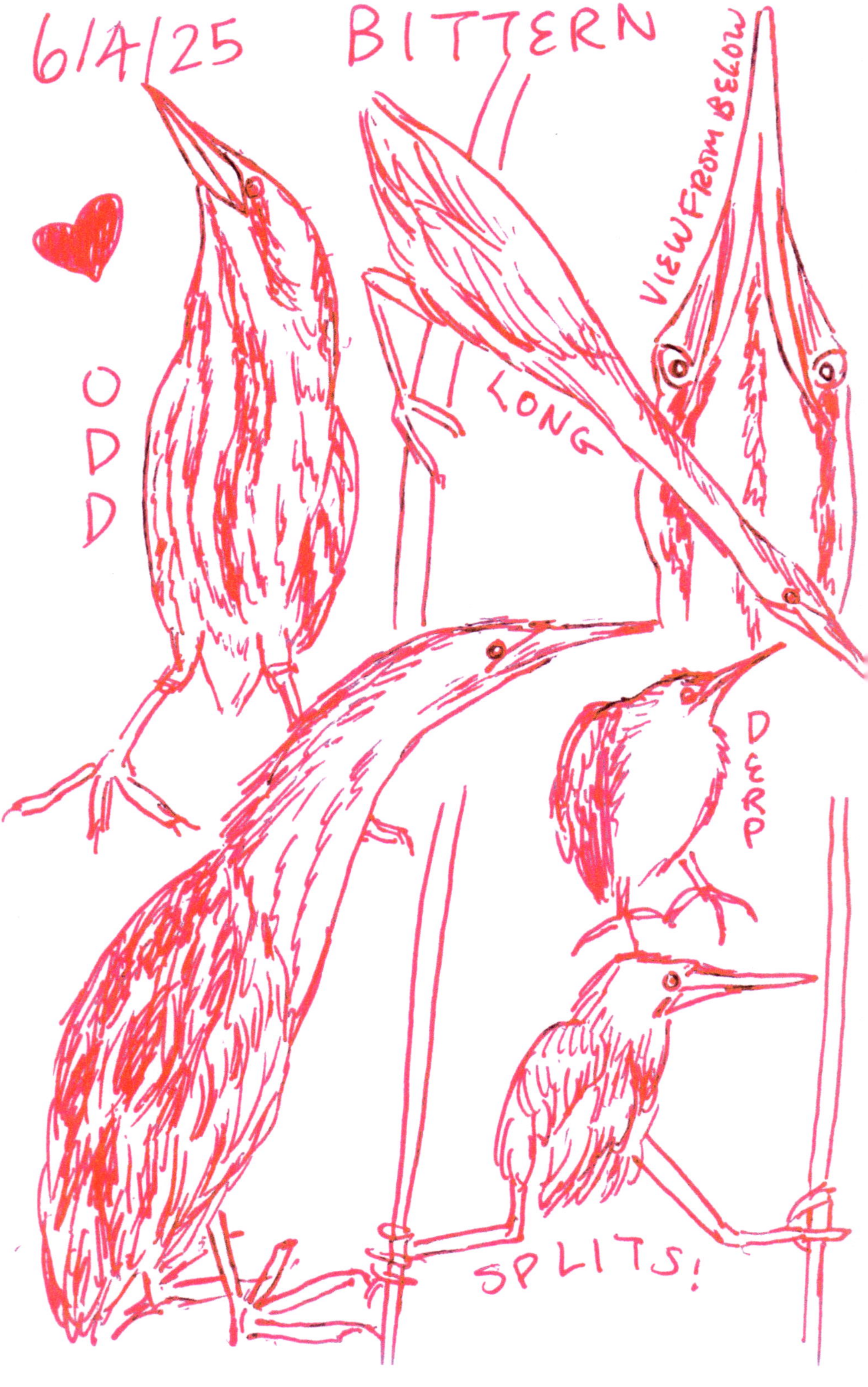
6/4/25
BITTERN
VIEW FROM BELOW
ODD
LONG
DERP
SPLITS!

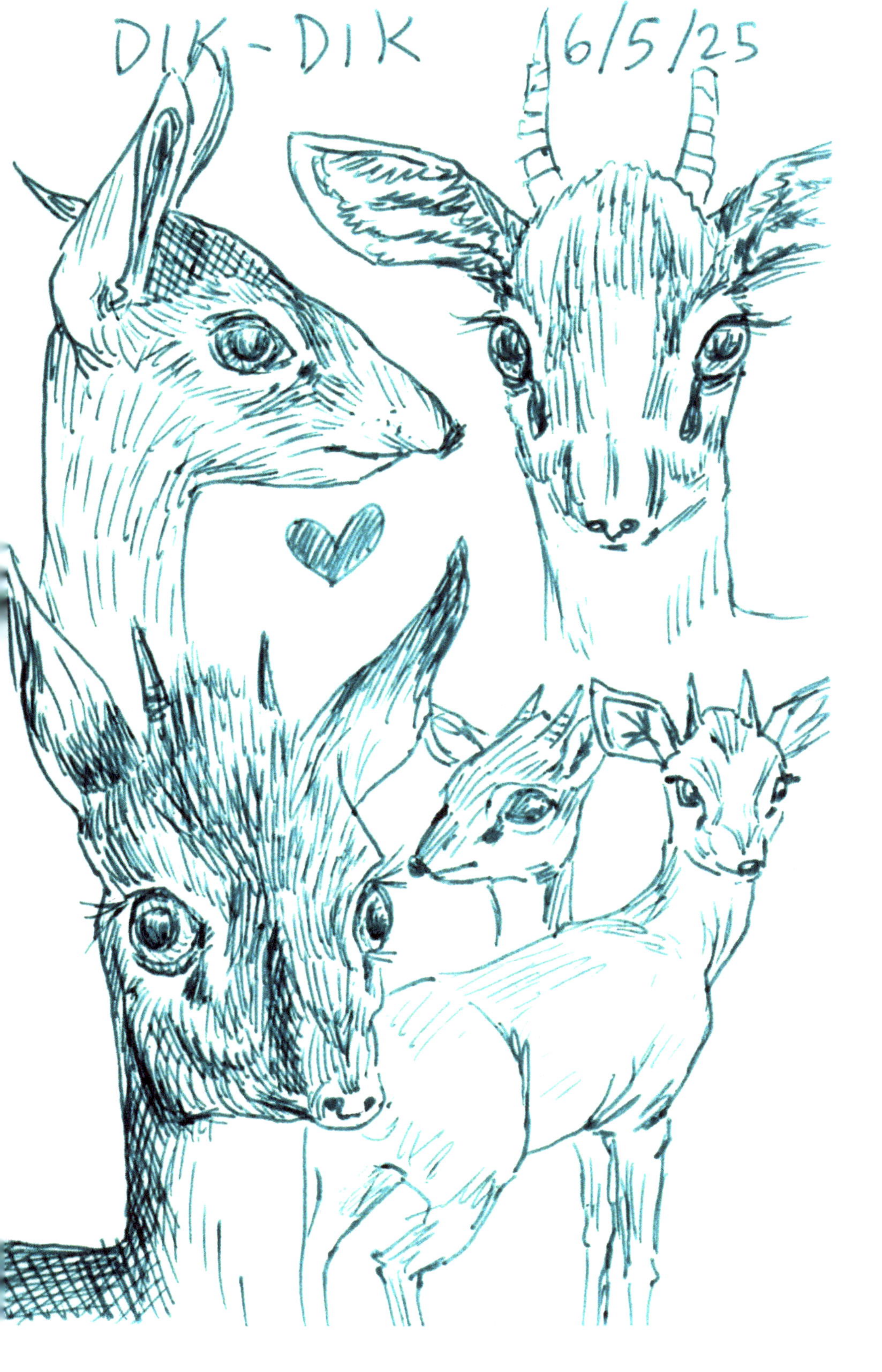
DIK-DIK
6/5/25

6/6/25 SEA TURTLES

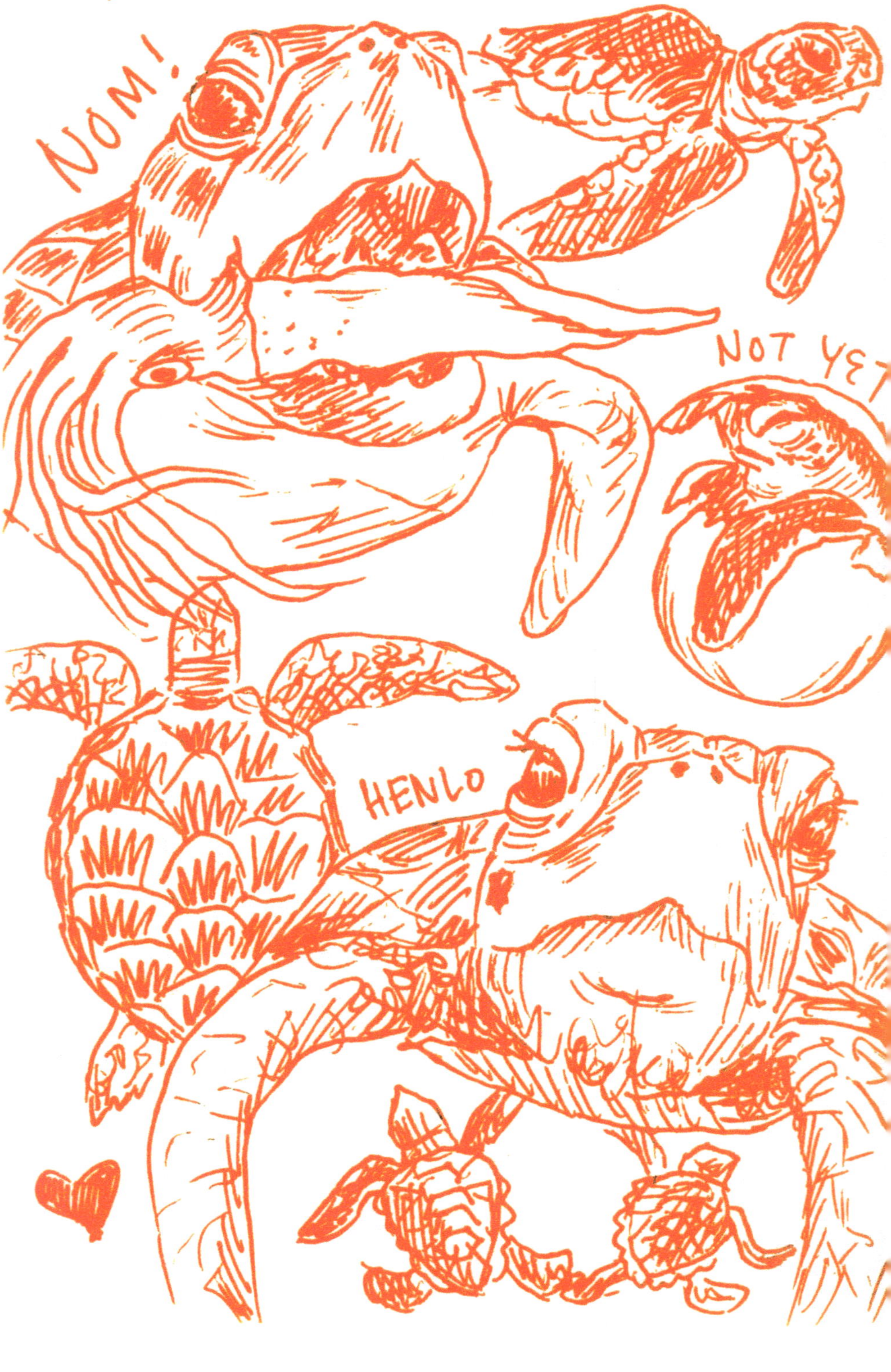

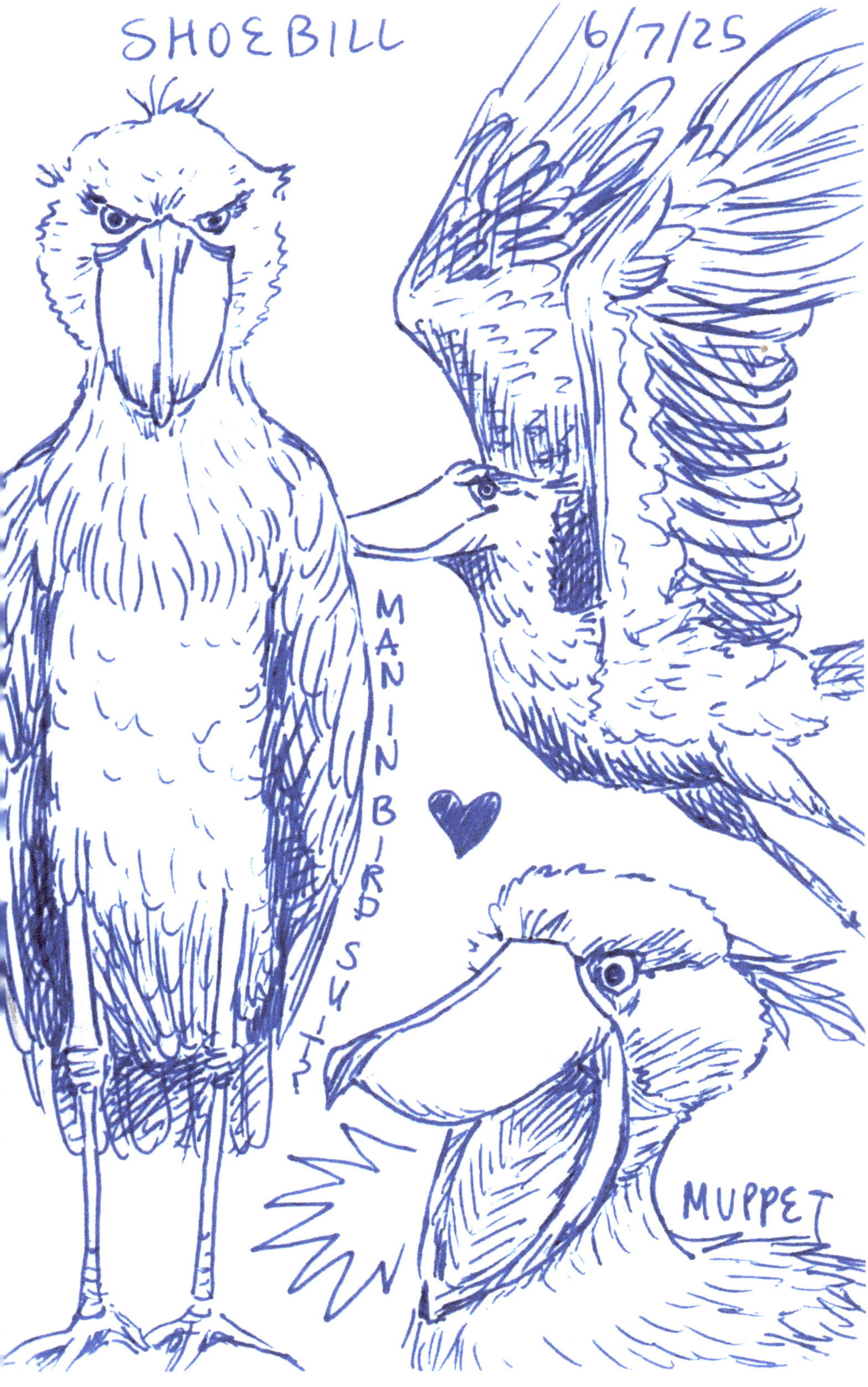
SHOEBILL
6/7/25
MANINBIRDSUIT
MUPPET

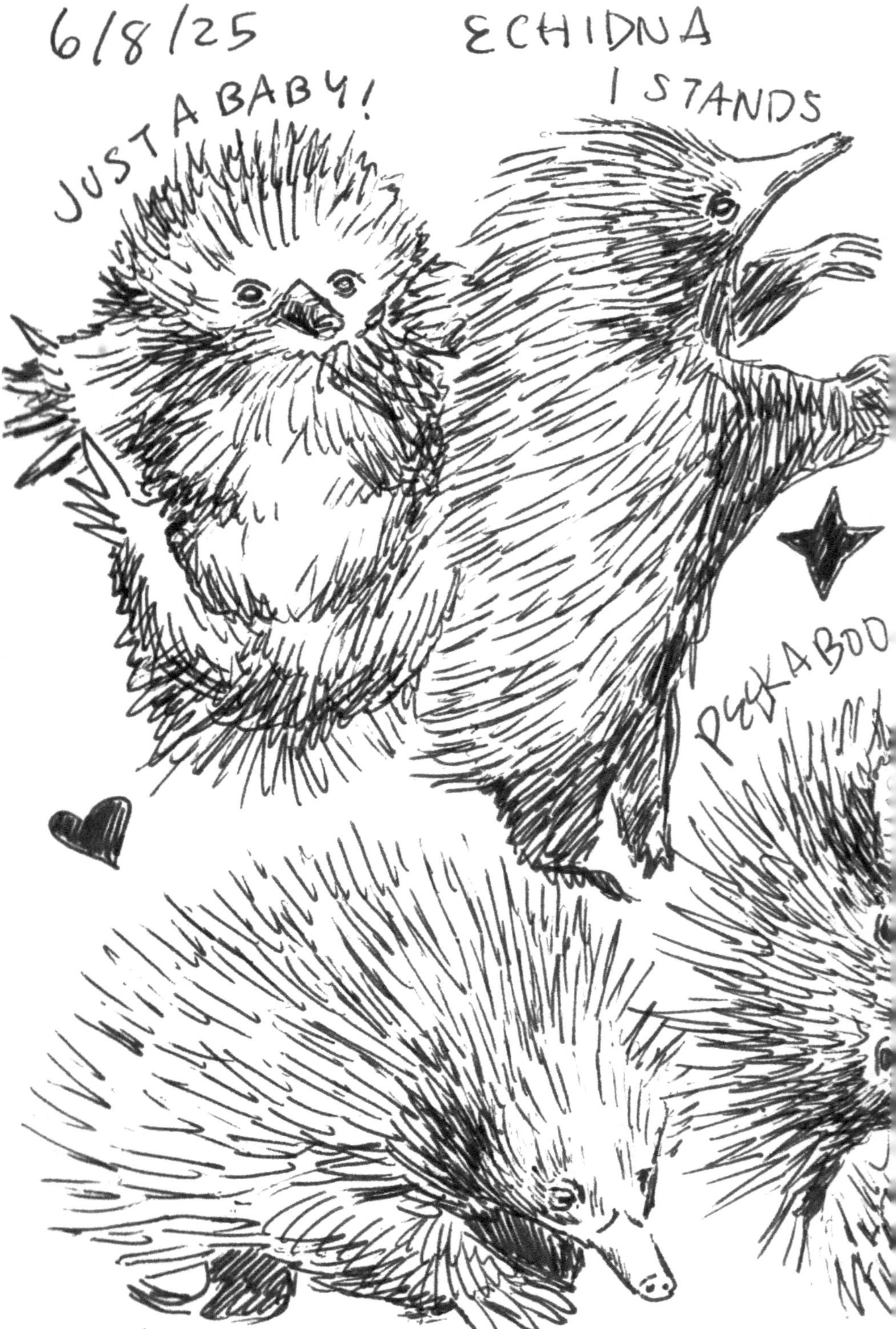

6/8/25
ECHIDNA
STANDS
JUST A BABY!
PEEKABOO
WADDLE WADDLE WADDLE

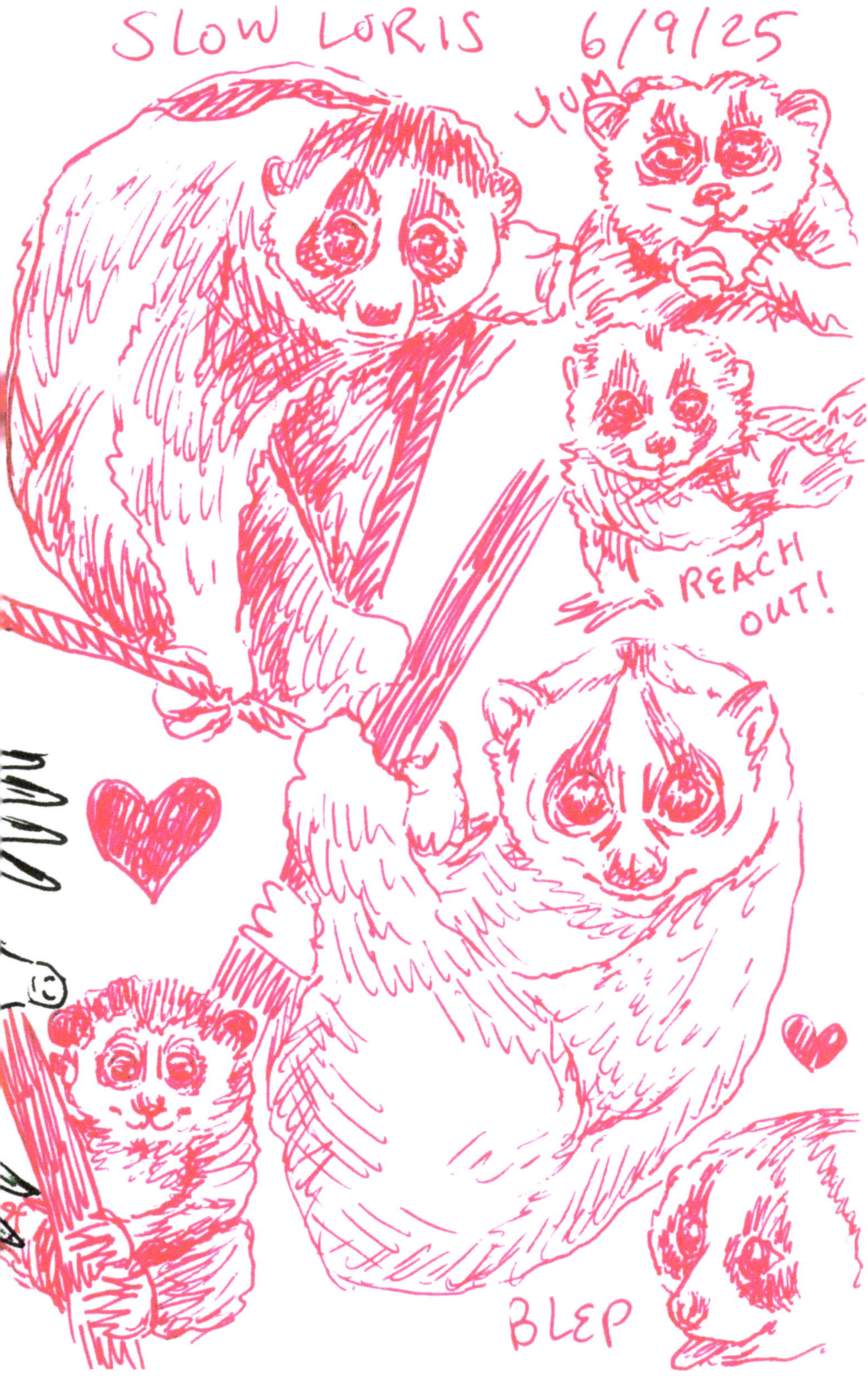

SLOW LORIS 6/9/25
REACH OUT!
BLEP

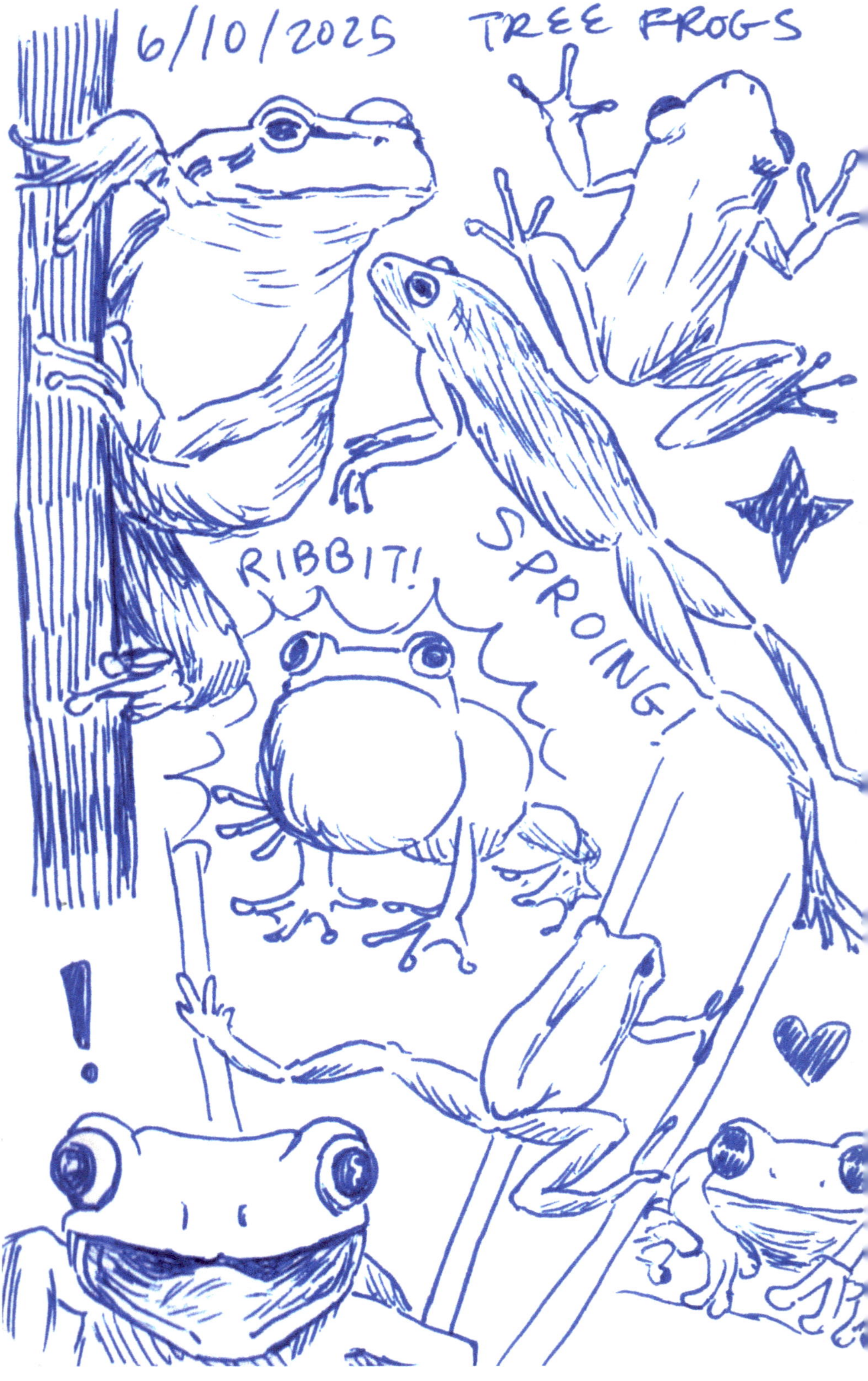
6/10/2025
TREE FROGS
RIBBIT!
SPROING!
!

CHICKENS 6/11/2025

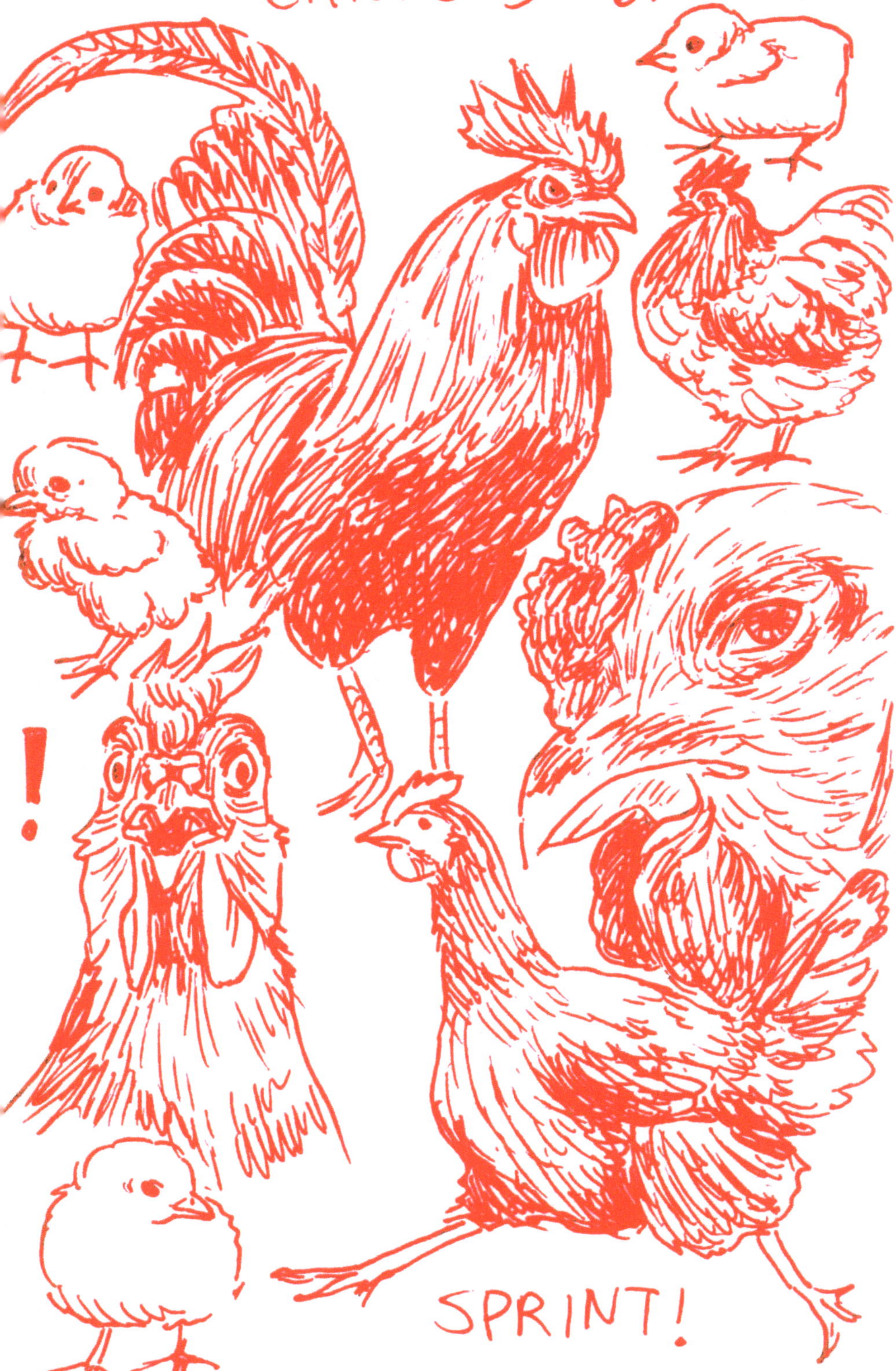

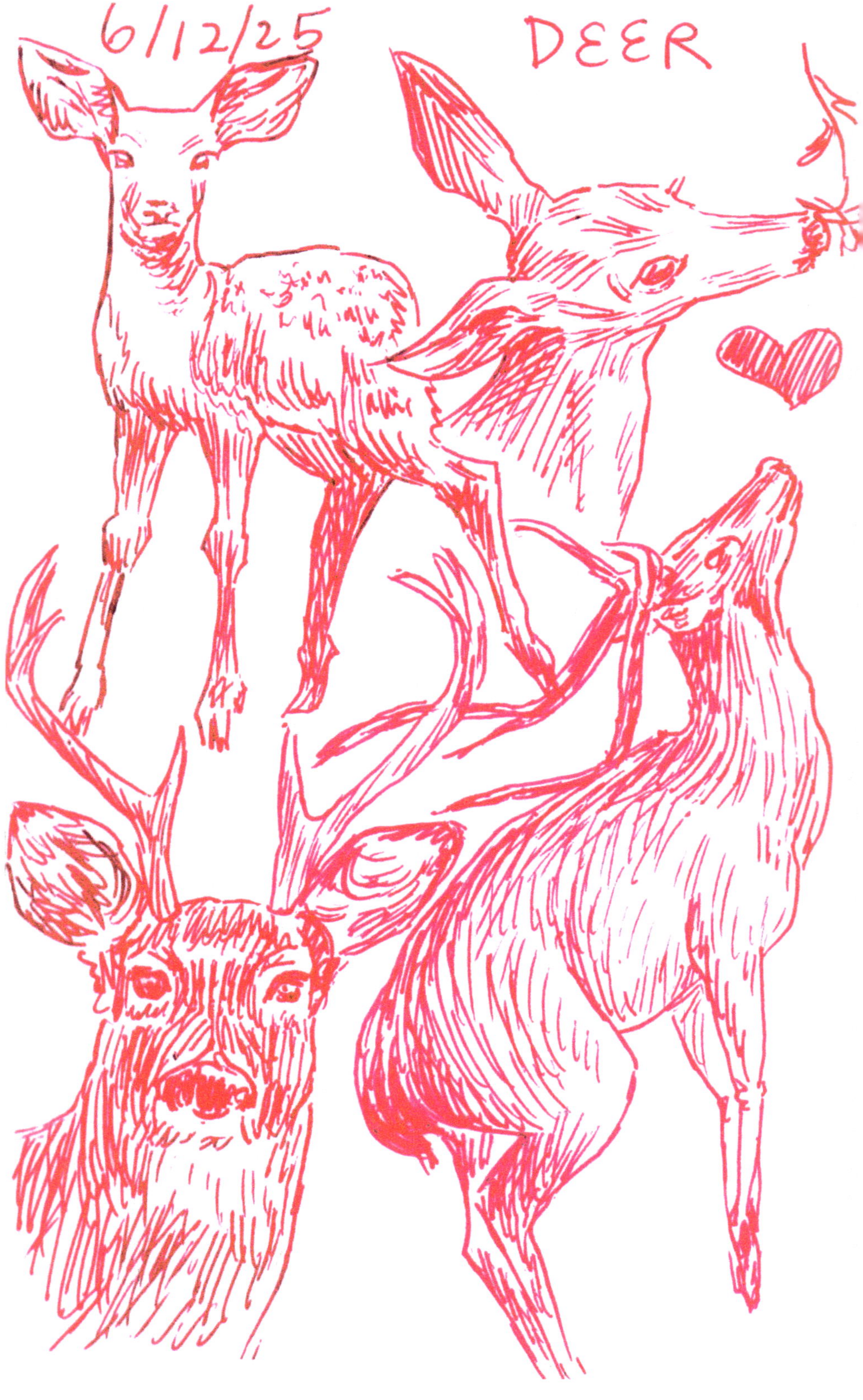
6/12/25
DEER

OTTERS 6/13/25

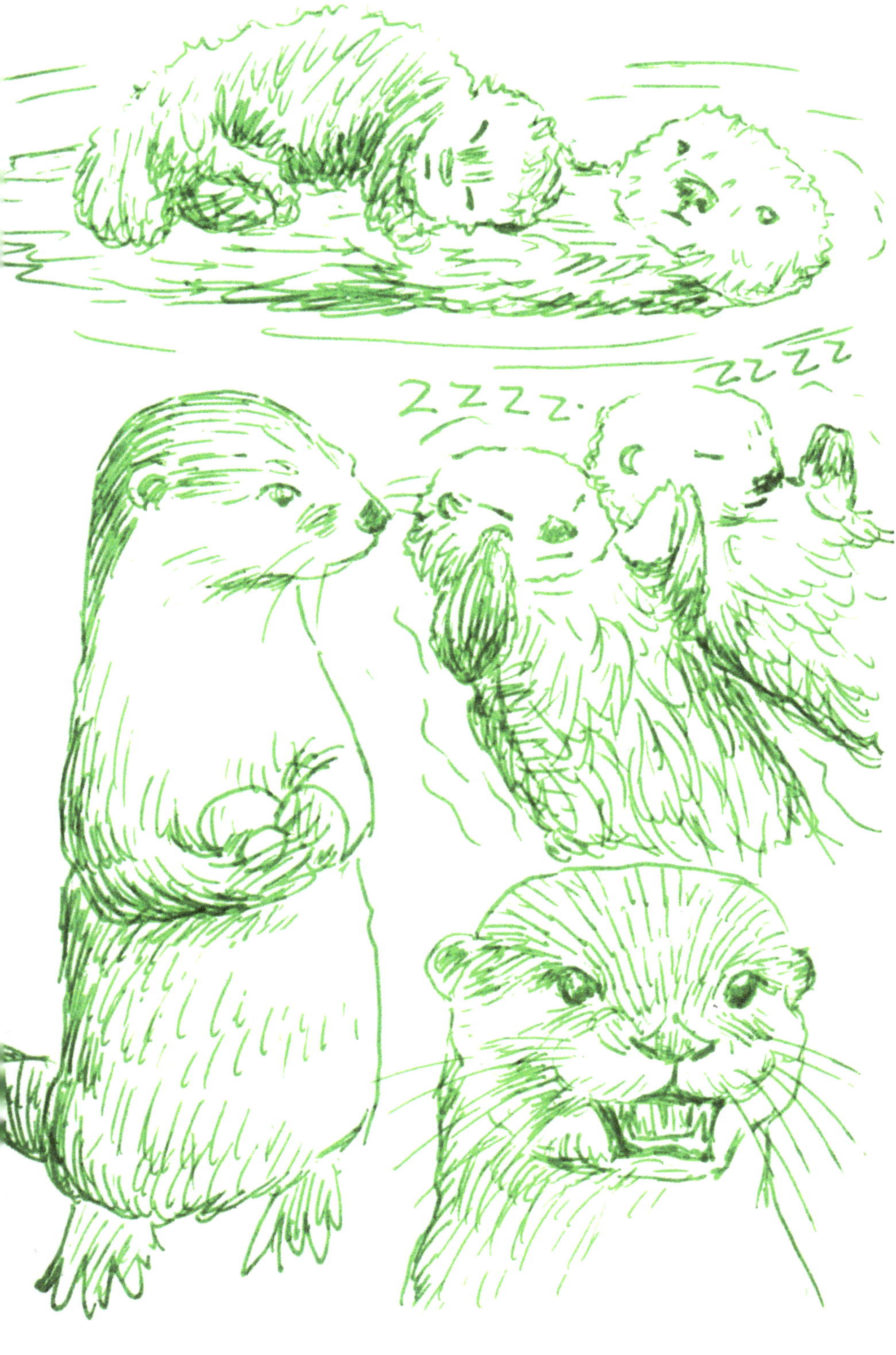

6/14/25 Canada Goose

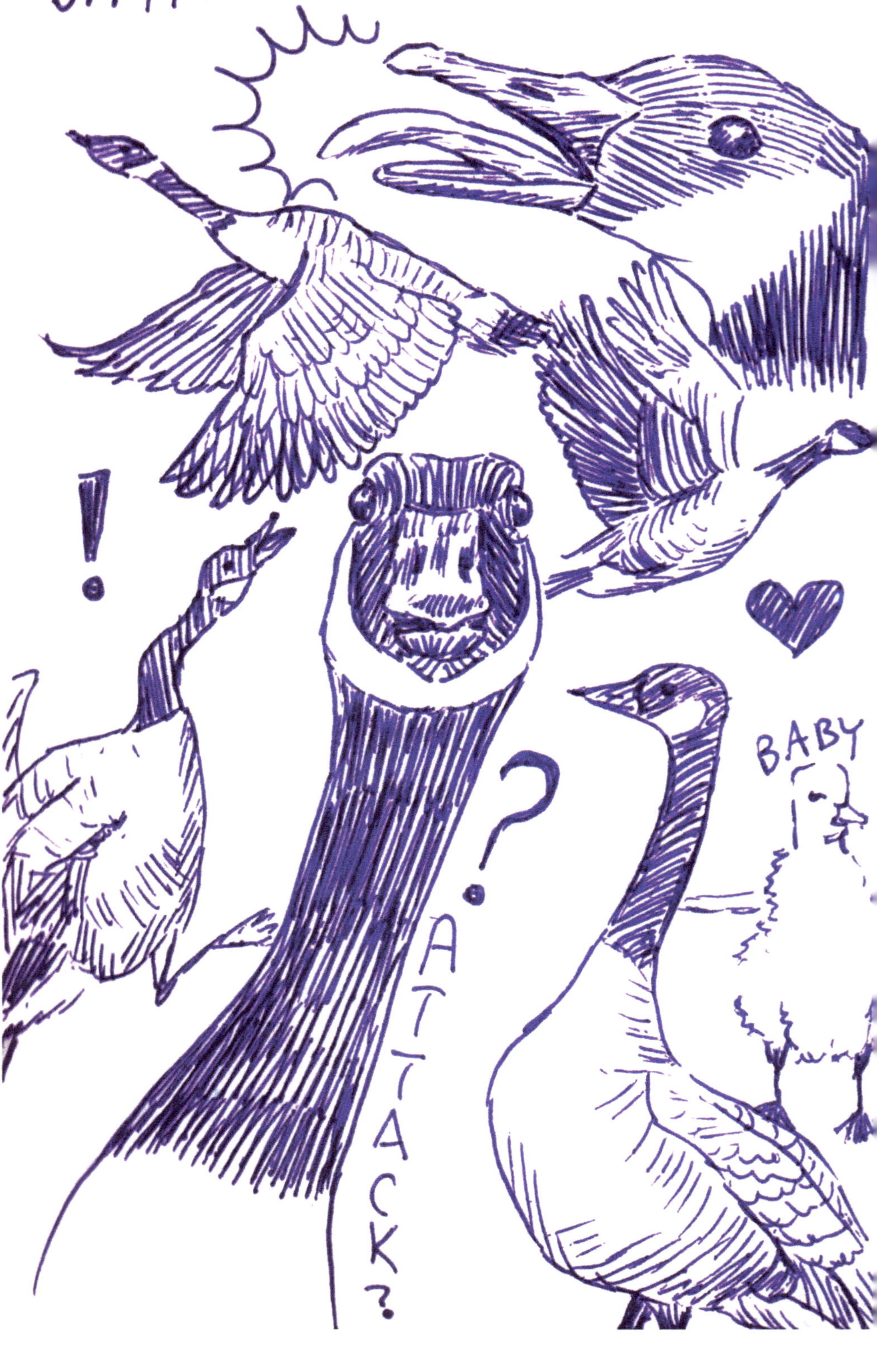

BOTTLENOSE DOLPHIN 6/15/25

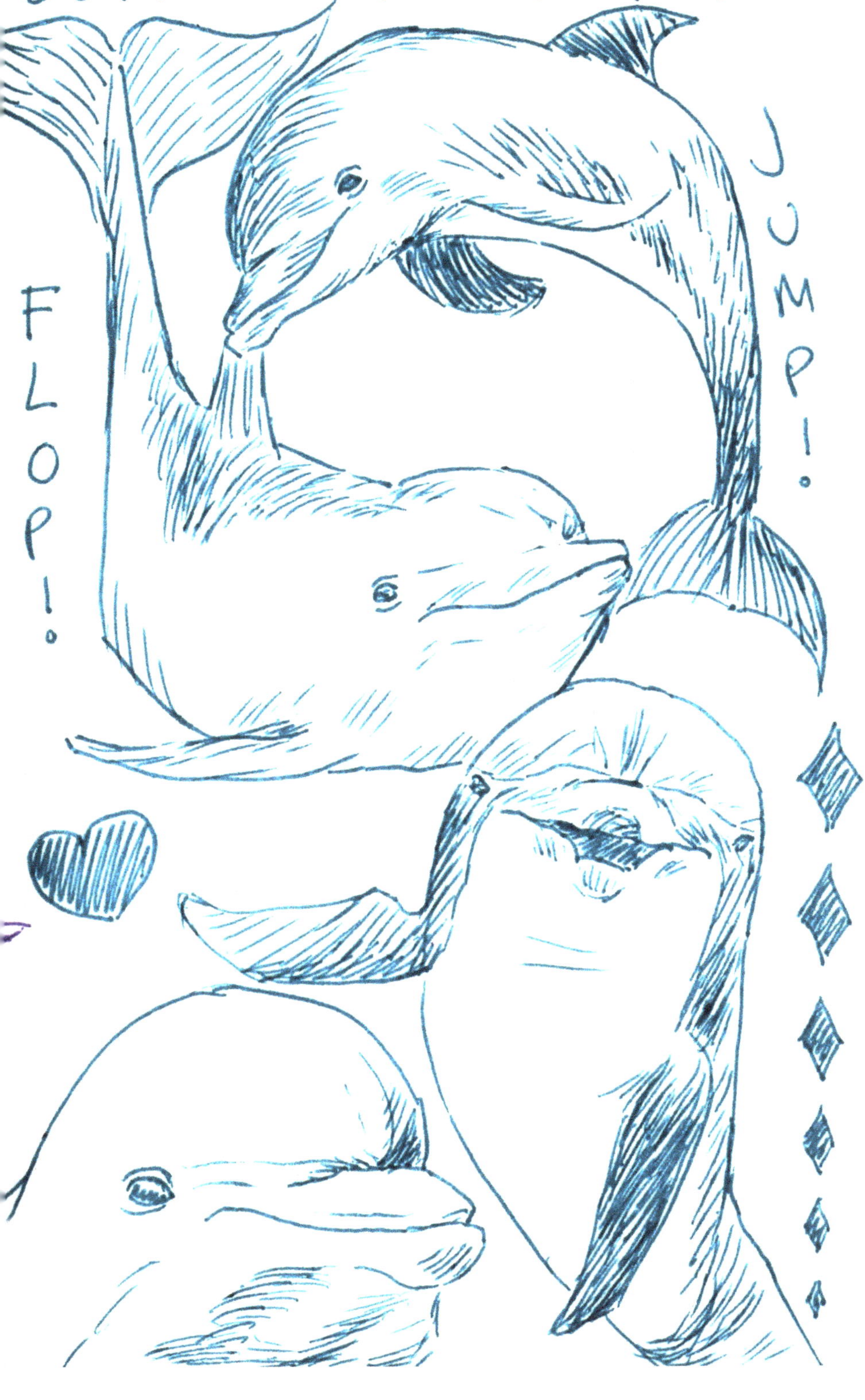

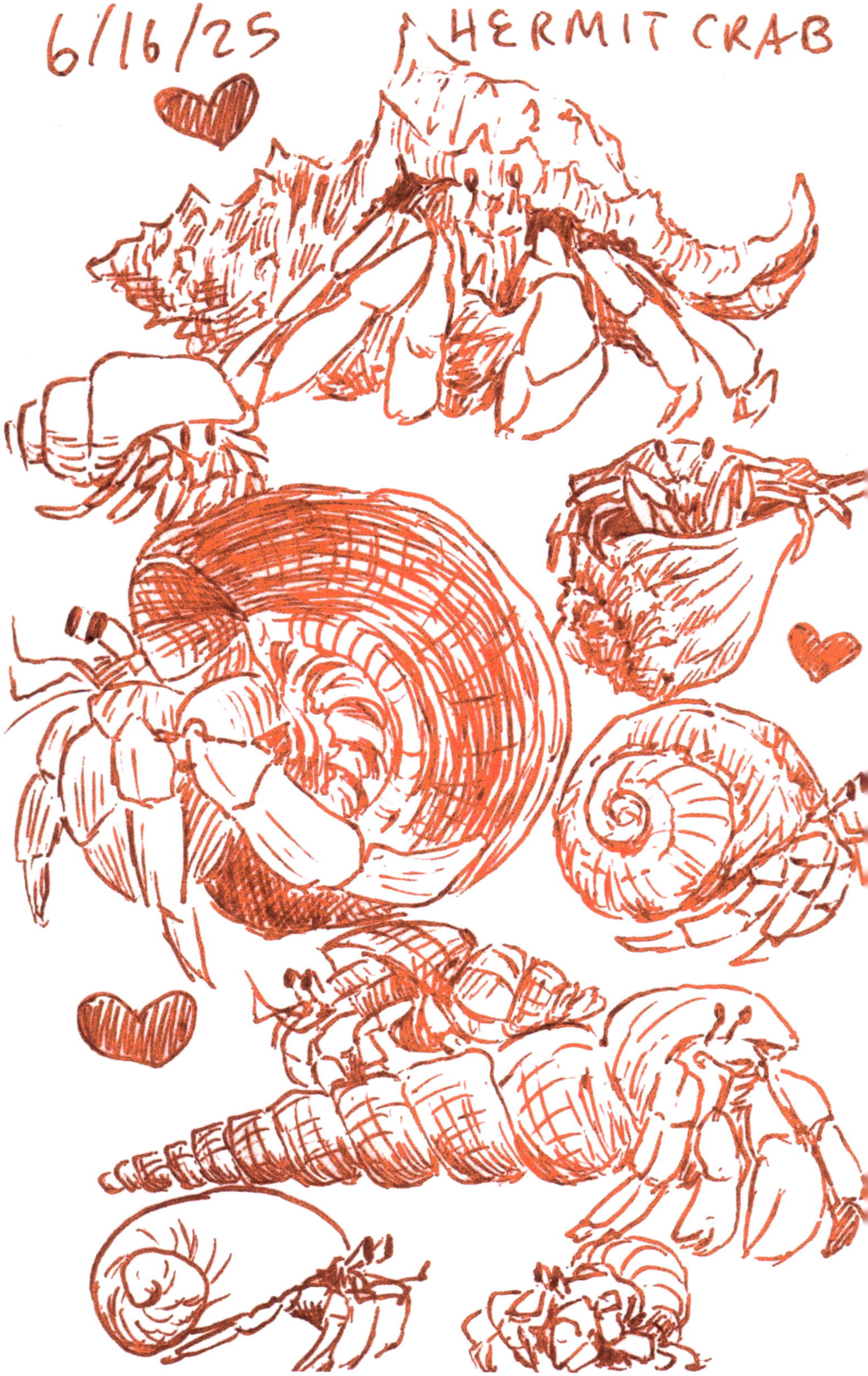
6/16/25
HERMIT CRAB

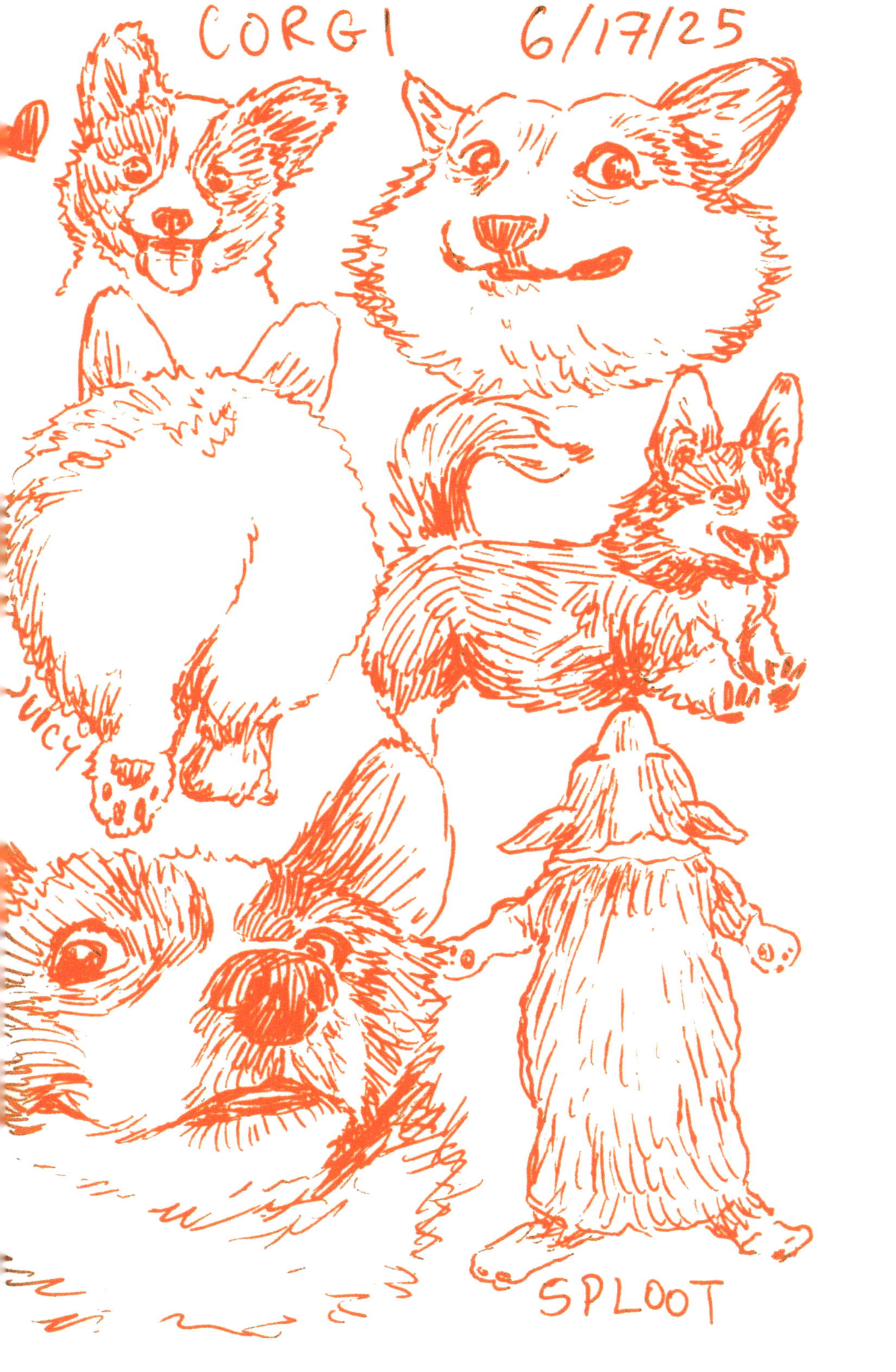
CORGI
6/17/25
JUICY
SPLOOT

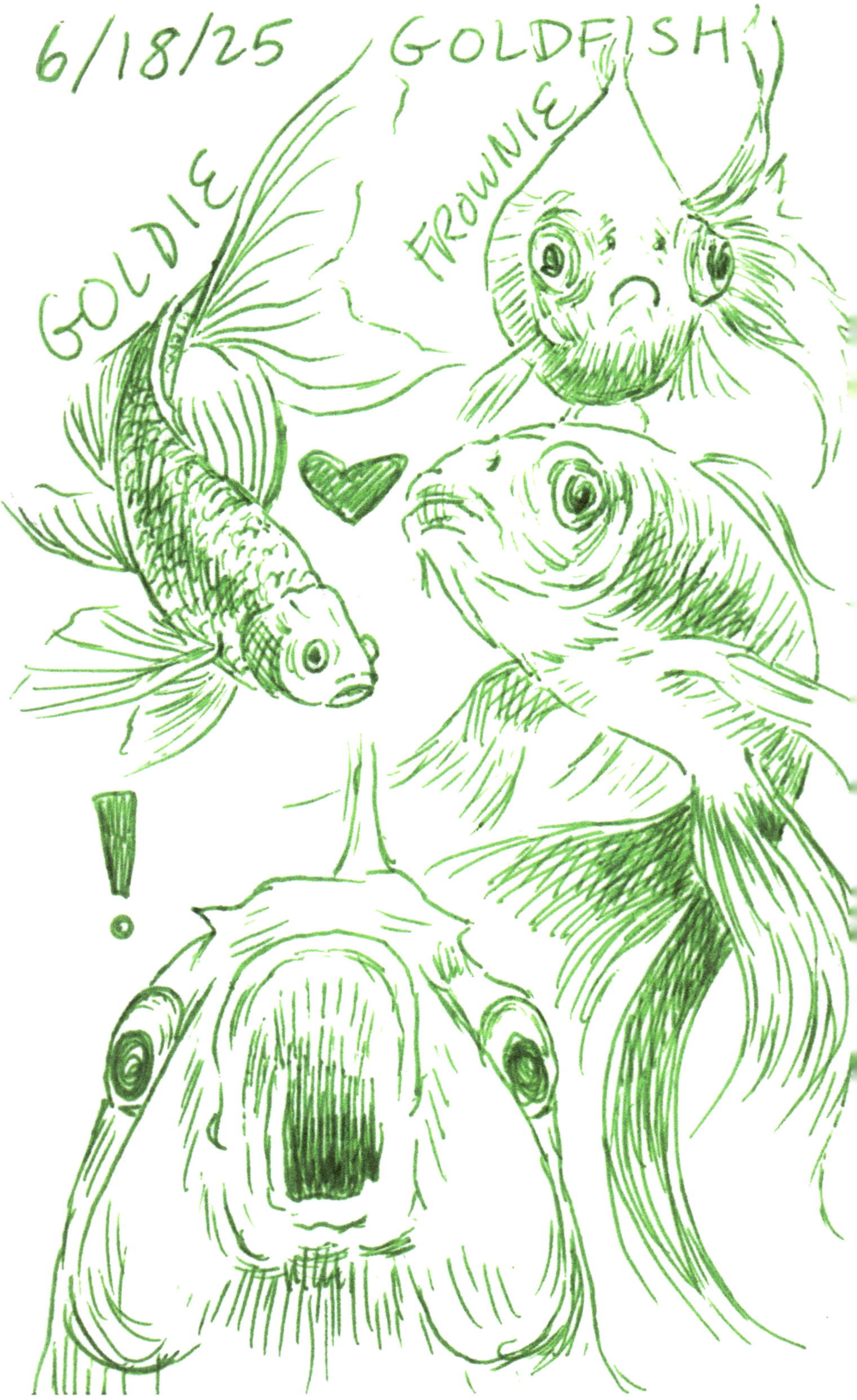
6/18/25 GOLDFISH
GOLDIE
FROWNIE
!

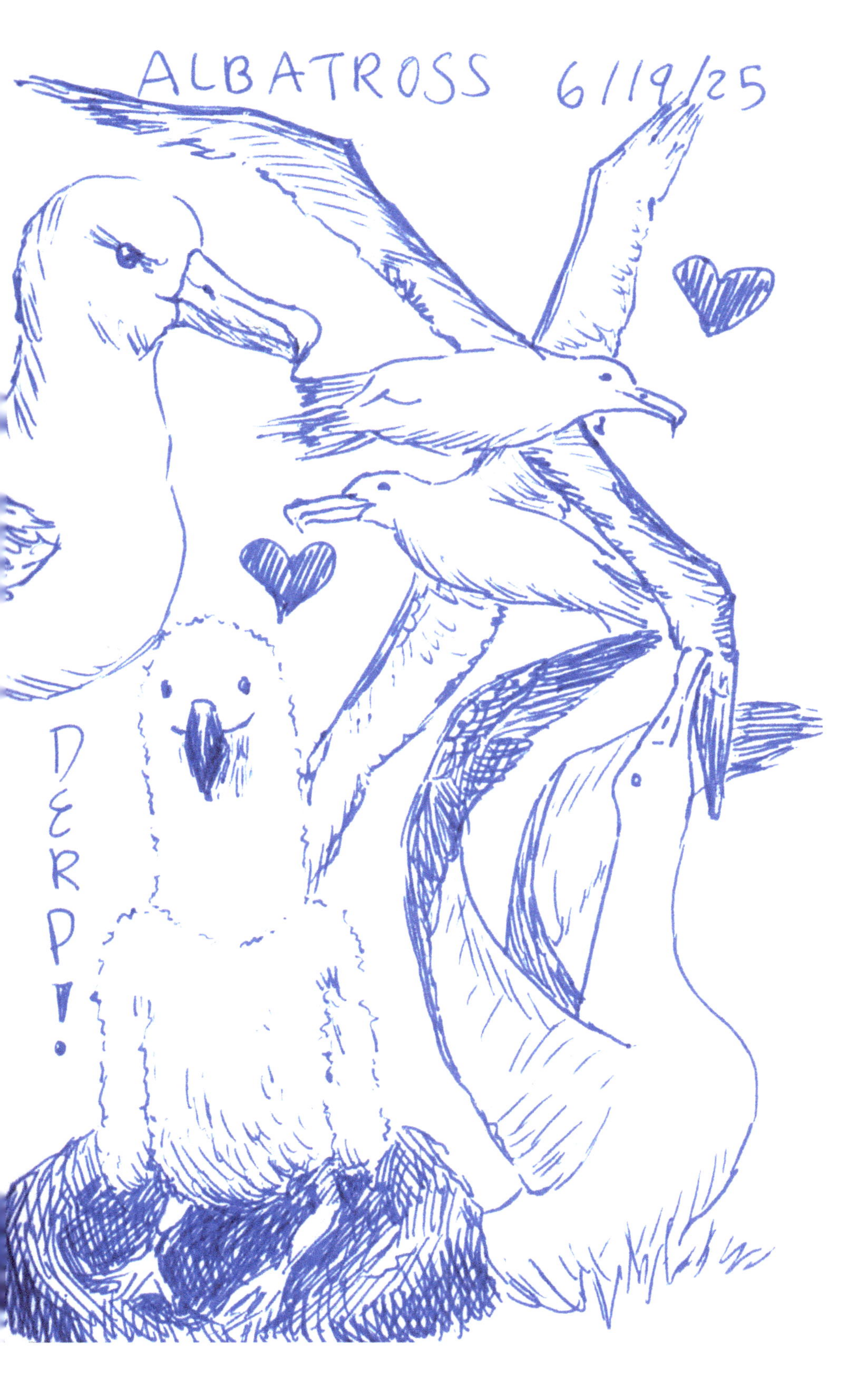
ALBATROSS 6/19/25
DERP!

6/20/25 GIANT PANDA

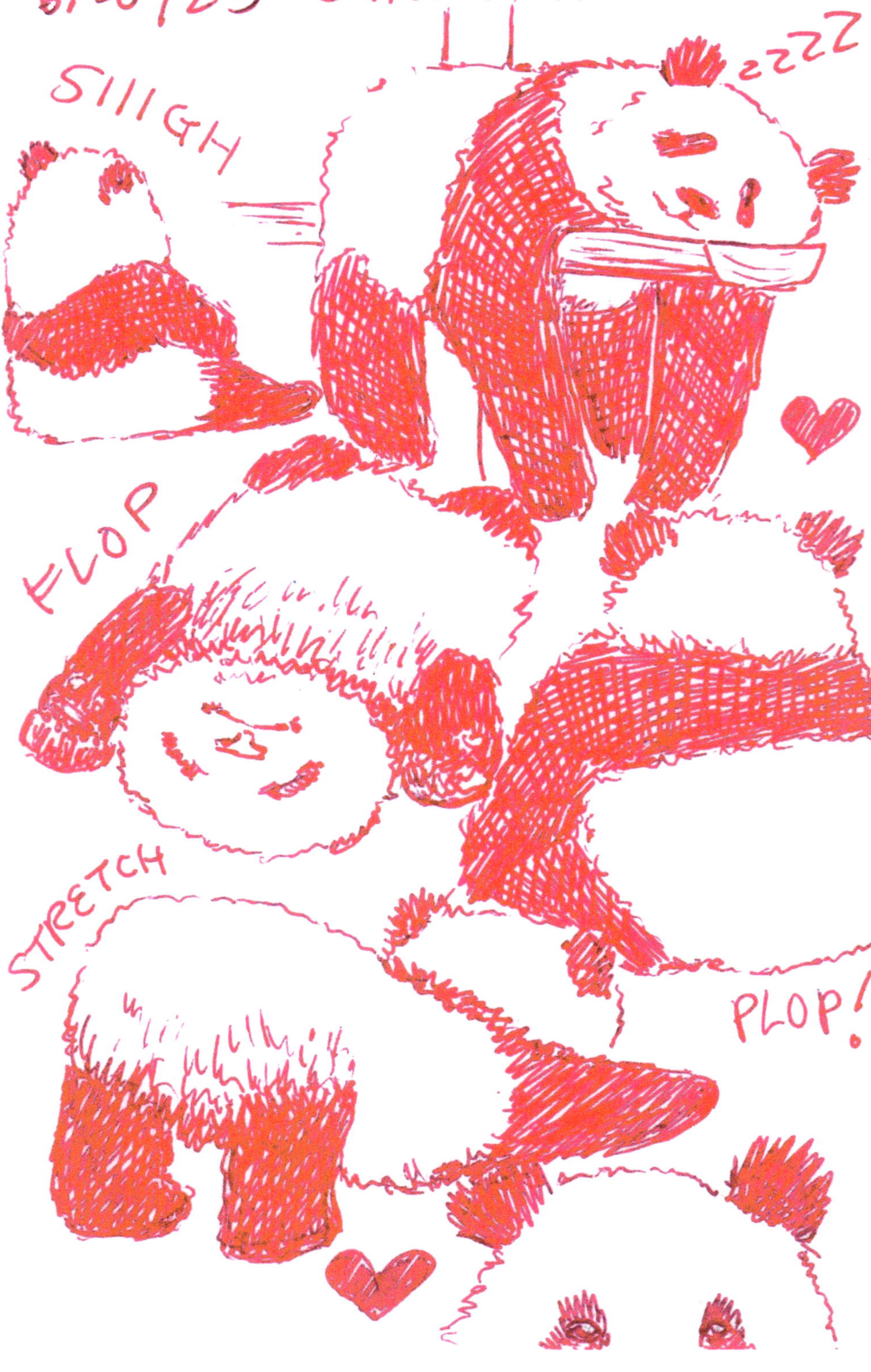

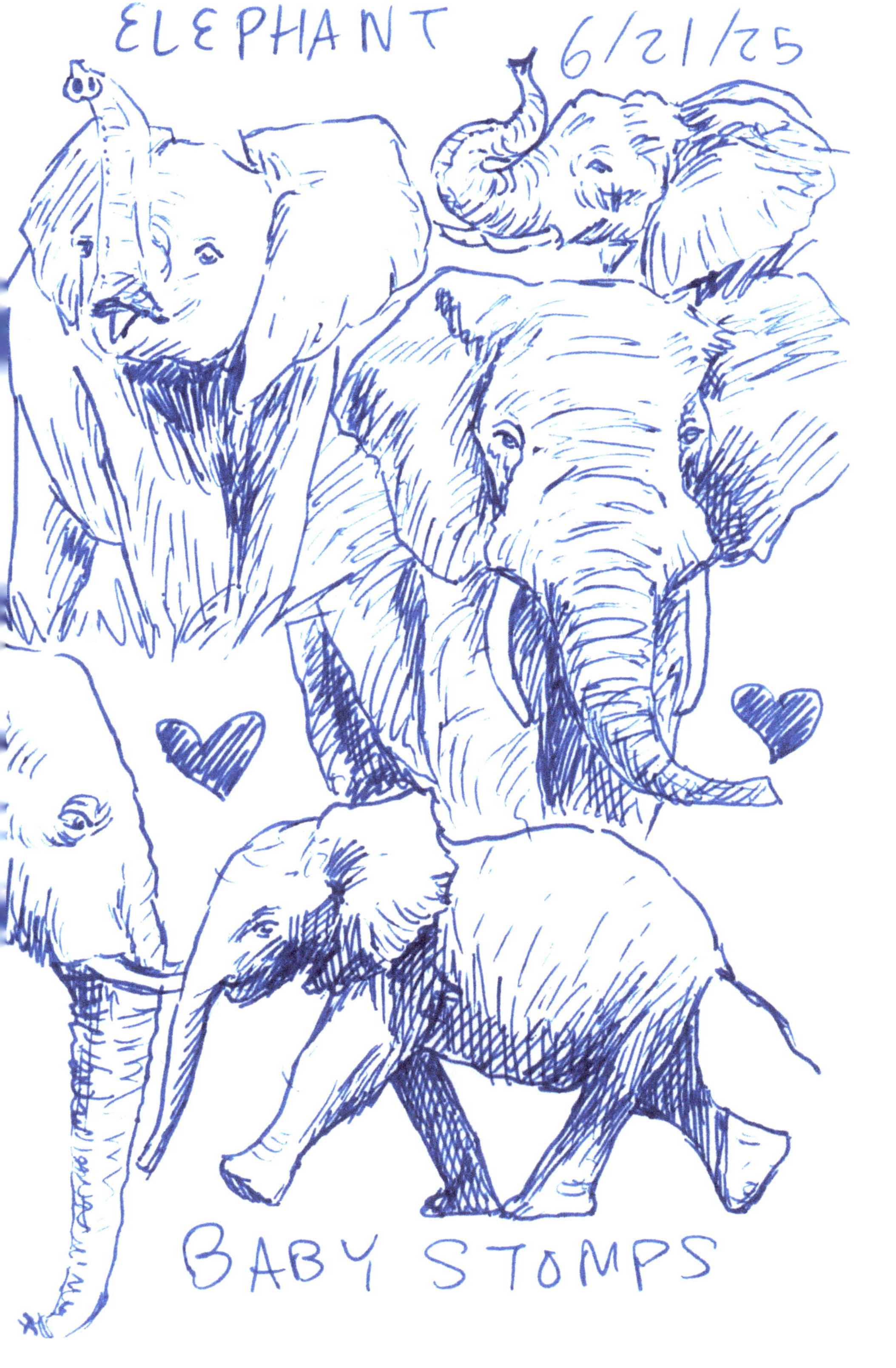
ELEPHANT
6/21/25
BABY STOMPS

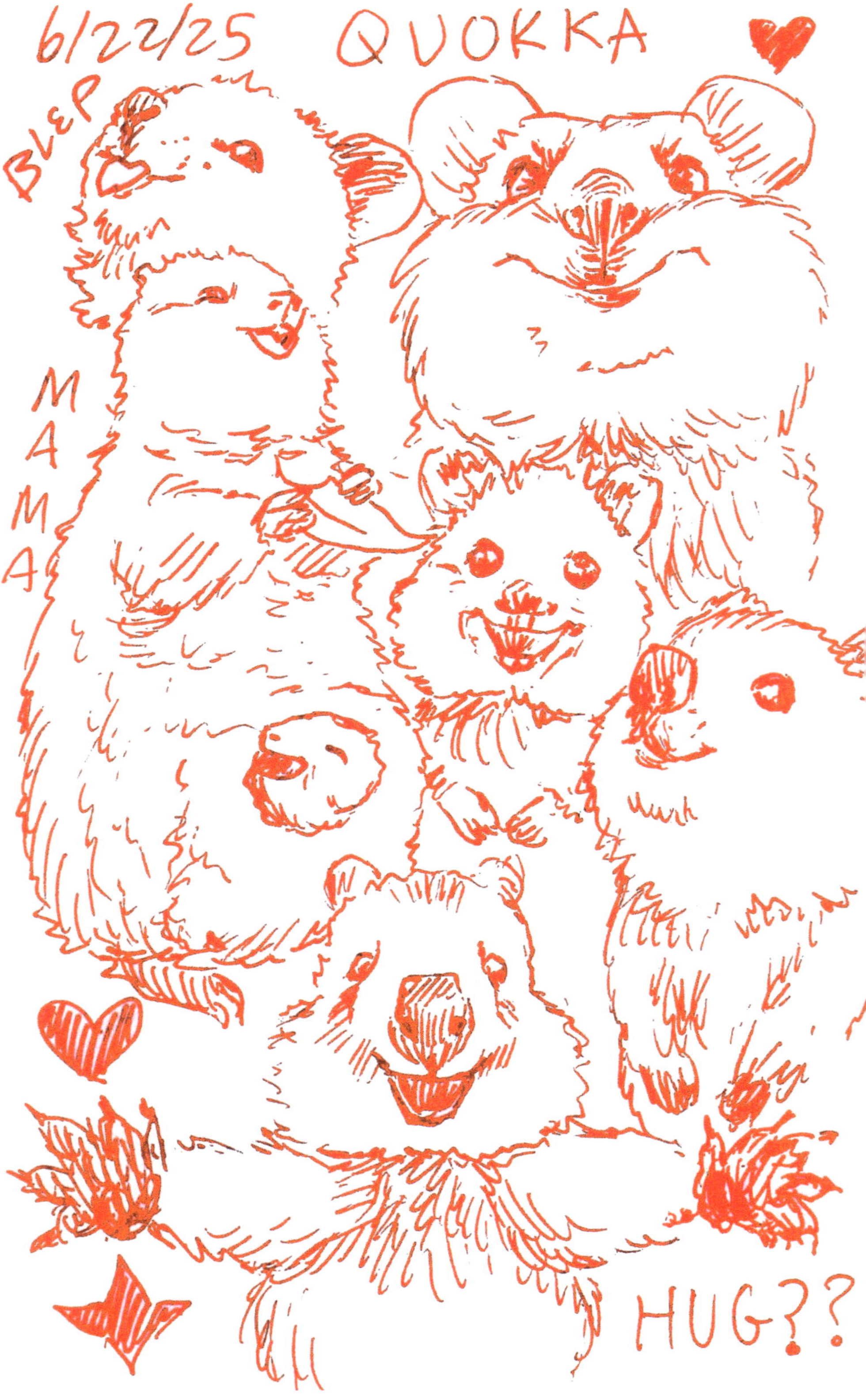
6/22/25
QUOKKA
BLEP
MAMA
HUG??

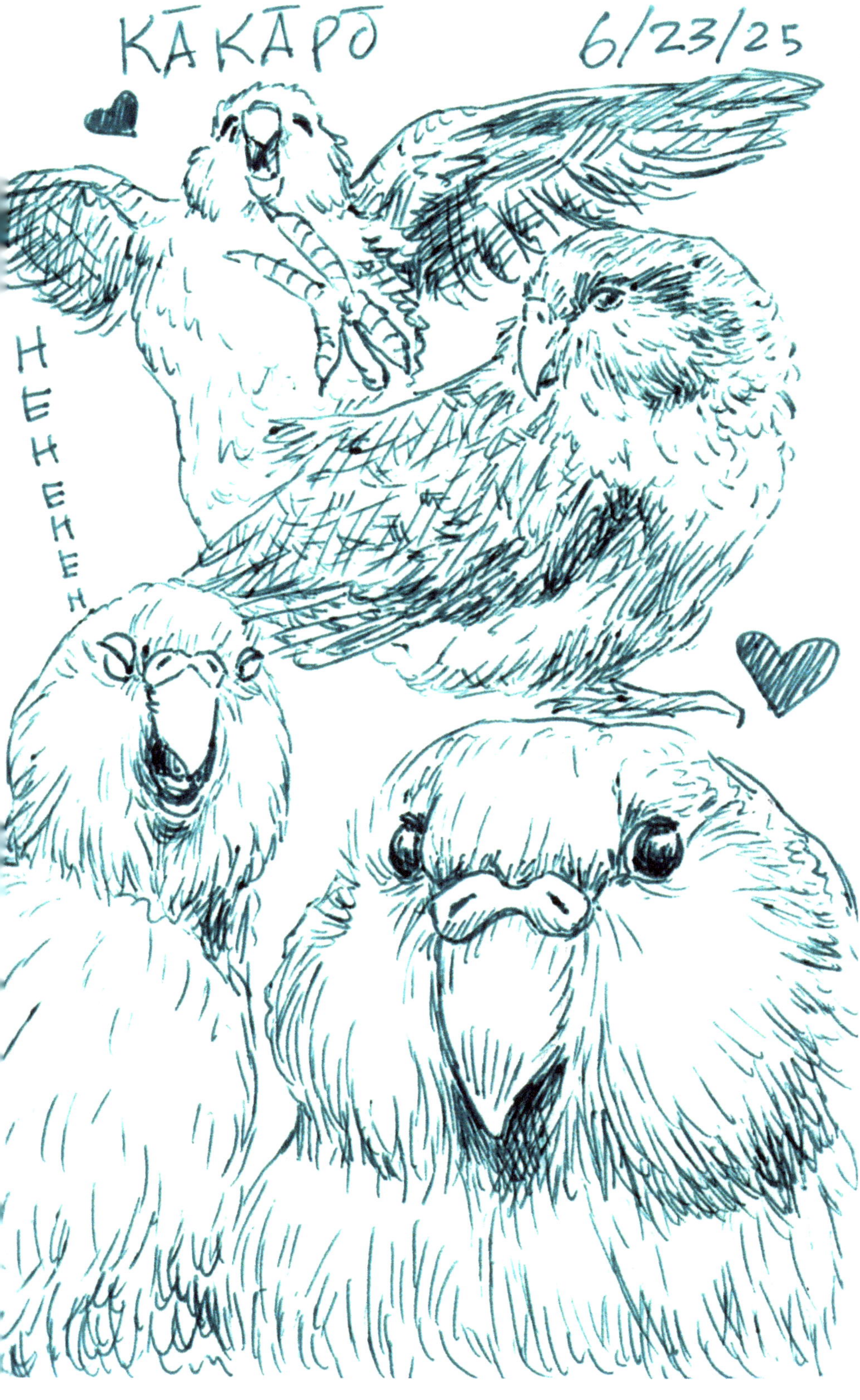
KĀKĀPŌ
6/23/25
HEHEHEH

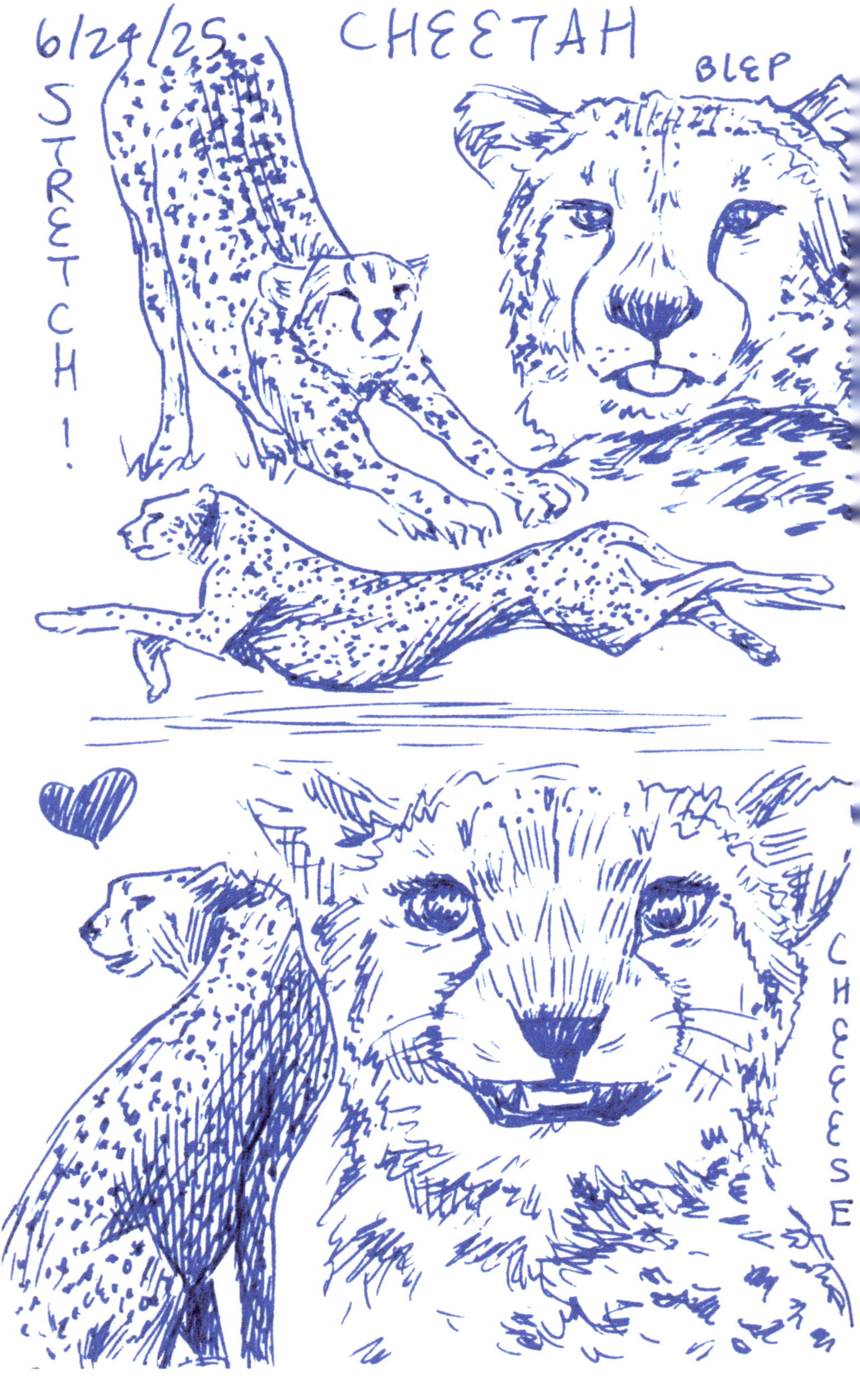

6/24/25.
CHEETAH
BLEP
STRETCH!
CHEEESE

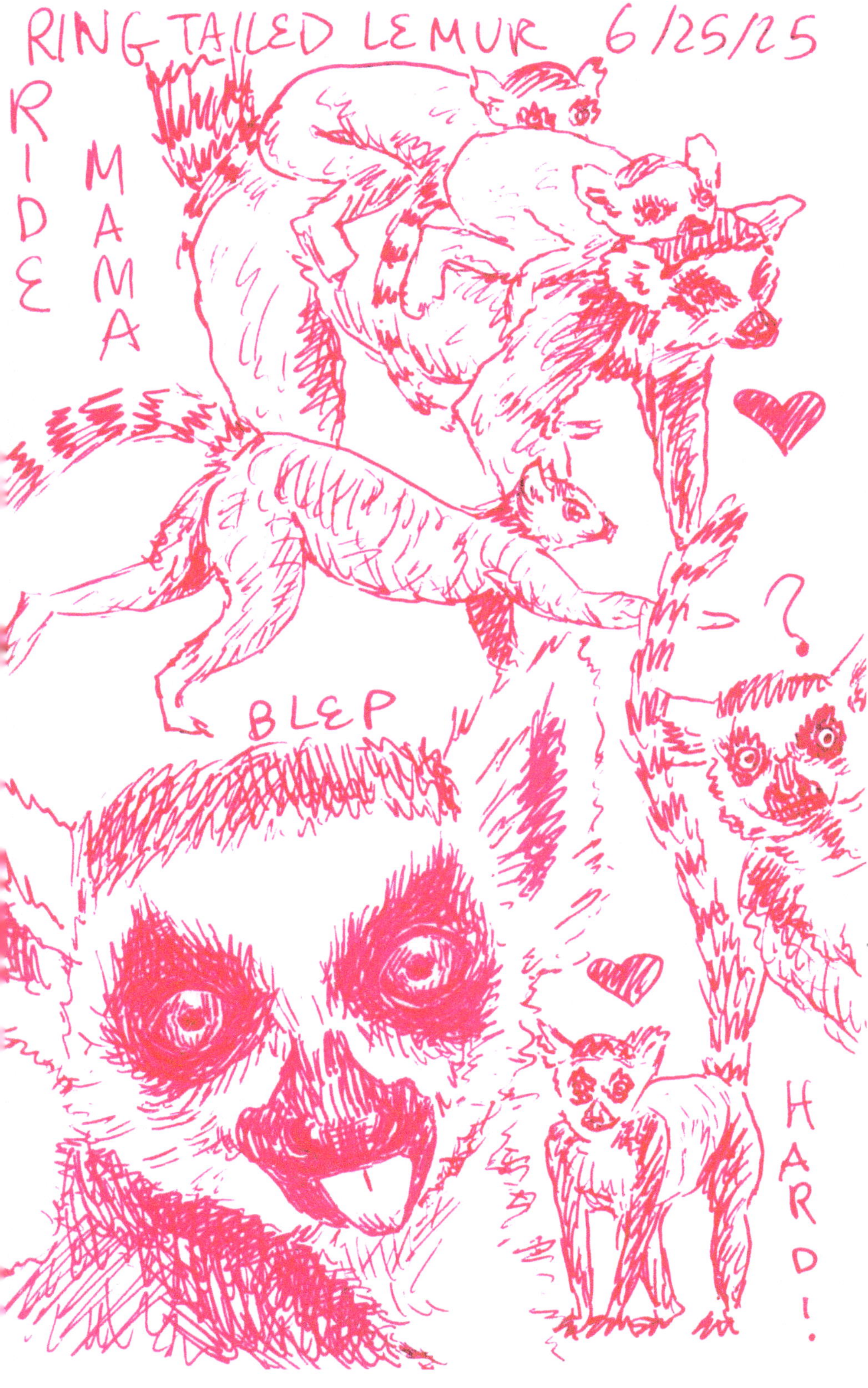
RING TAILED LEMUR 6/25/25
RIDE MAMA
BLEP
HARD!

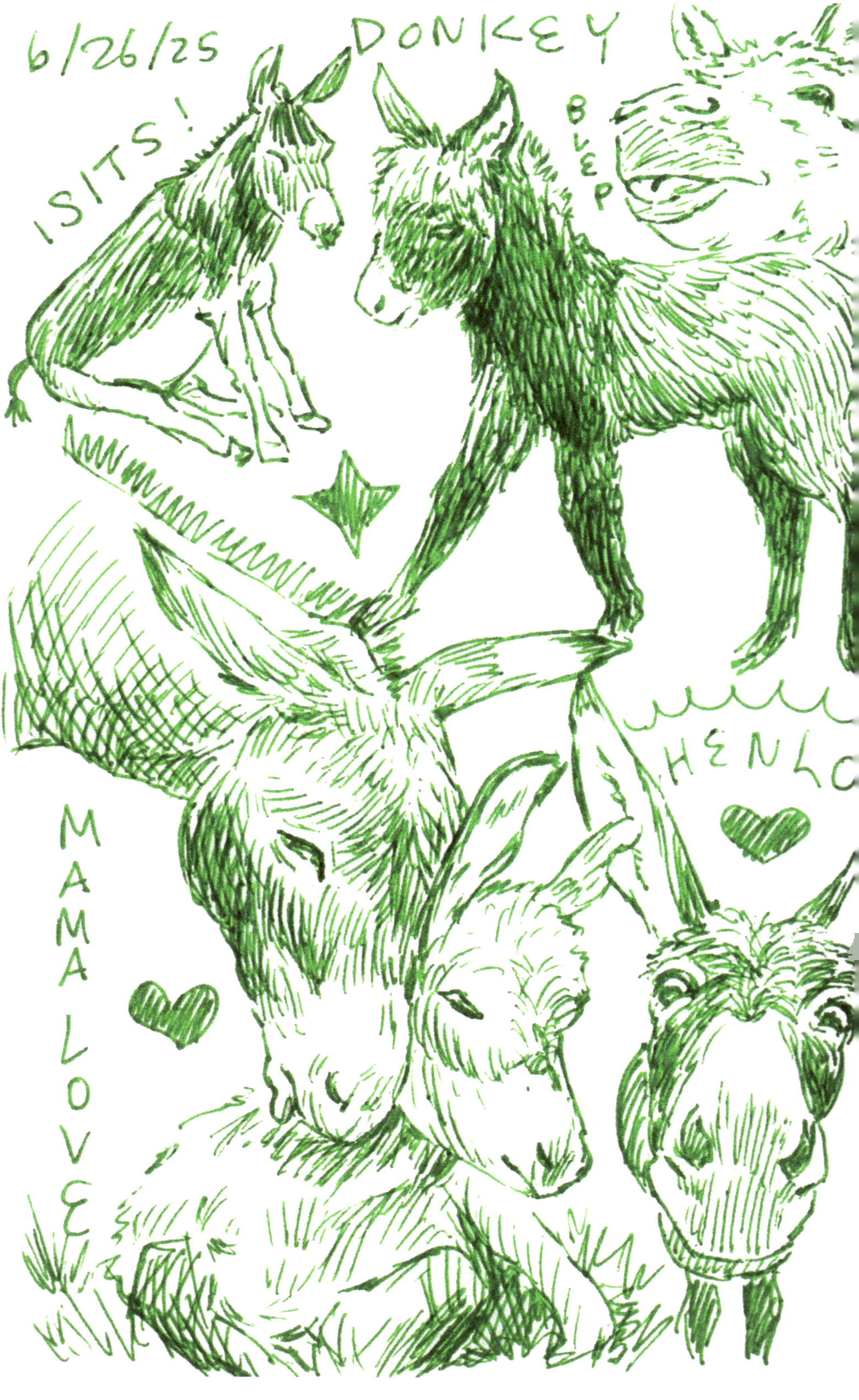

6/26/25
DONKEY
SITS!
BLEP
HENLO
MAMA LOVE

WHALE SHARK 6/27/25

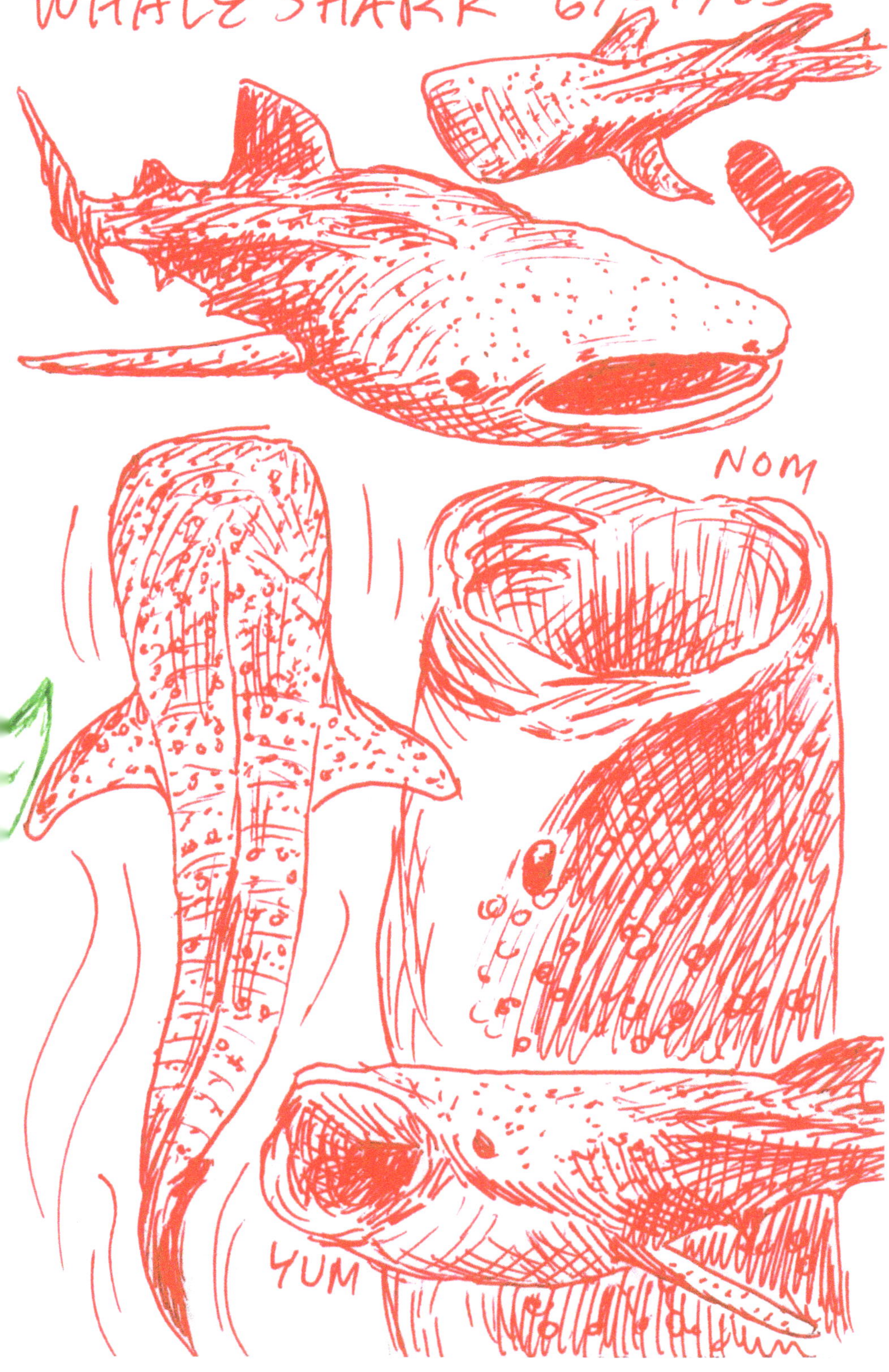

6/28/25 CALIFORNIA QUAIL

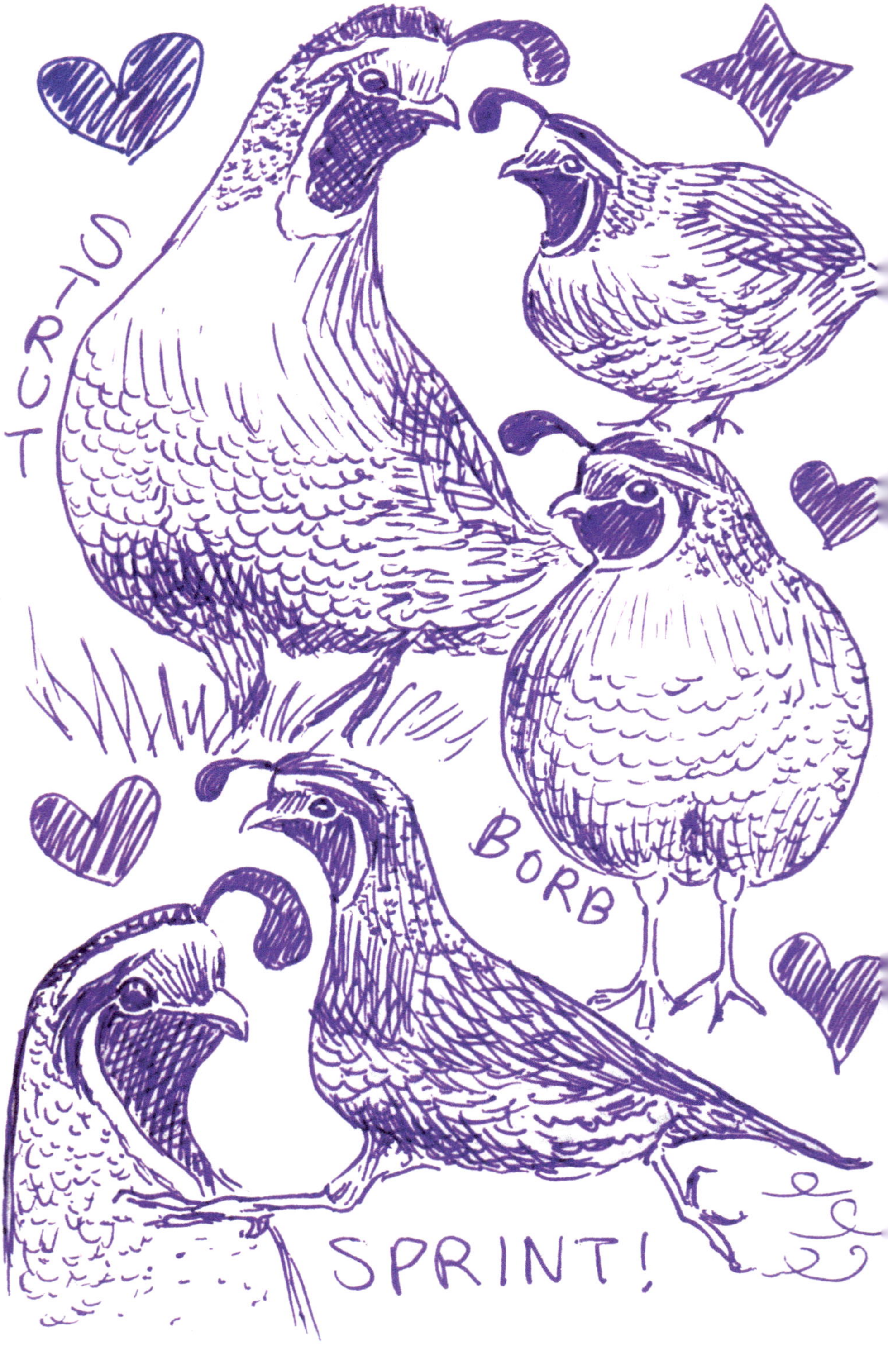

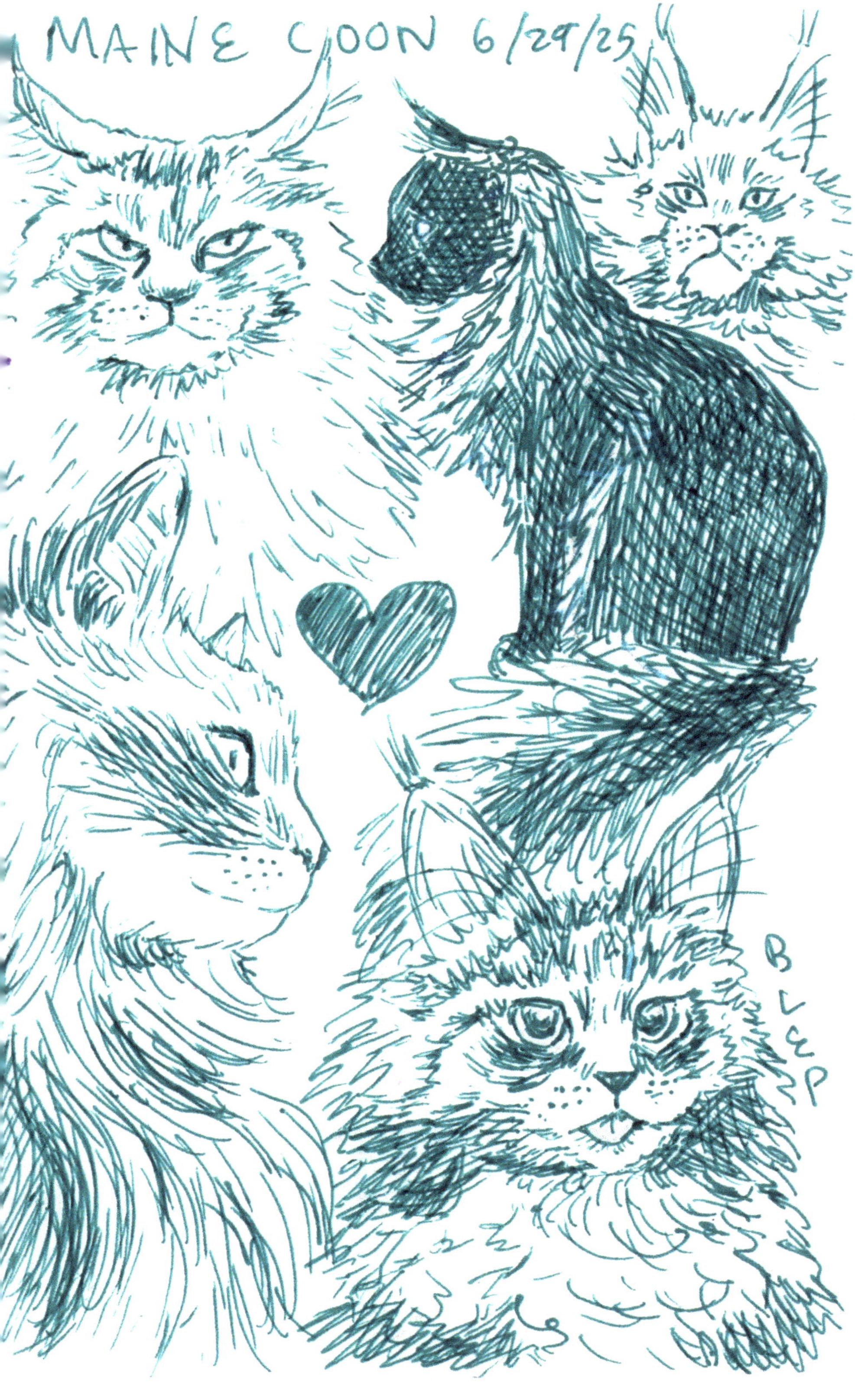
MAINE COON 6/29/25
BLEP

6/30/25 HARE

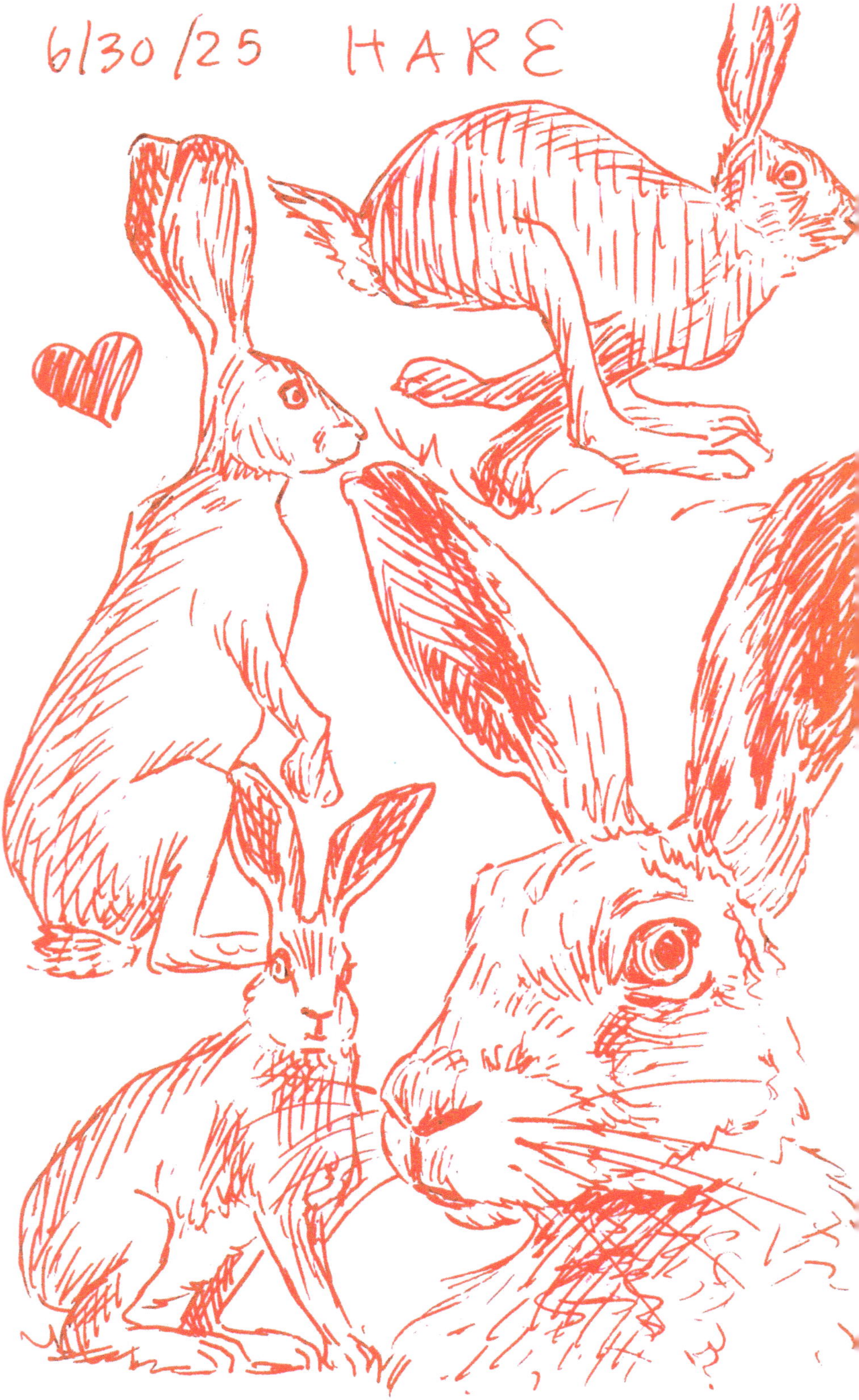

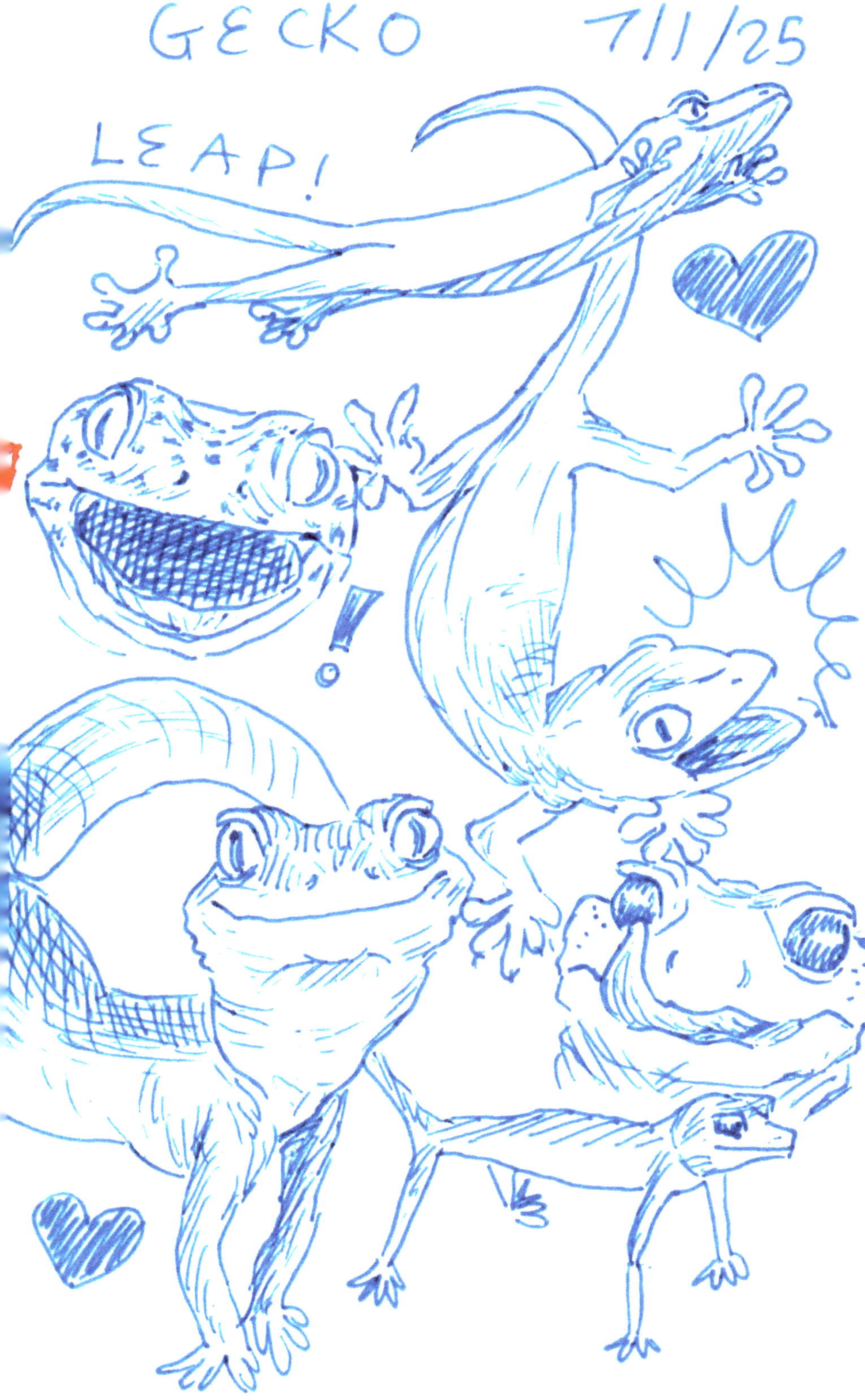
GECKO
7/11/25
LEAP!

7/2/25 SAIGAANTELOPE

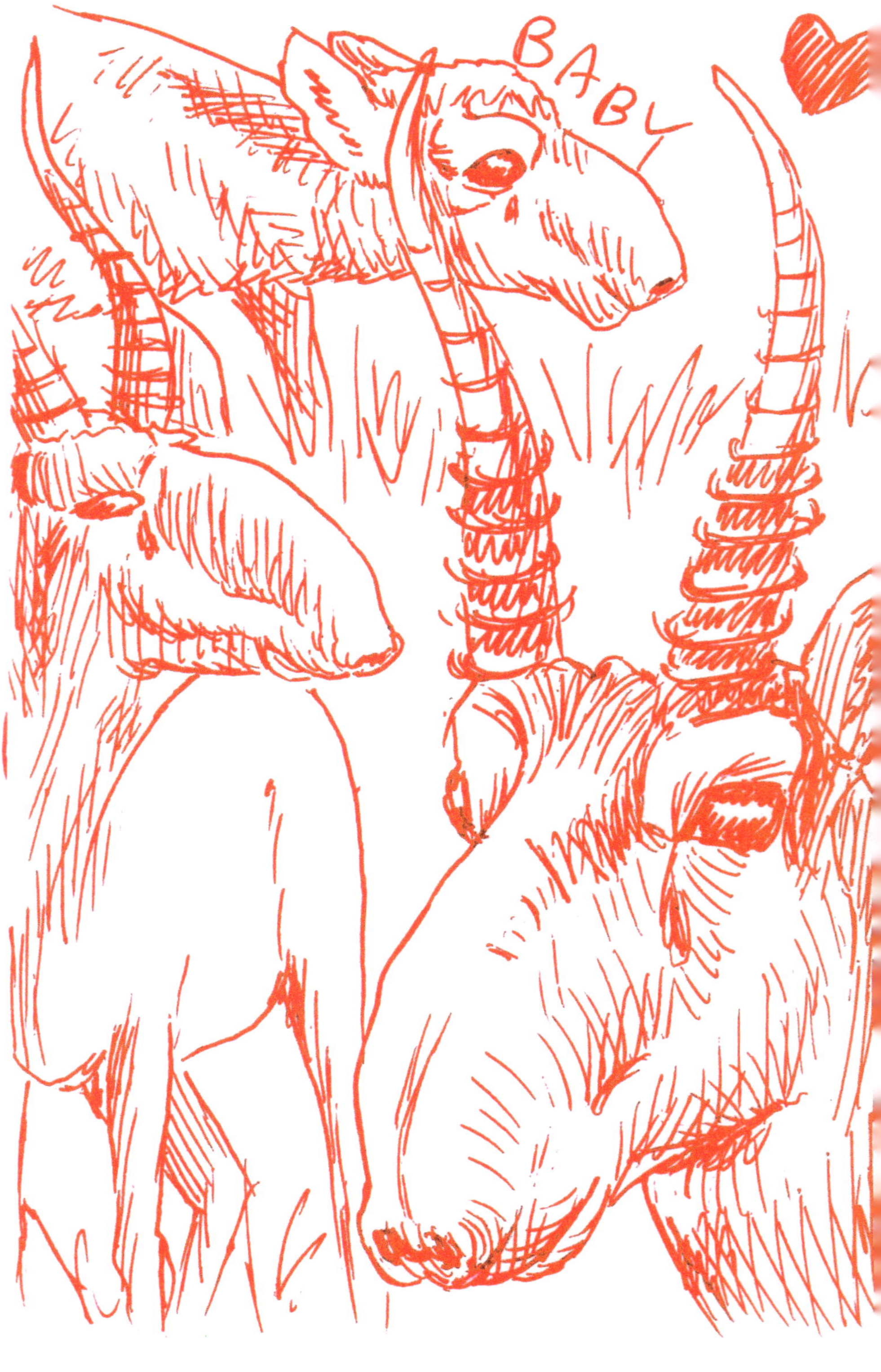

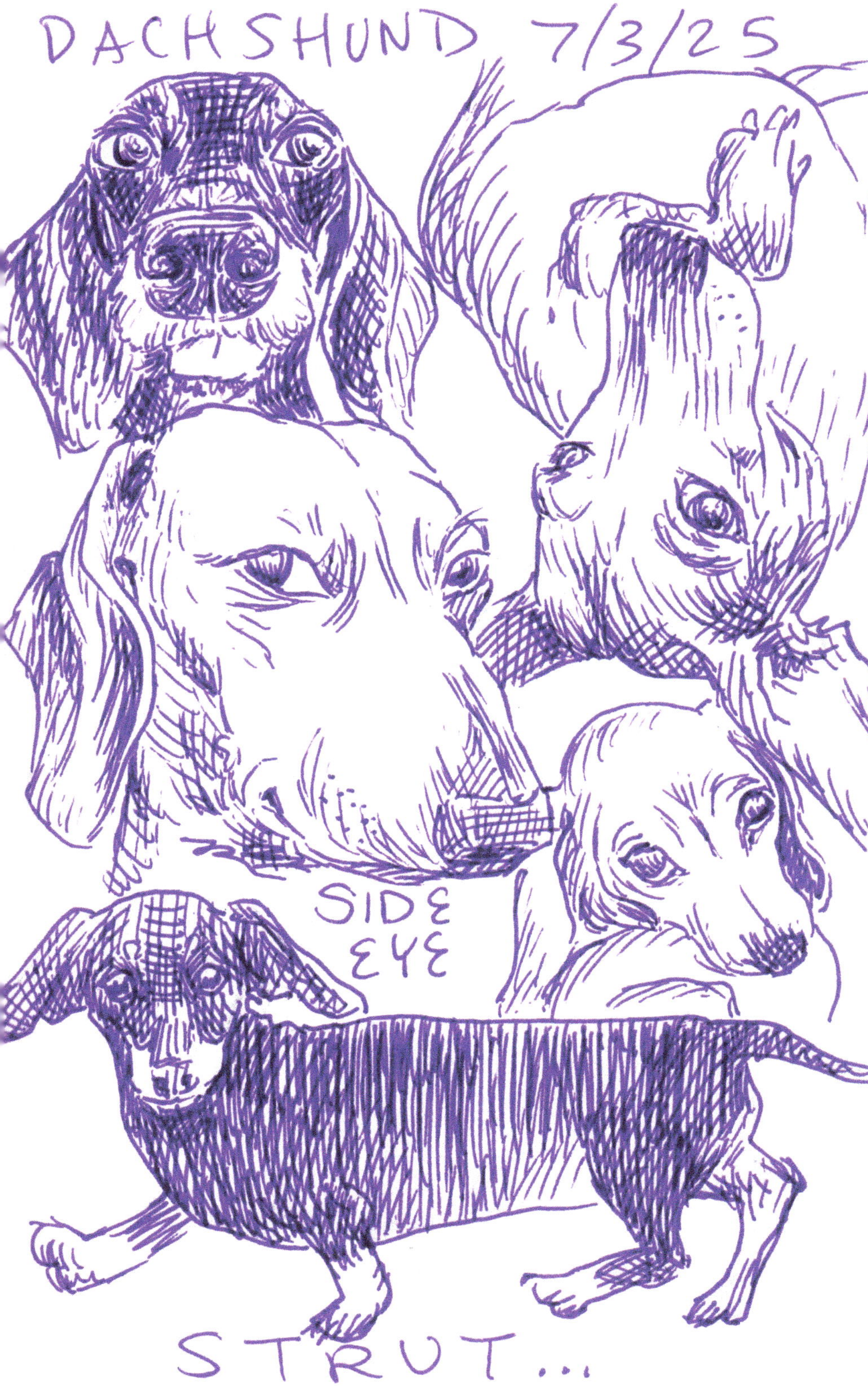
DACHSHUND 7/3/25
SIDE EYE
STRUT...

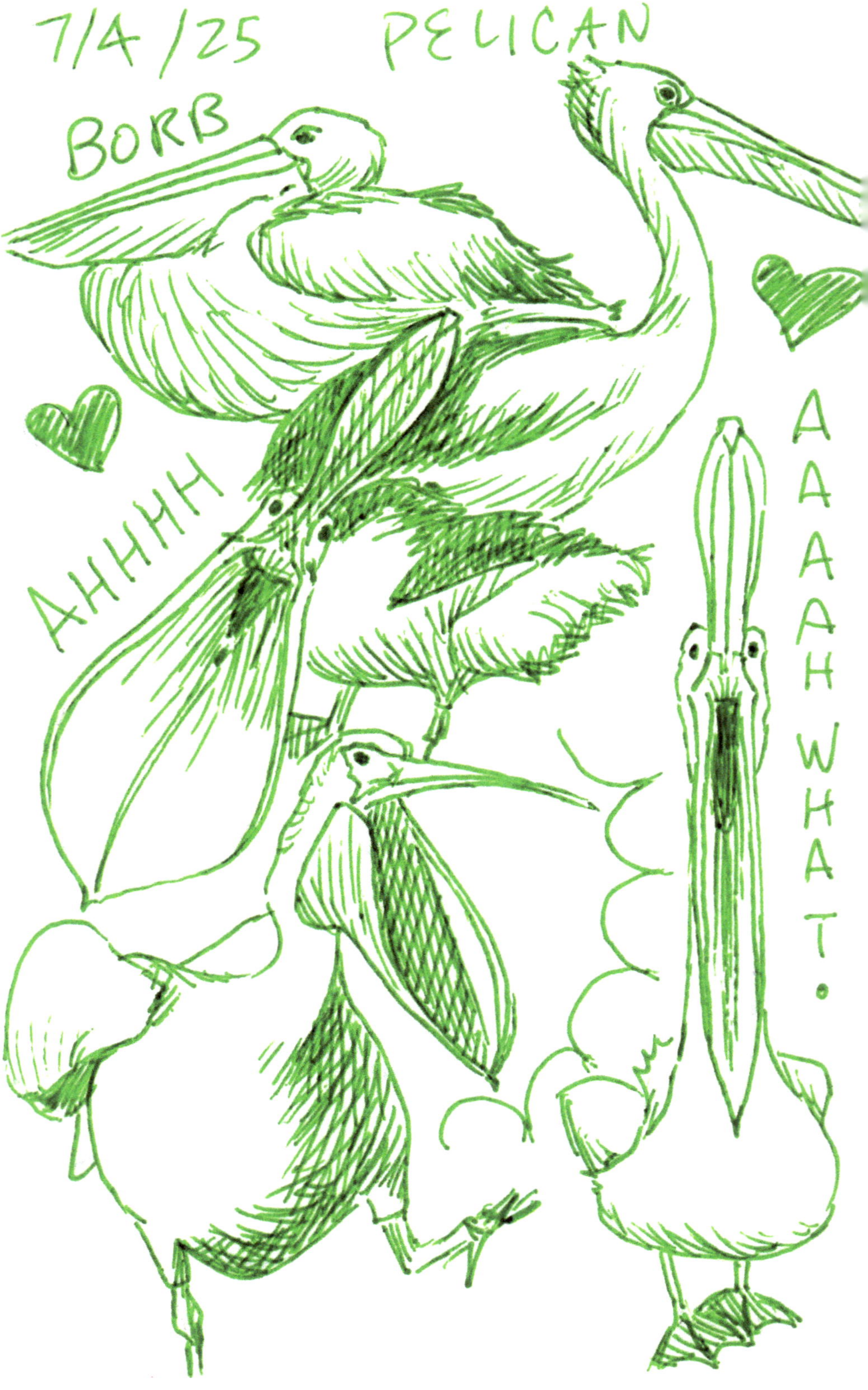
7/4/25
PELICAN
BORB
AHHHH
AAAAHWHAT.

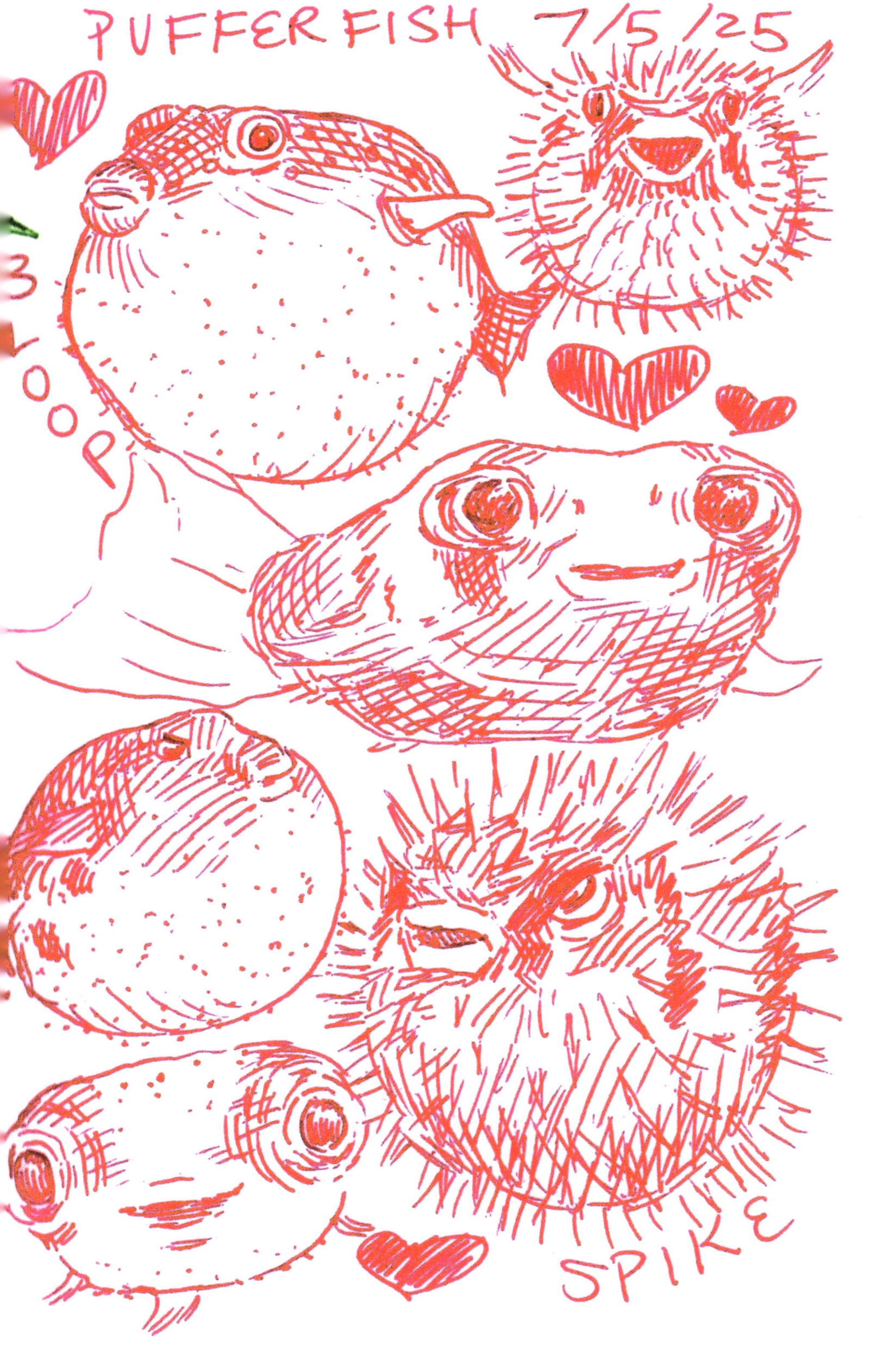
PUFFER FISH
7/5/25
BLOOP
SPIKE

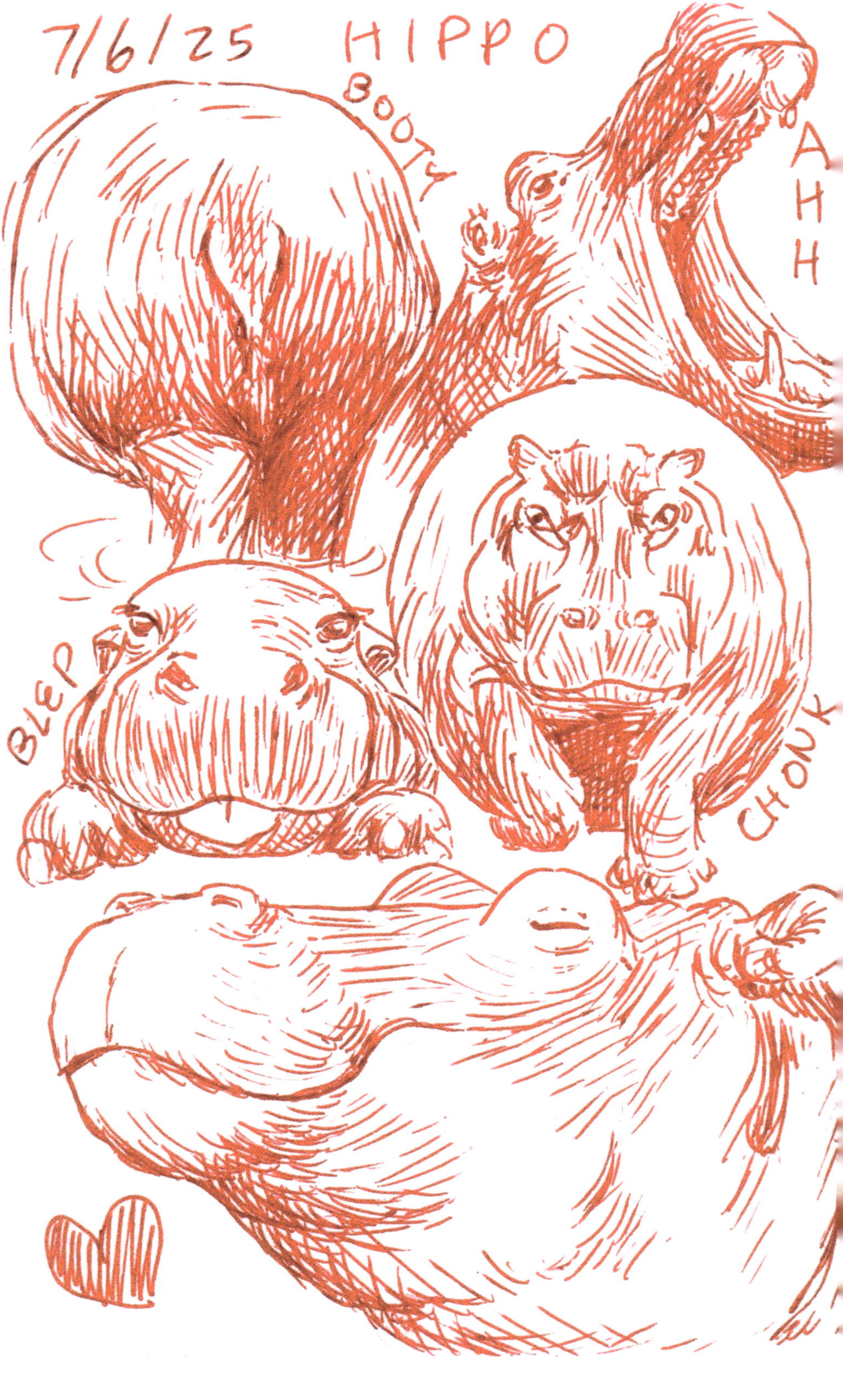
7/6/25
HIPPO
BOOTY
AHH
BLEP
CHONK

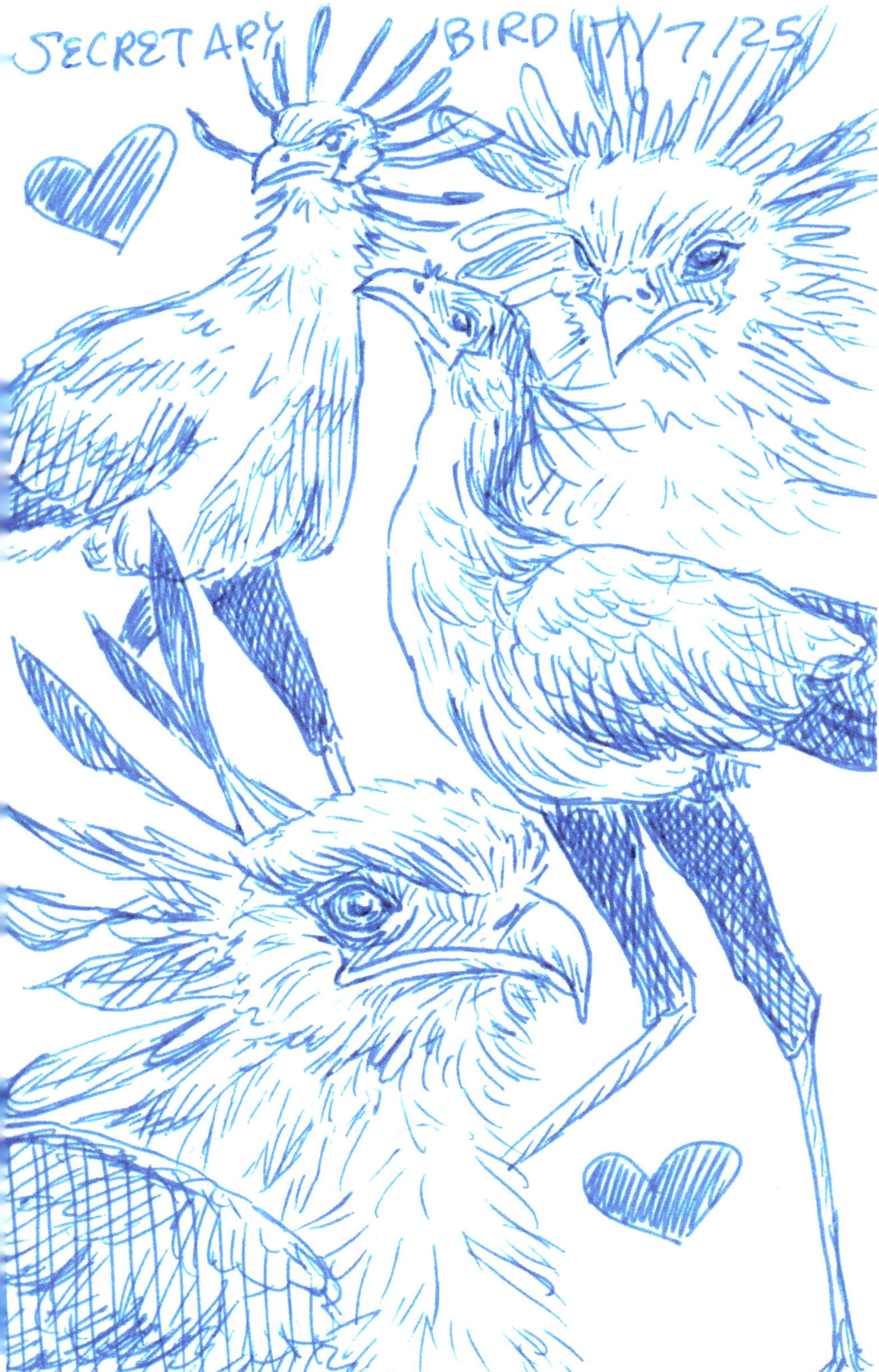
SECRETARY BIRD
7/25

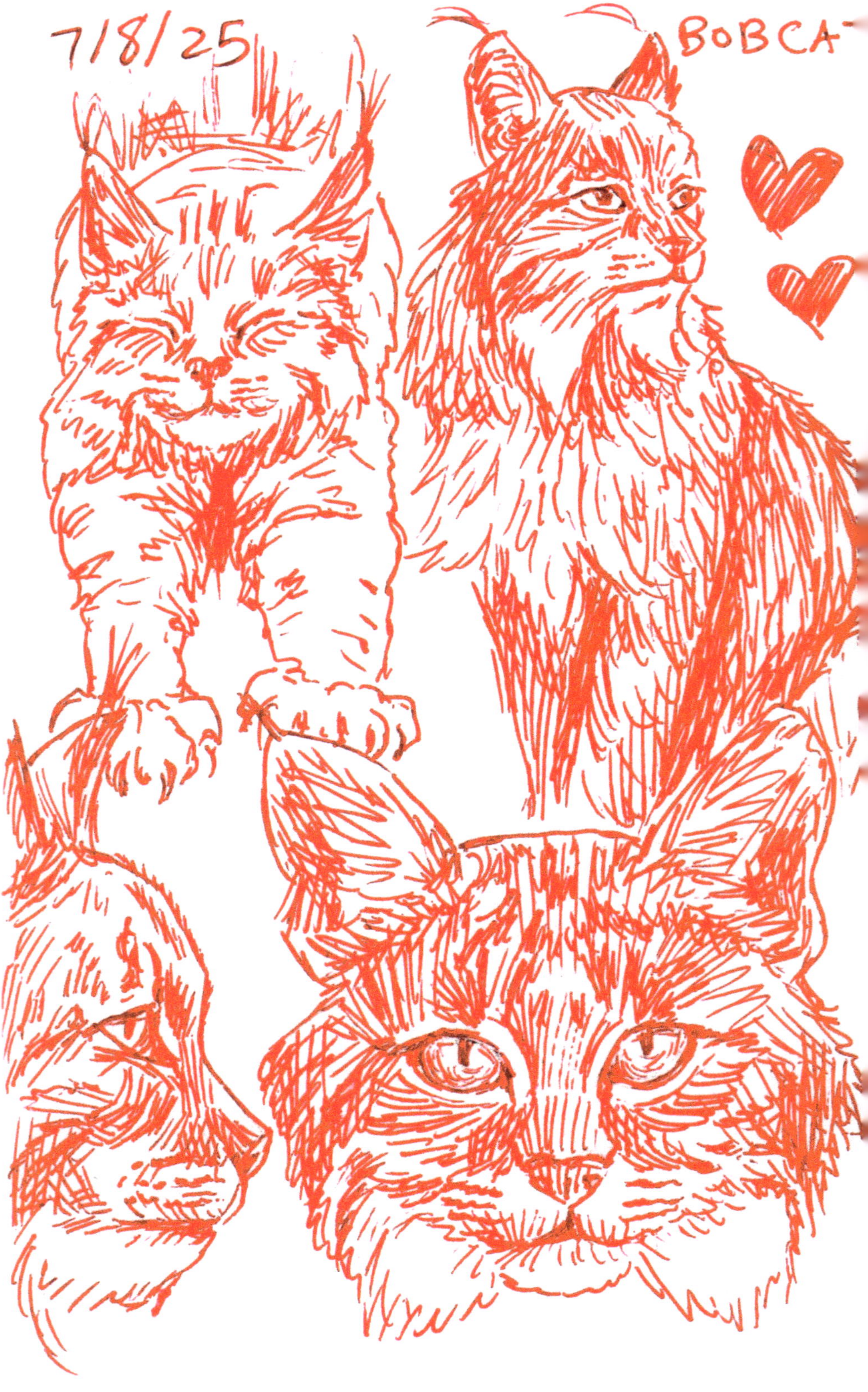
7/8/25
BOBCAT

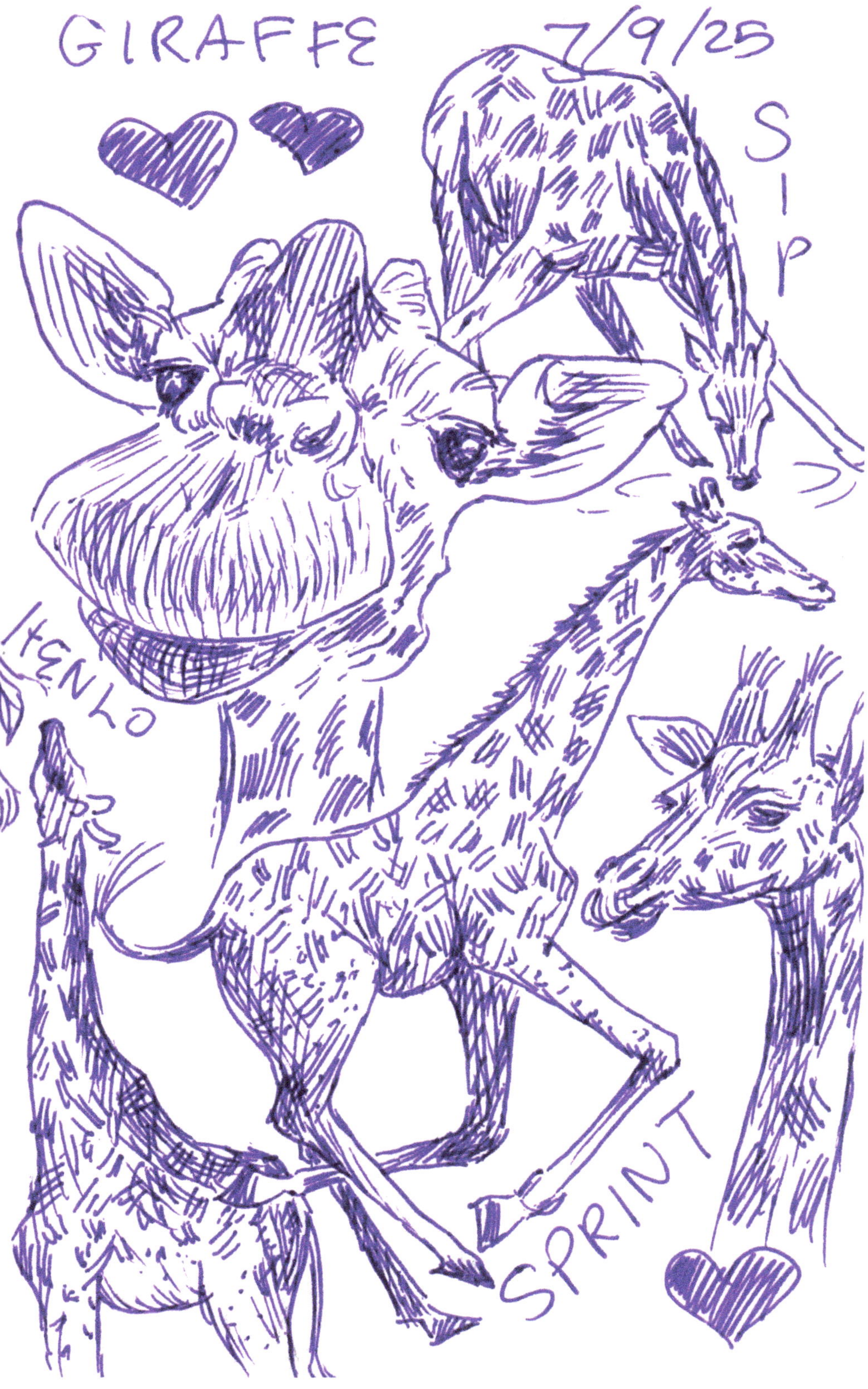
GIRAFFE
7/9/25
SIP
HENLO
SPRINT

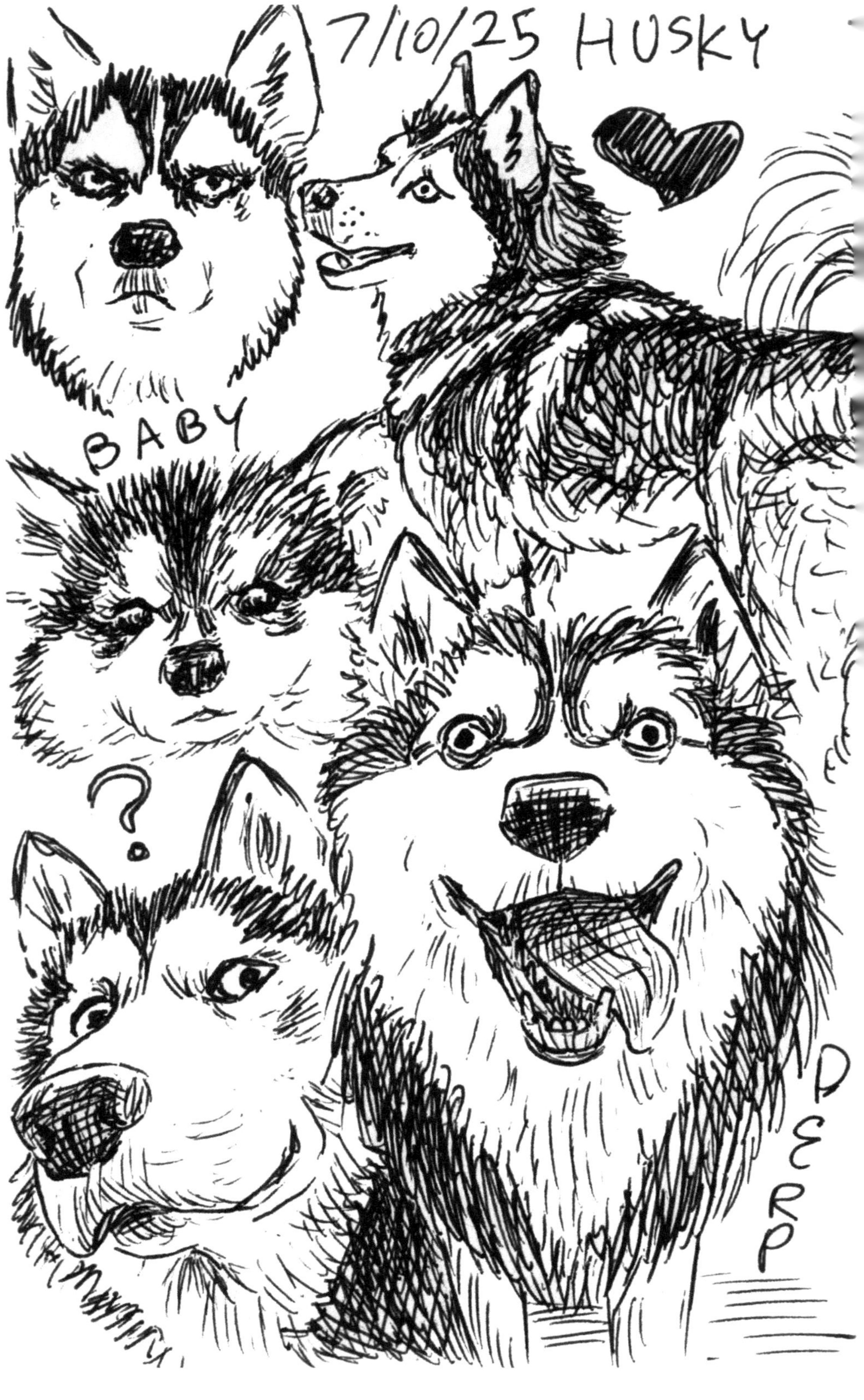
7/10/25 HUSKY
BABY
?
DERP

BLUEFOOTED BOOBY 7/11/25

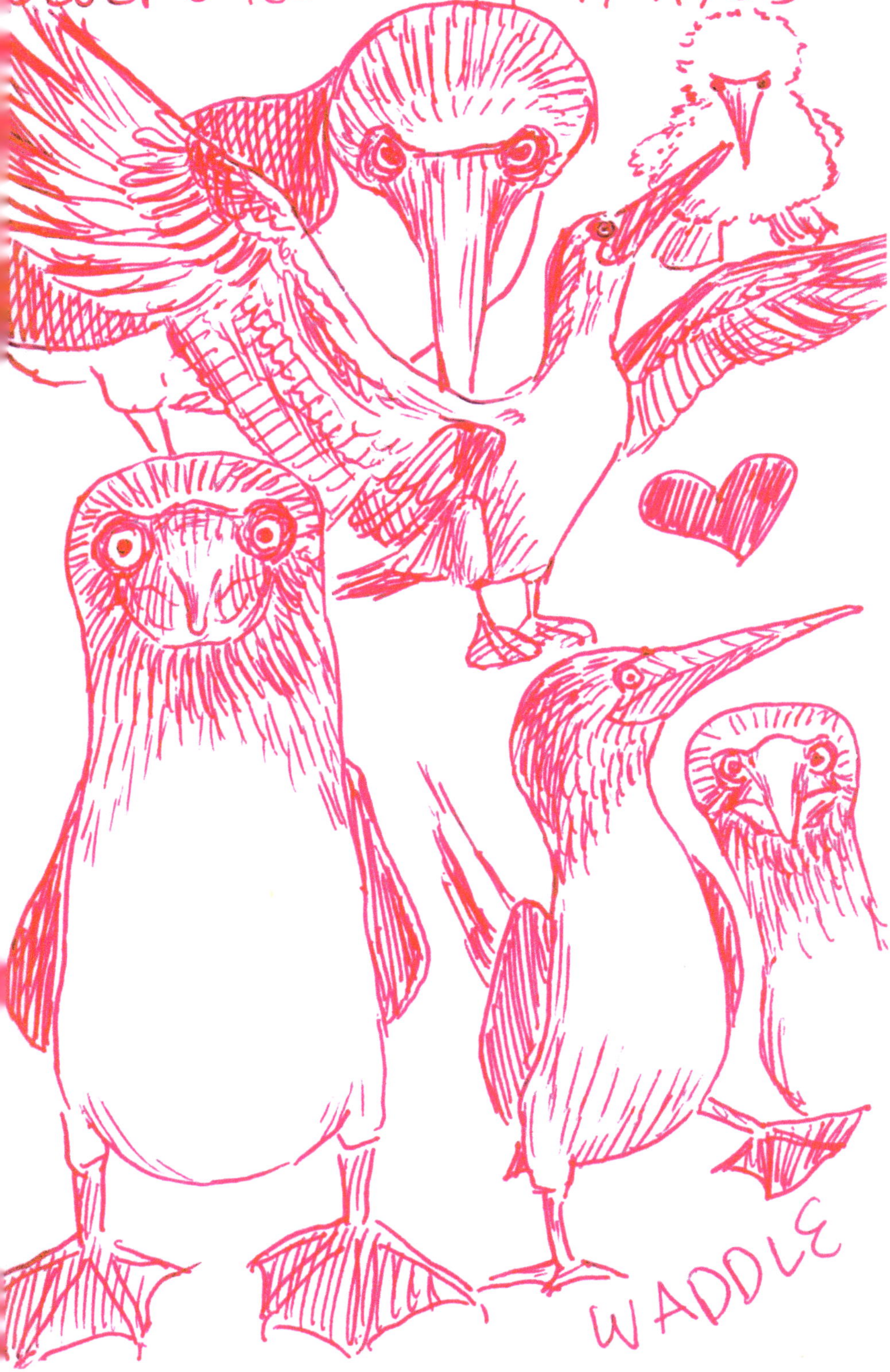

7/12/25 LEAFY SEA DRAGON

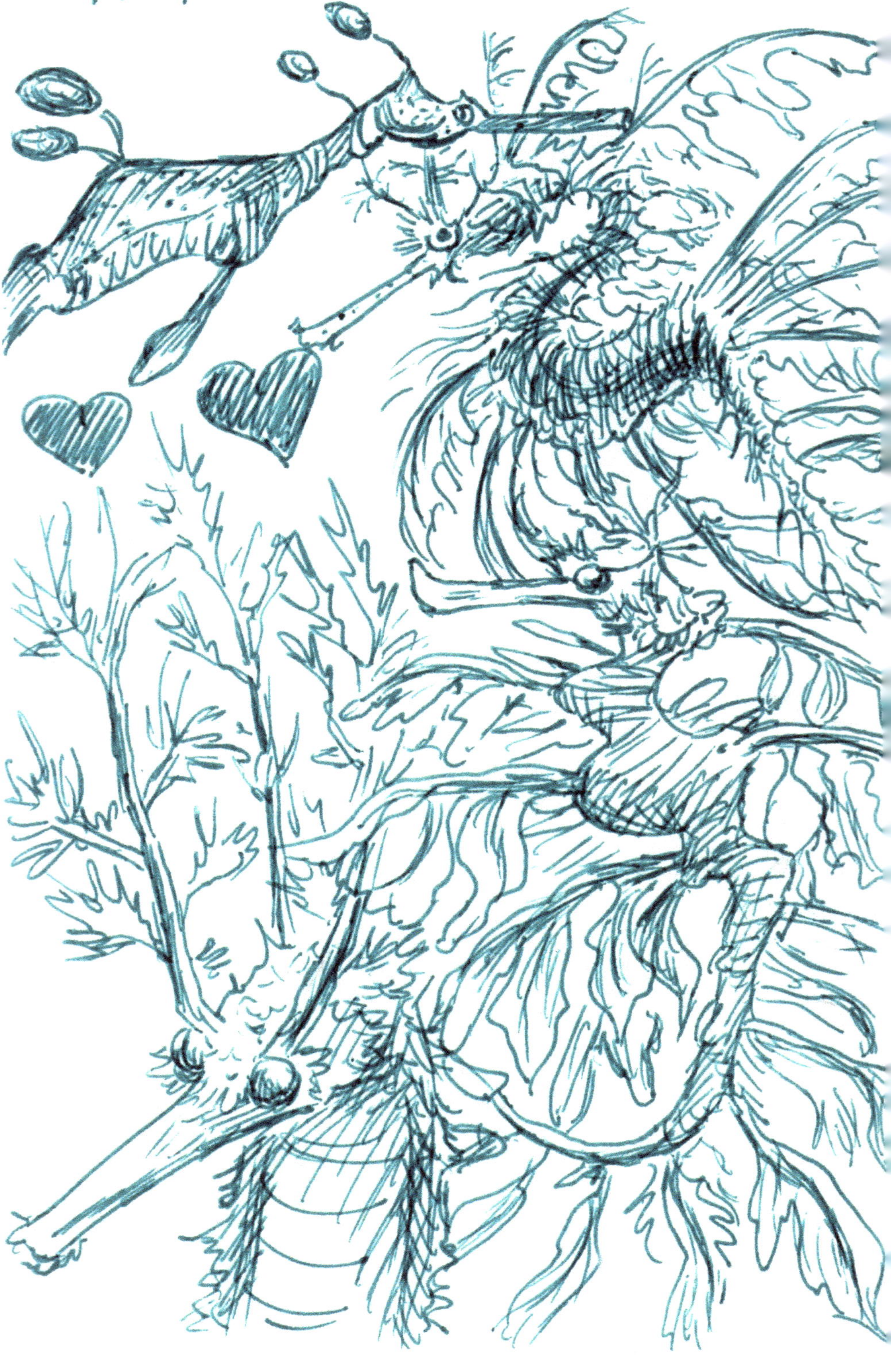

ZEBRA 7/13/25

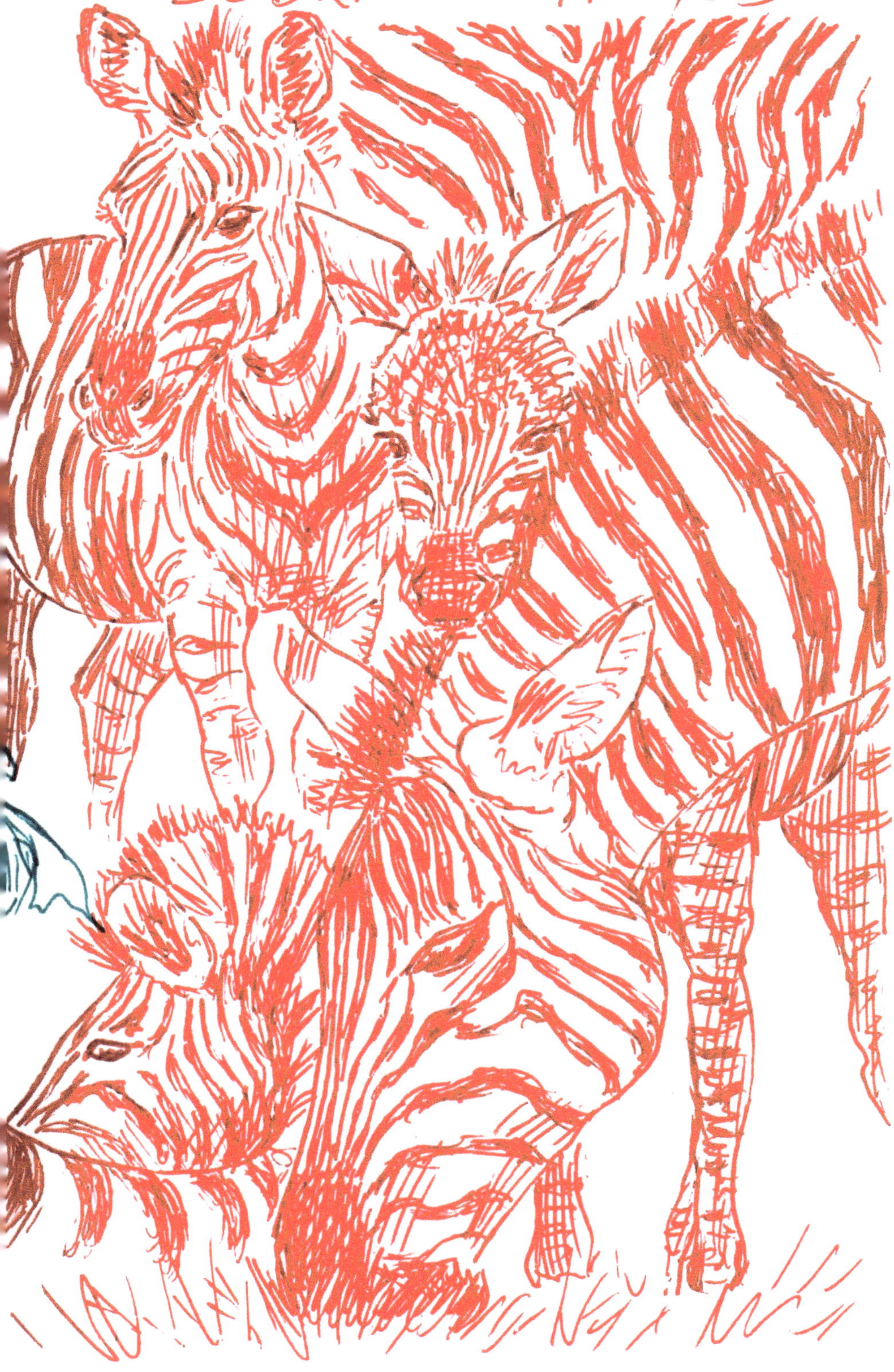

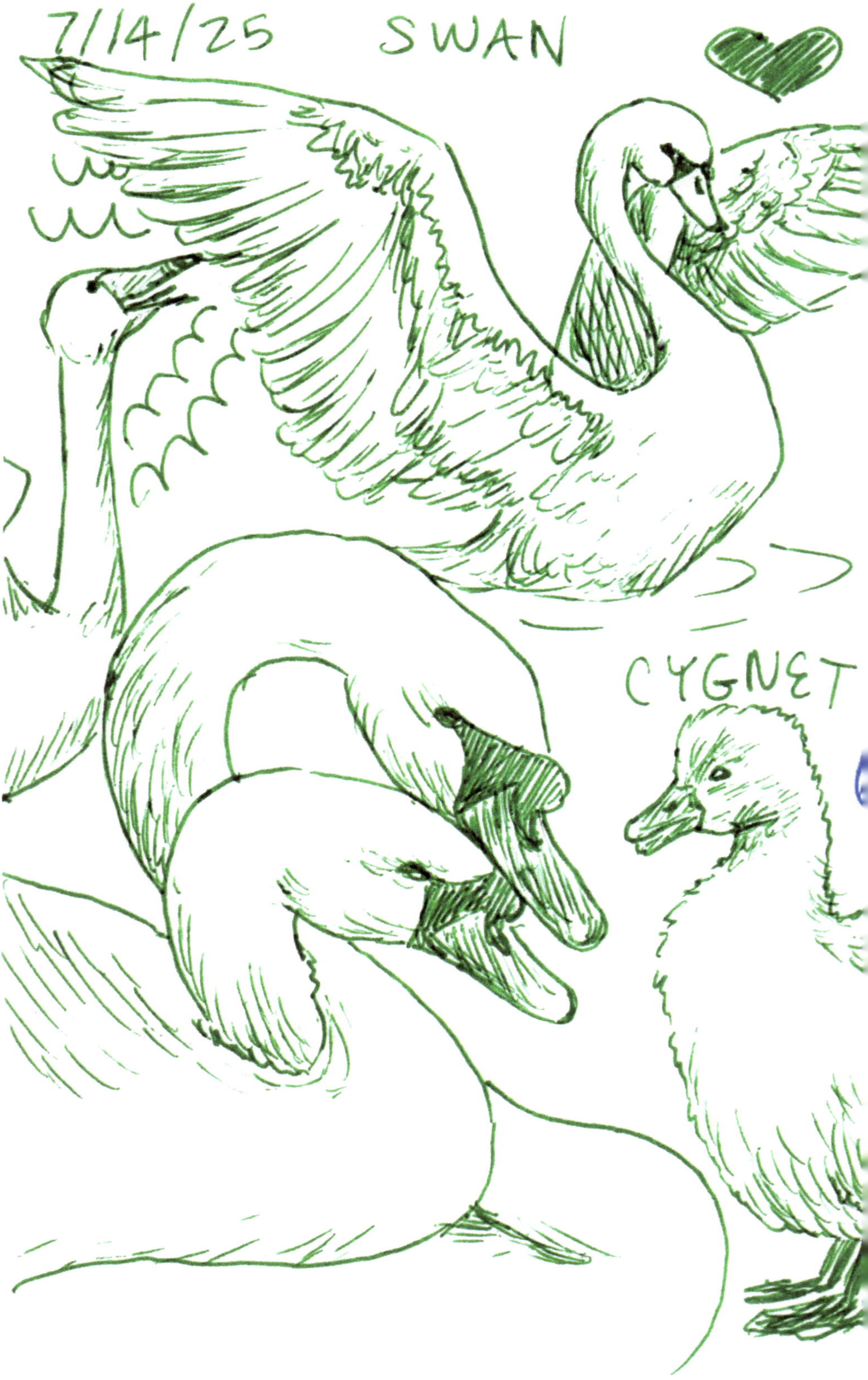
7/14/25
SWAN
CYGNET

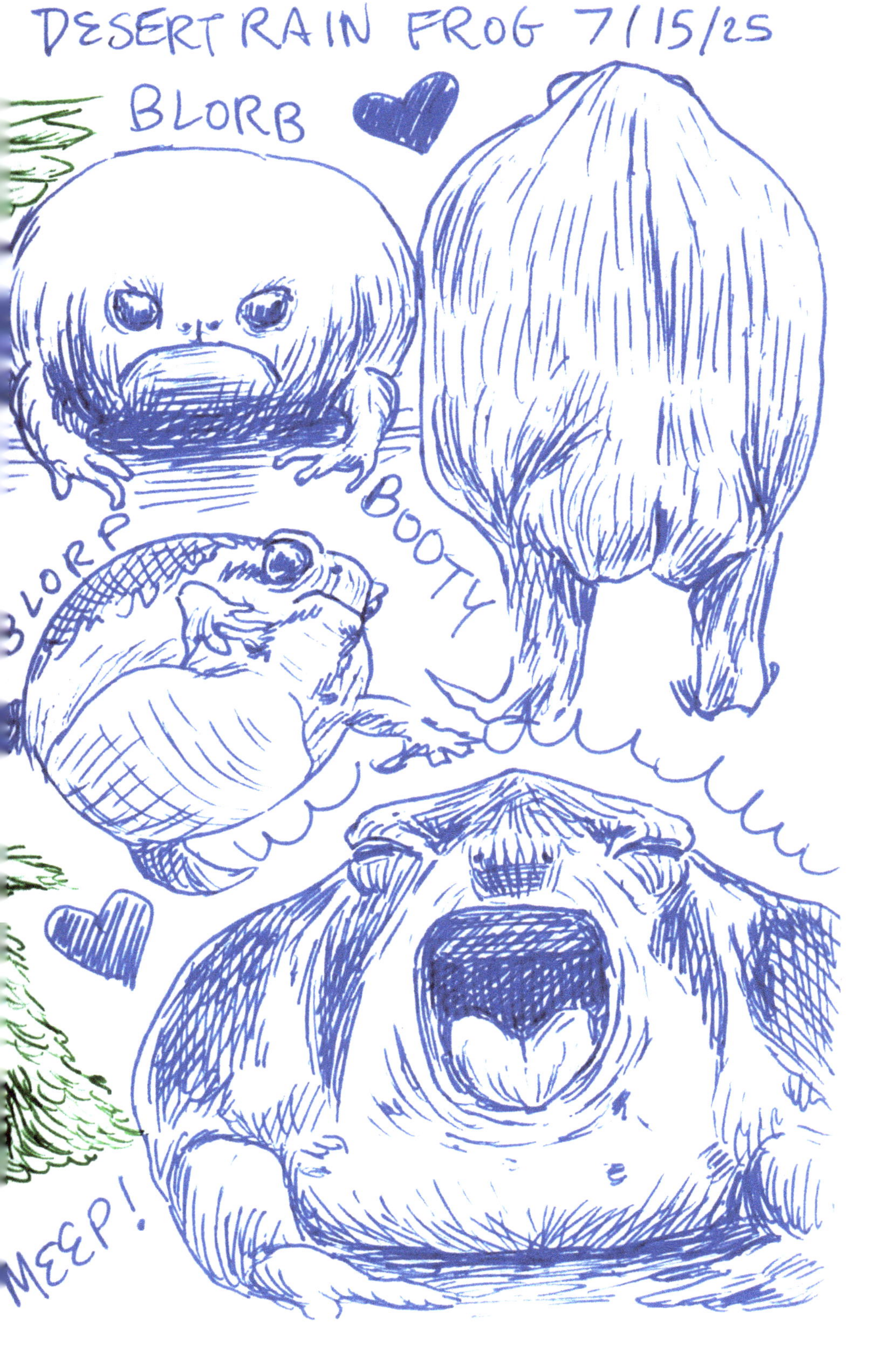
DESERT RAIN FROG 7/15/25
BLORB
BOOTY
BLORP
MEEP!

7/16/25 CAMEL

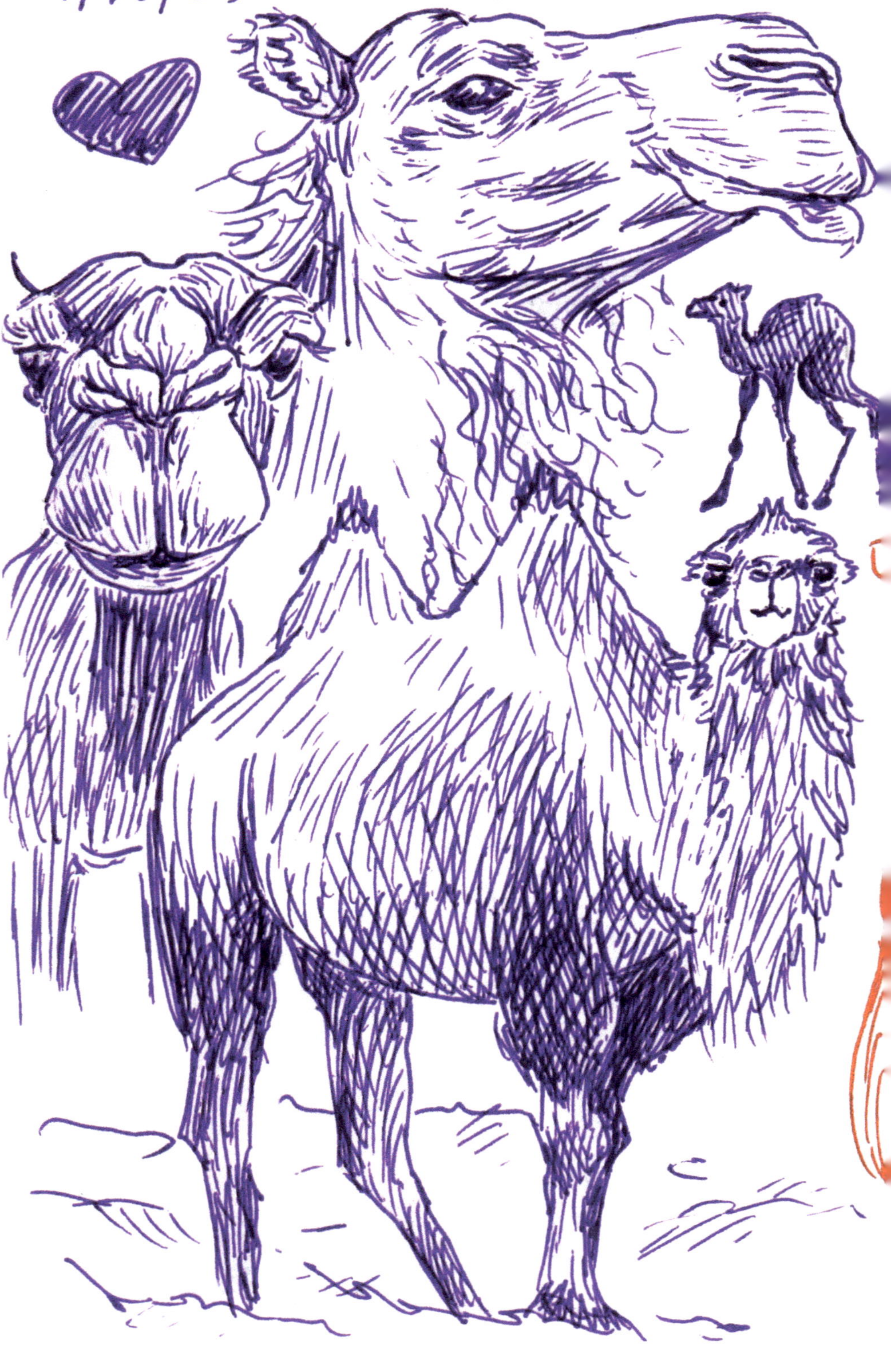

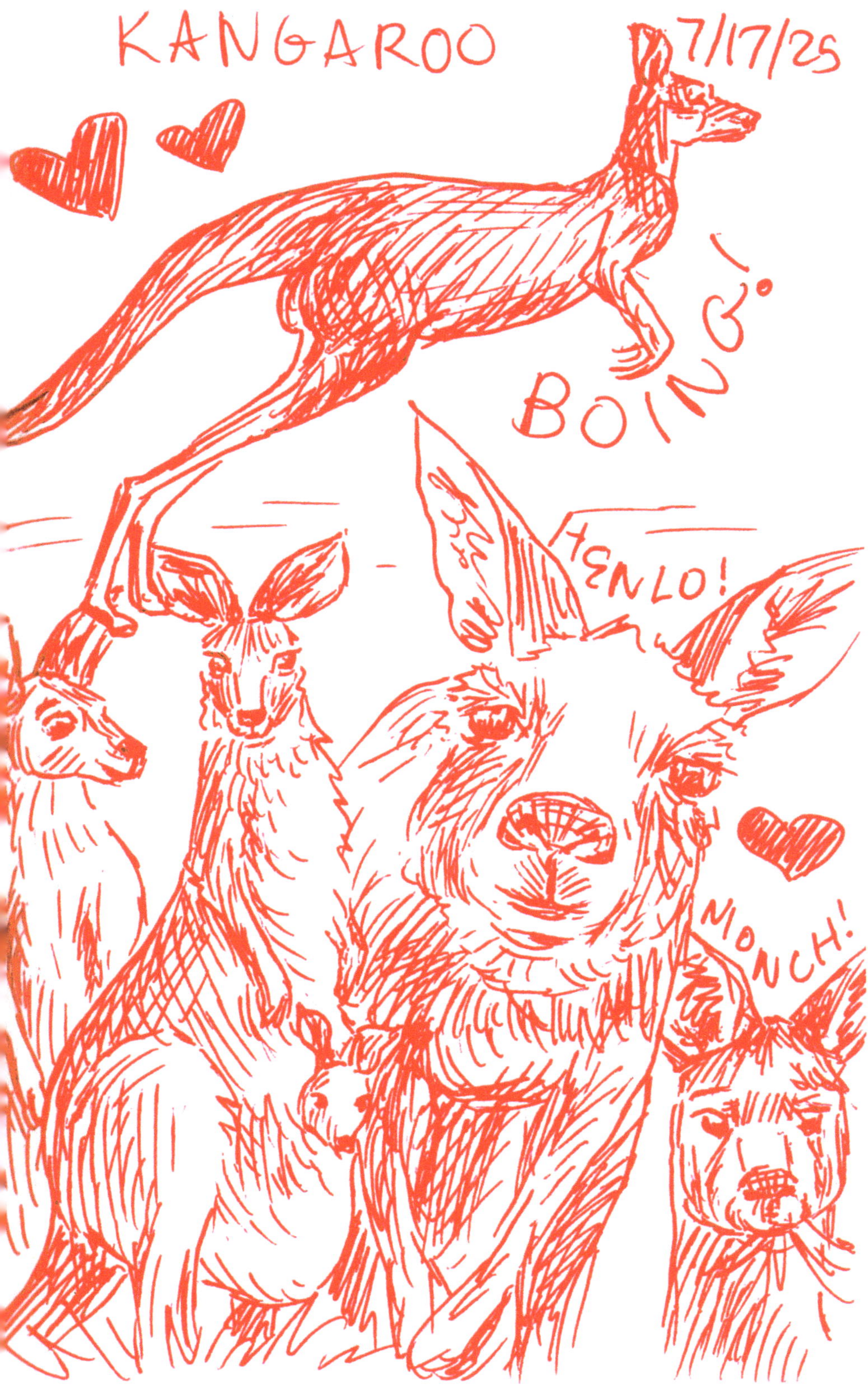
KANGAROO
7/17/25
BOING!
HENLO!
MONCH!

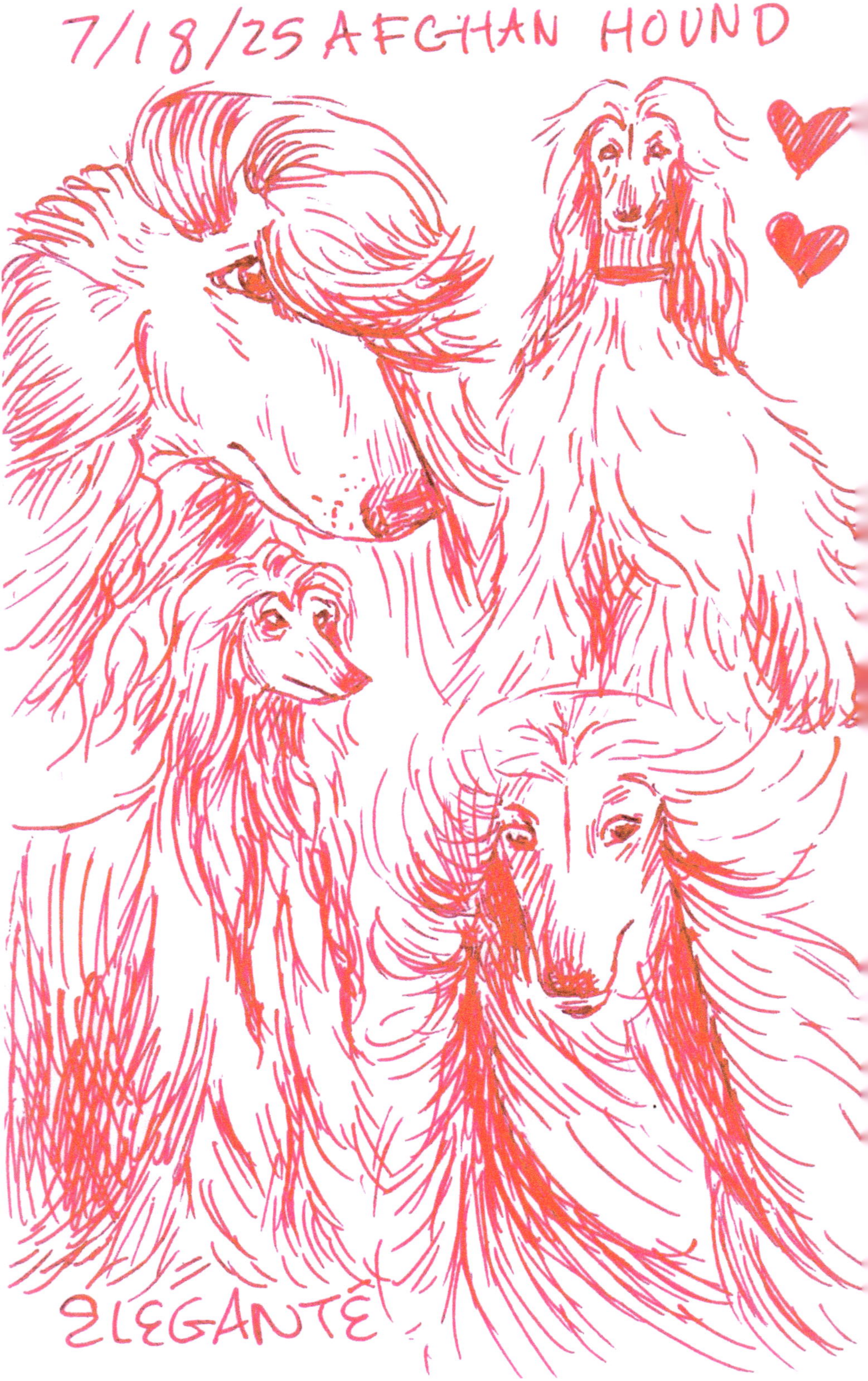
7/18/25 AFGHAN HOUND
ELEGANTE

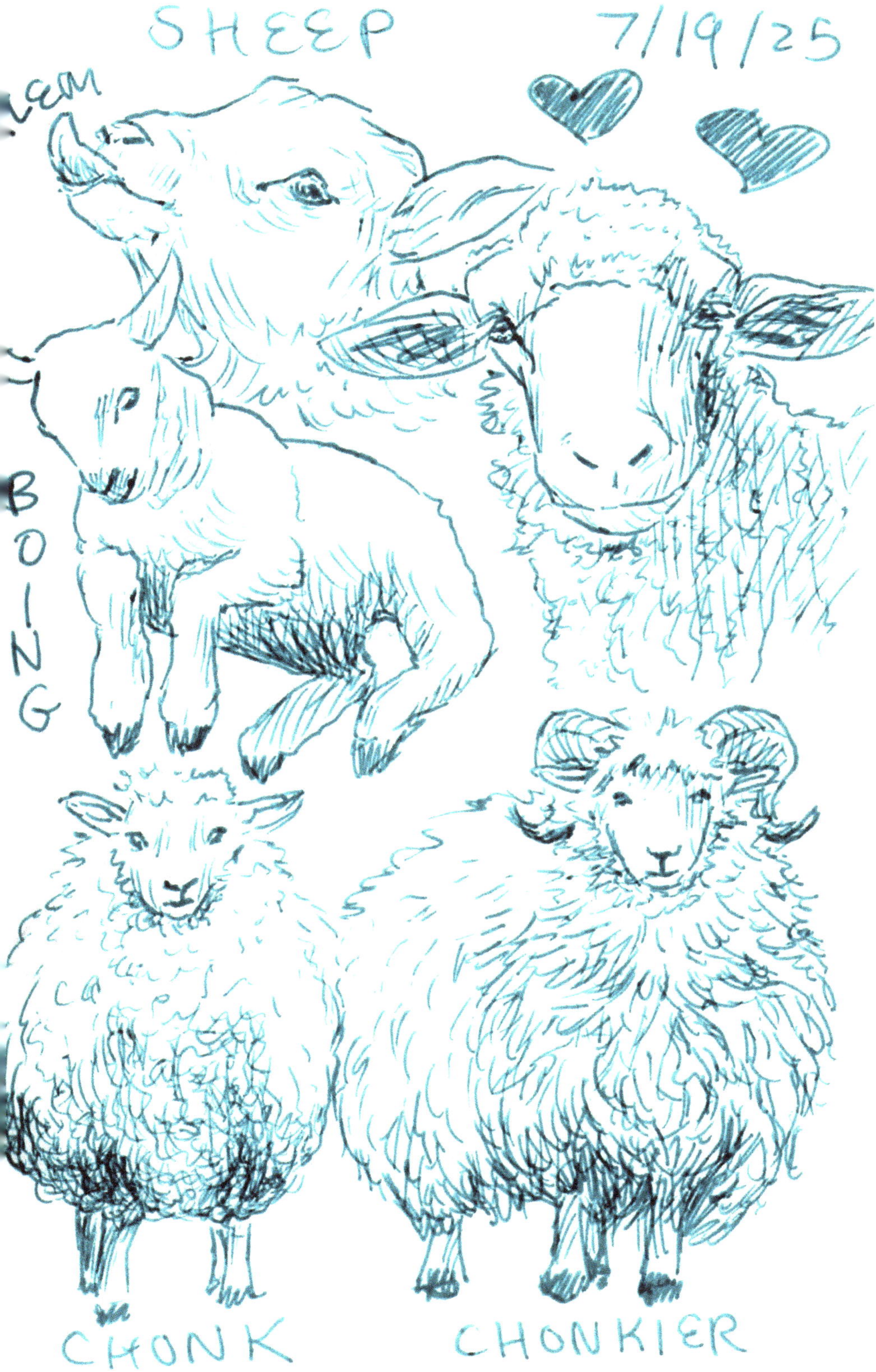
SHEEP
7/19/25
BOING
CHONK
CHONKIER

7/20/25 CASSOWARY

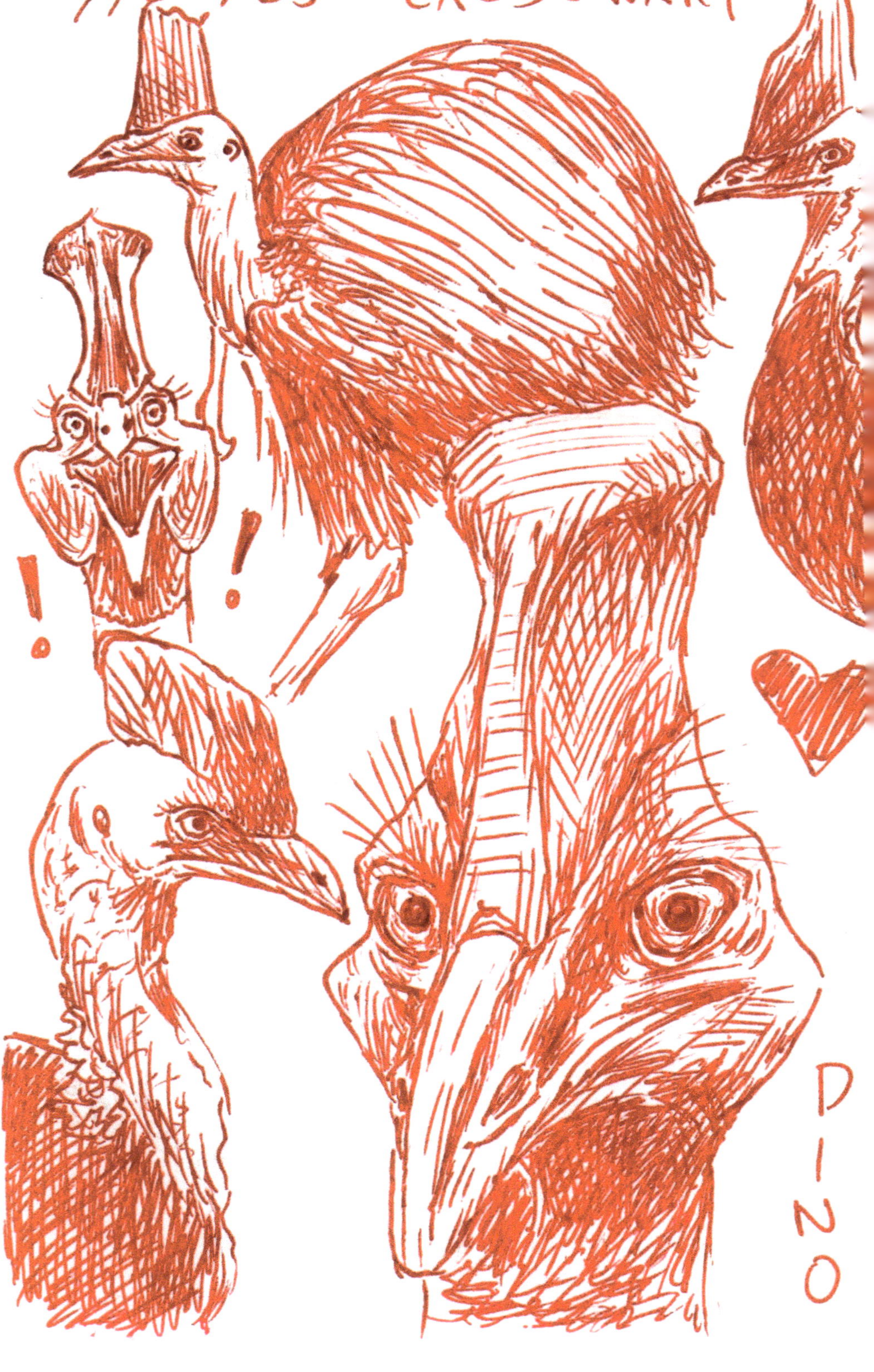

MANTA RAY 7/21/25

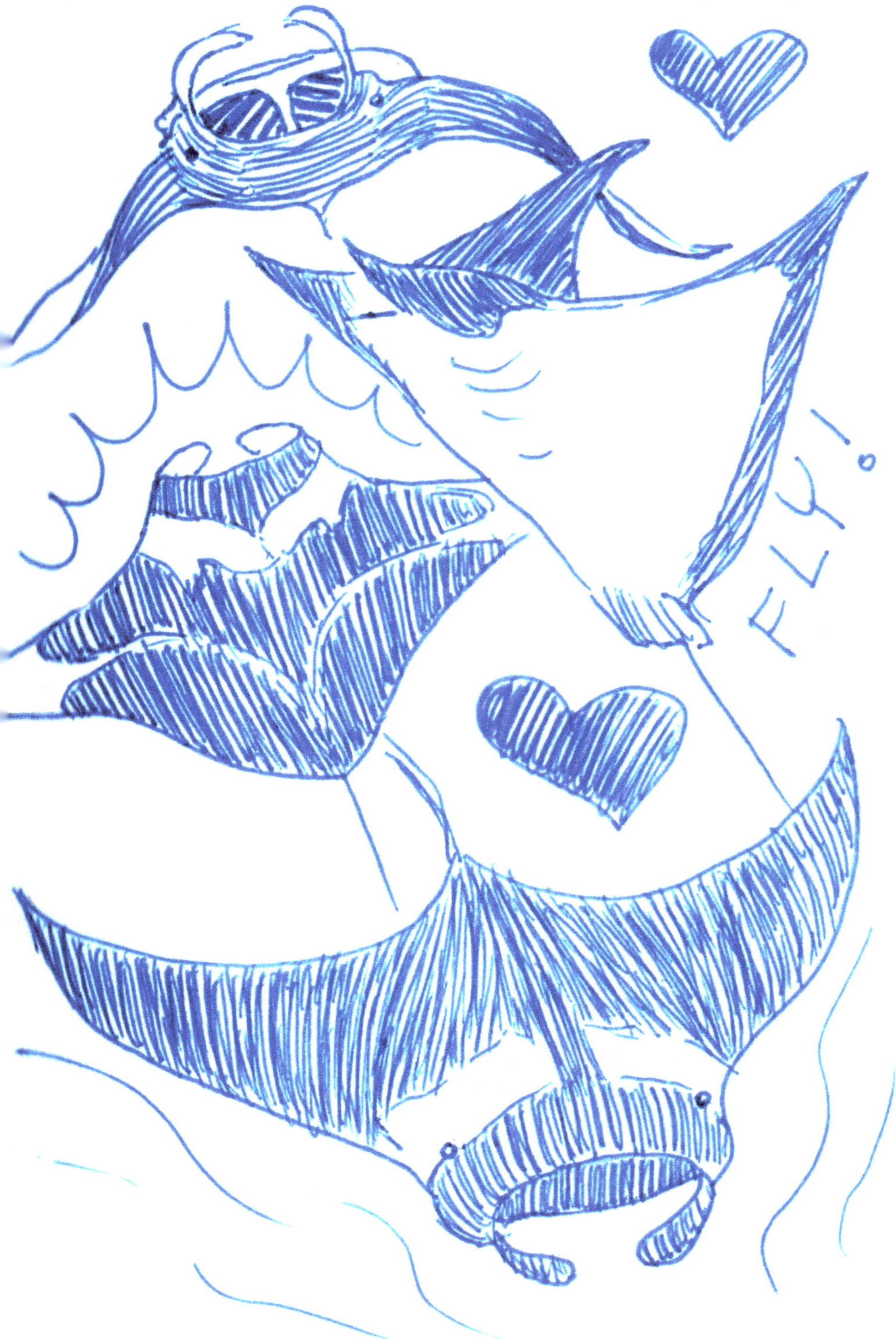

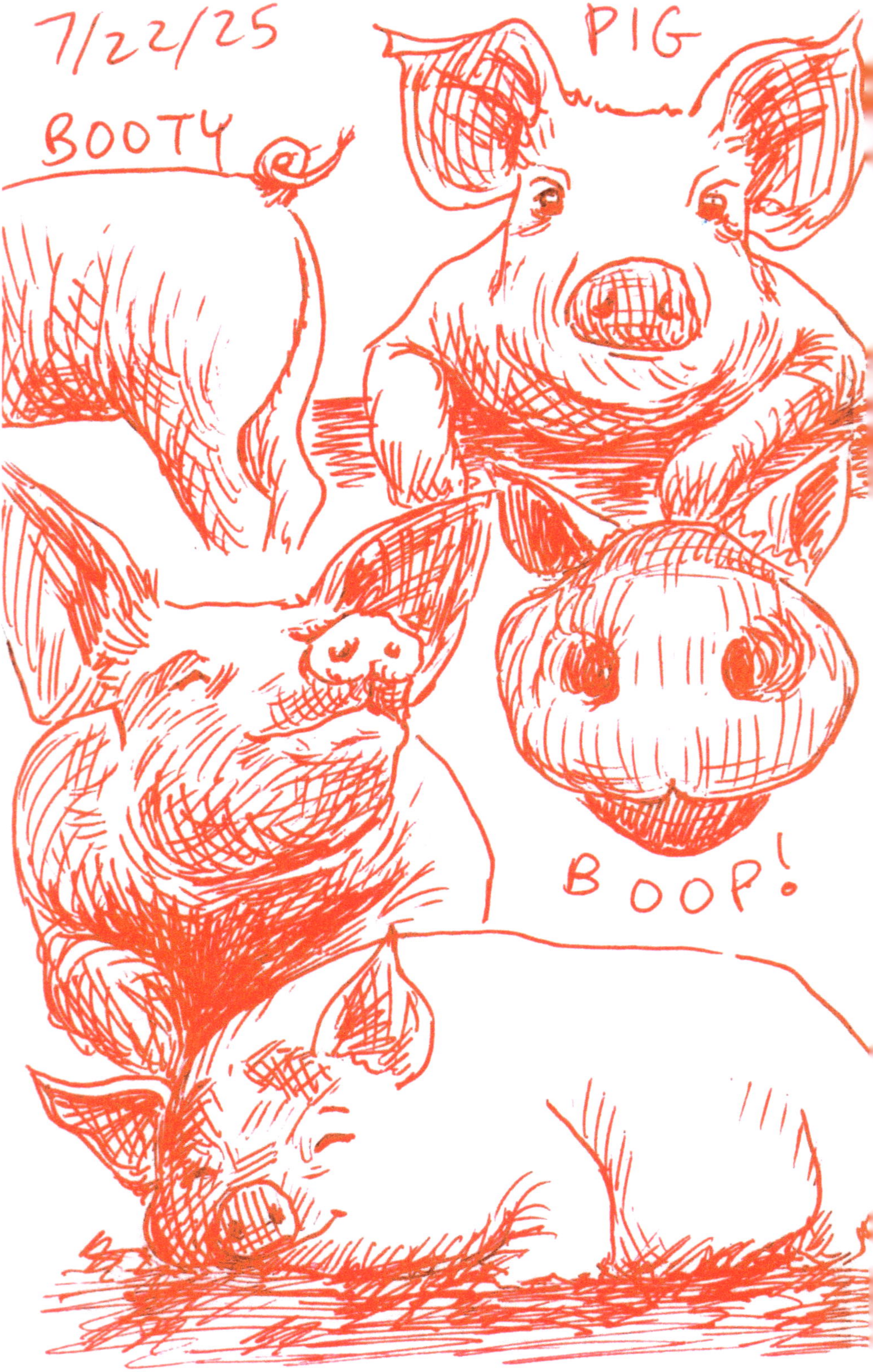
7/22/25
PIG
BOOTY
BOOP!

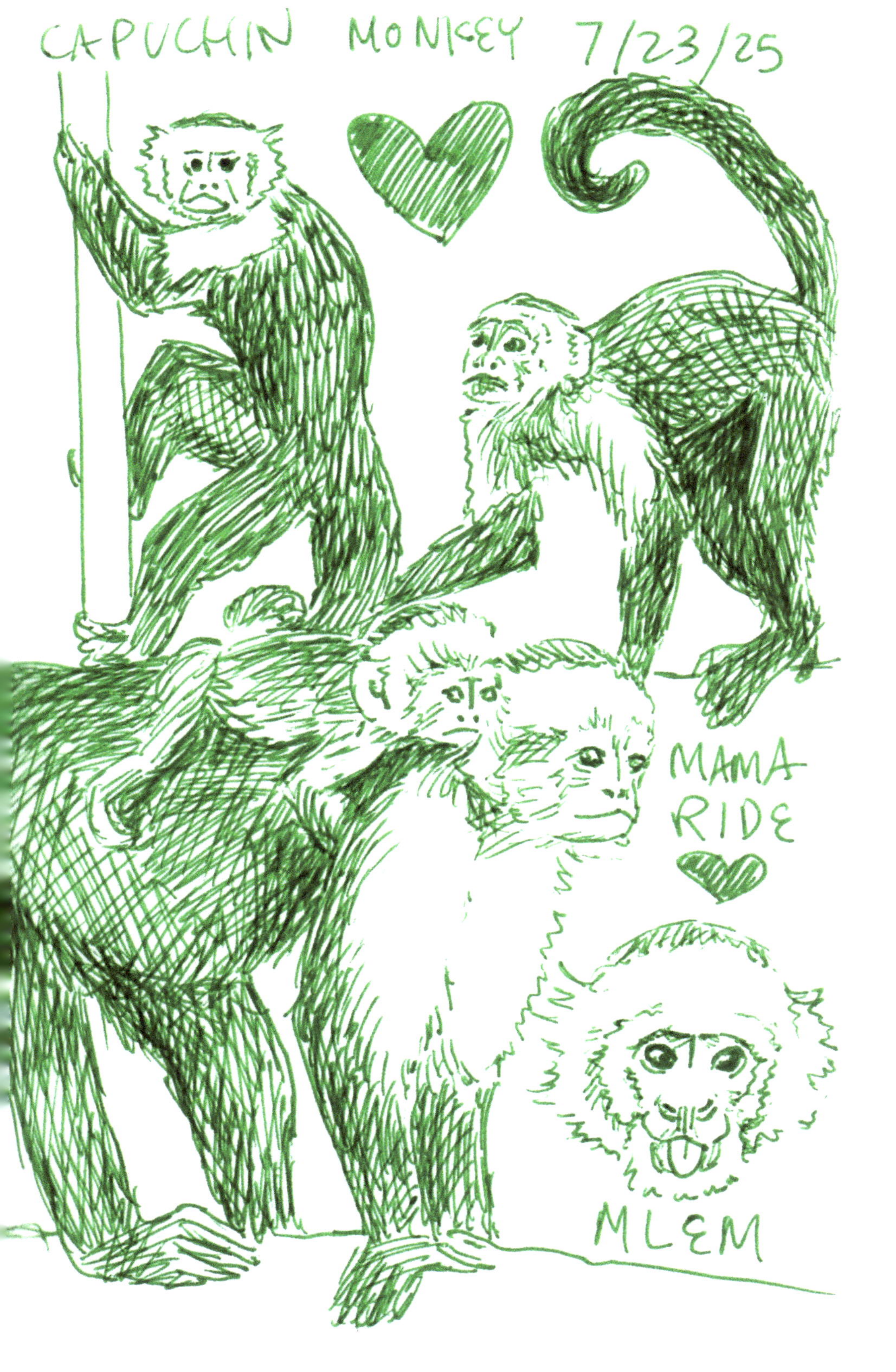
CAPUCHIN MONKEY 7/23/25
MAMA RIDE
MLEM

7/24/25 ADÉLIE PENGUIN

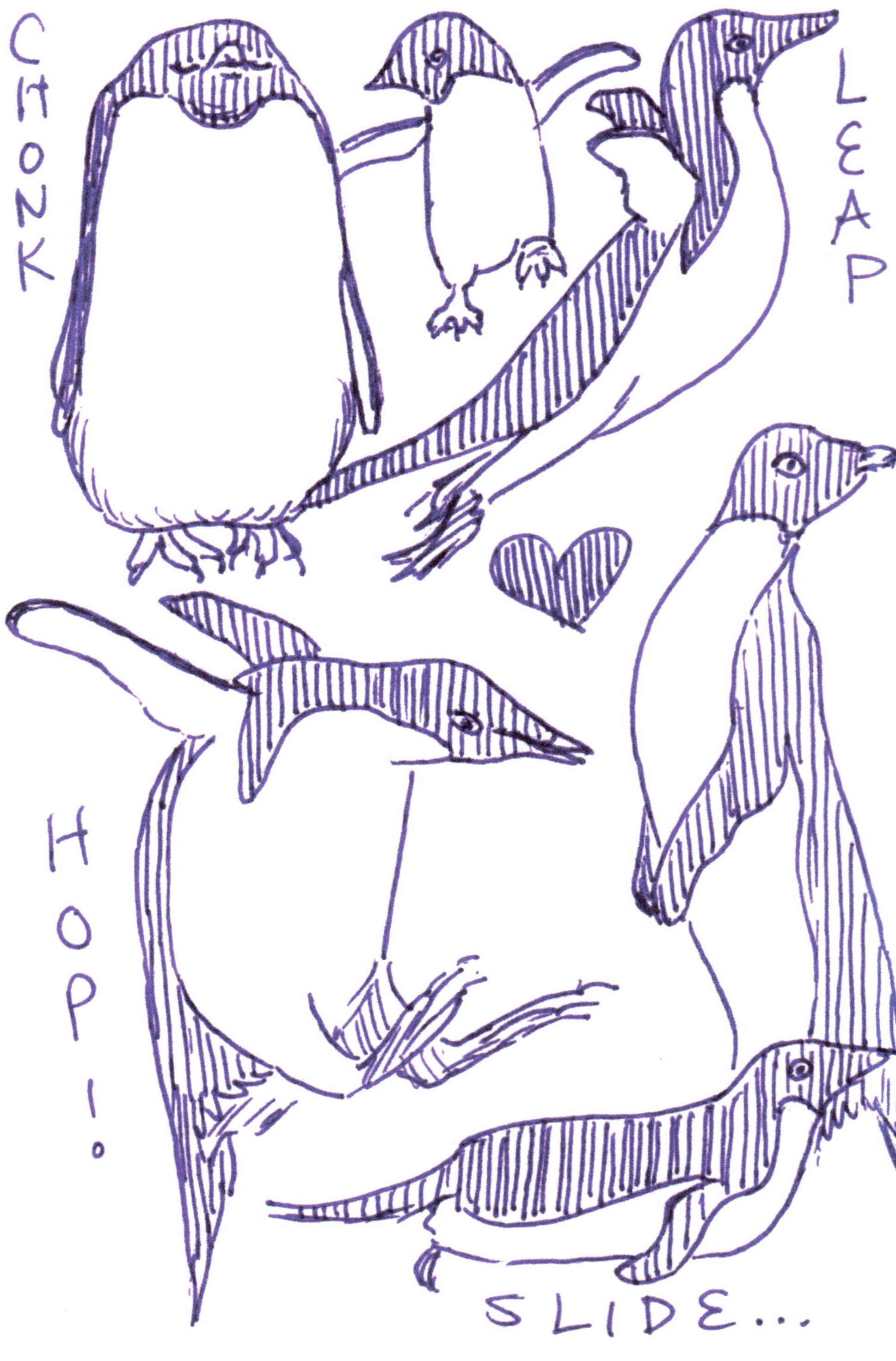

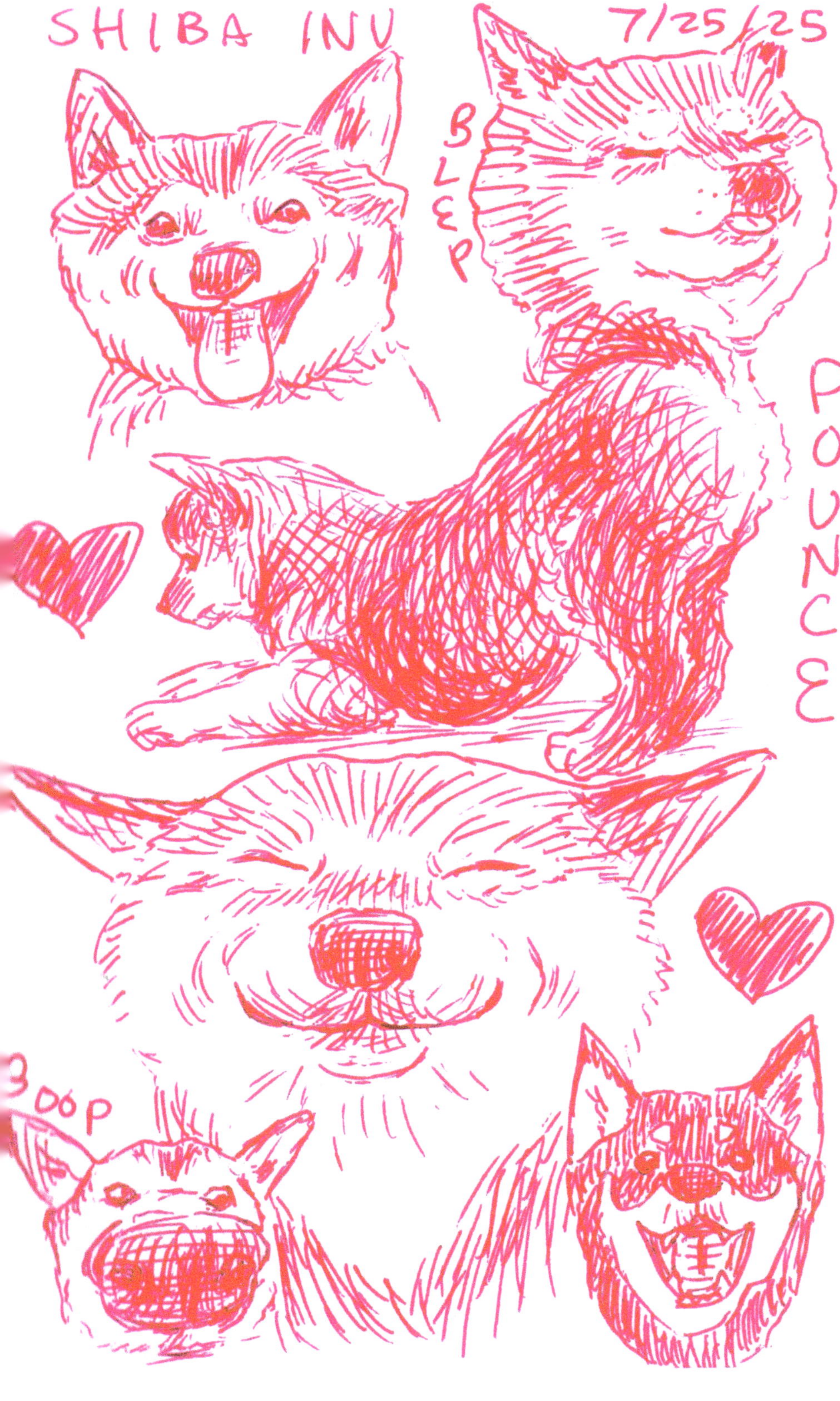
SHIBA INU
7/25/25
BLEP
POUNCE
BOOP

7/26/25 MUDSKKIPPERS

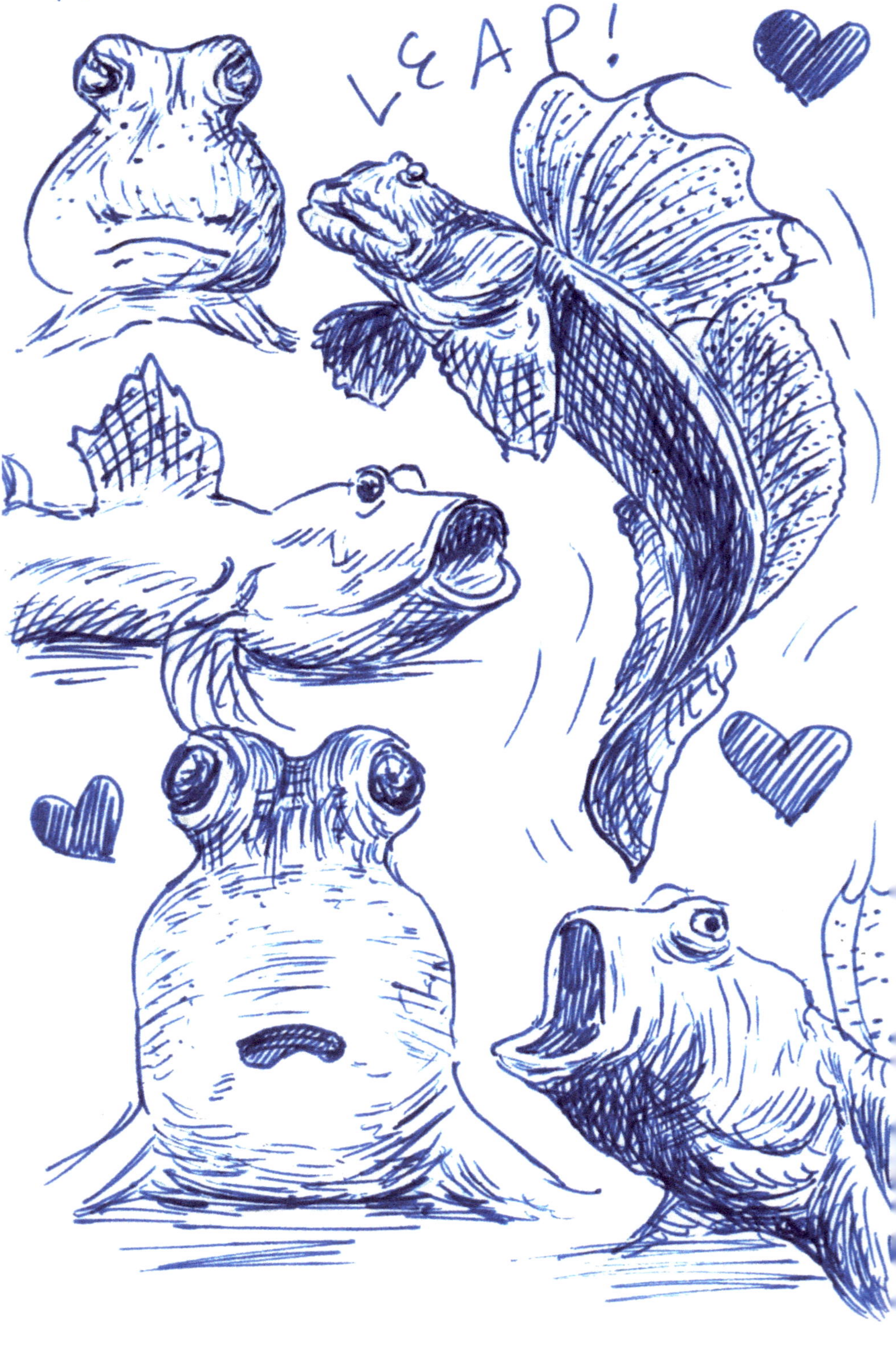

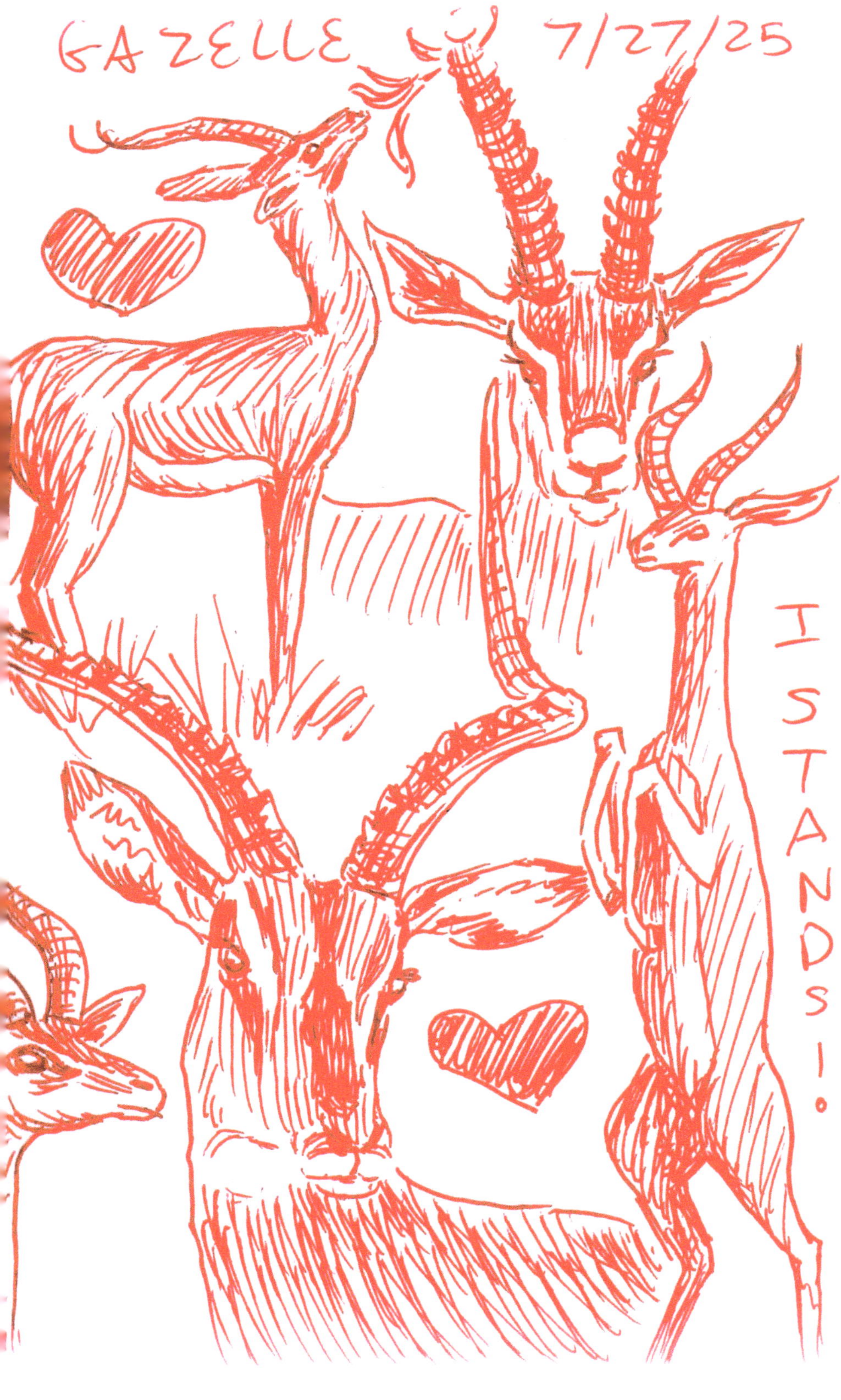
GAZELLE
7/27/25
I STANDS!

7/28/25 MANATEE

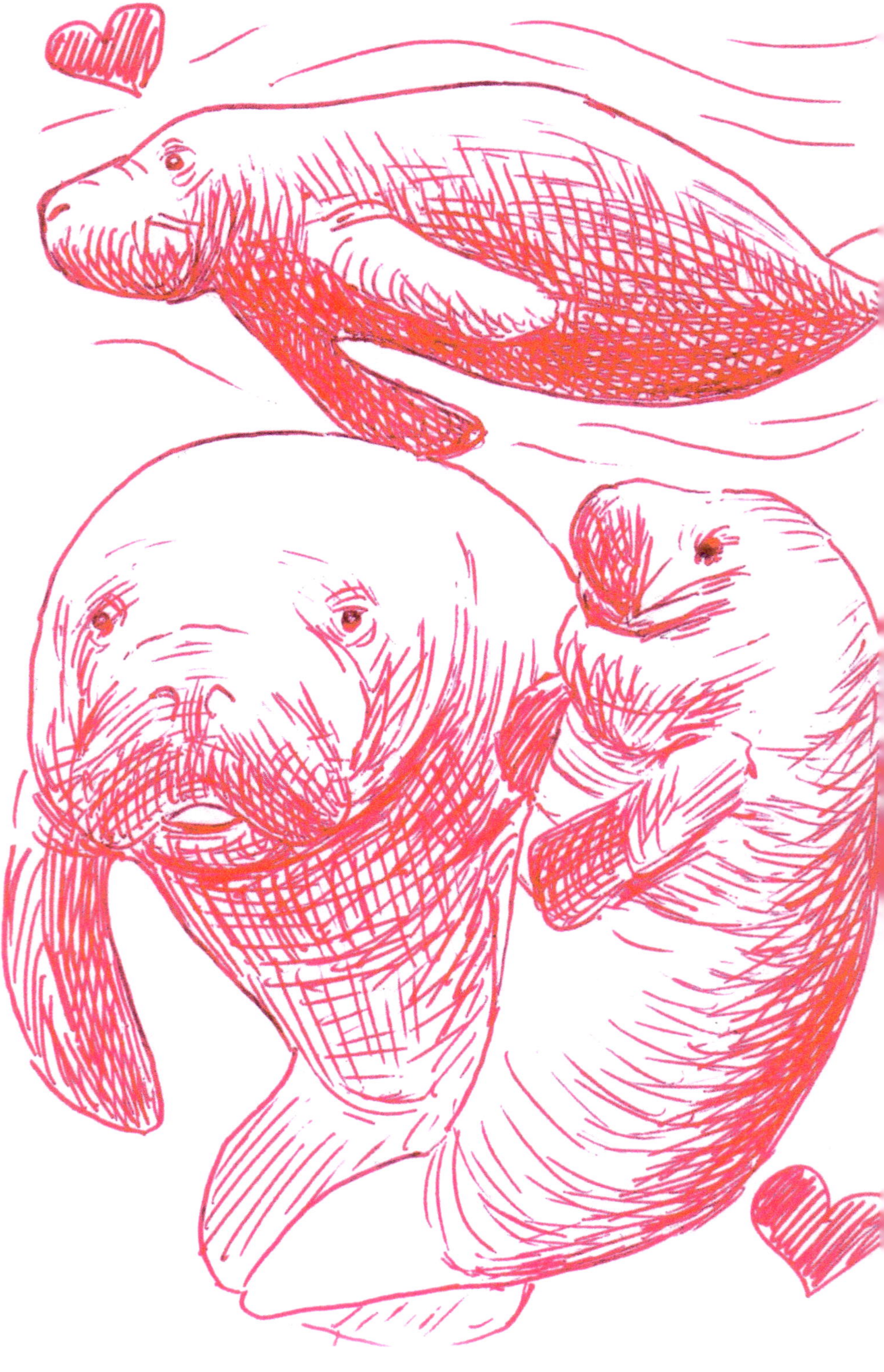

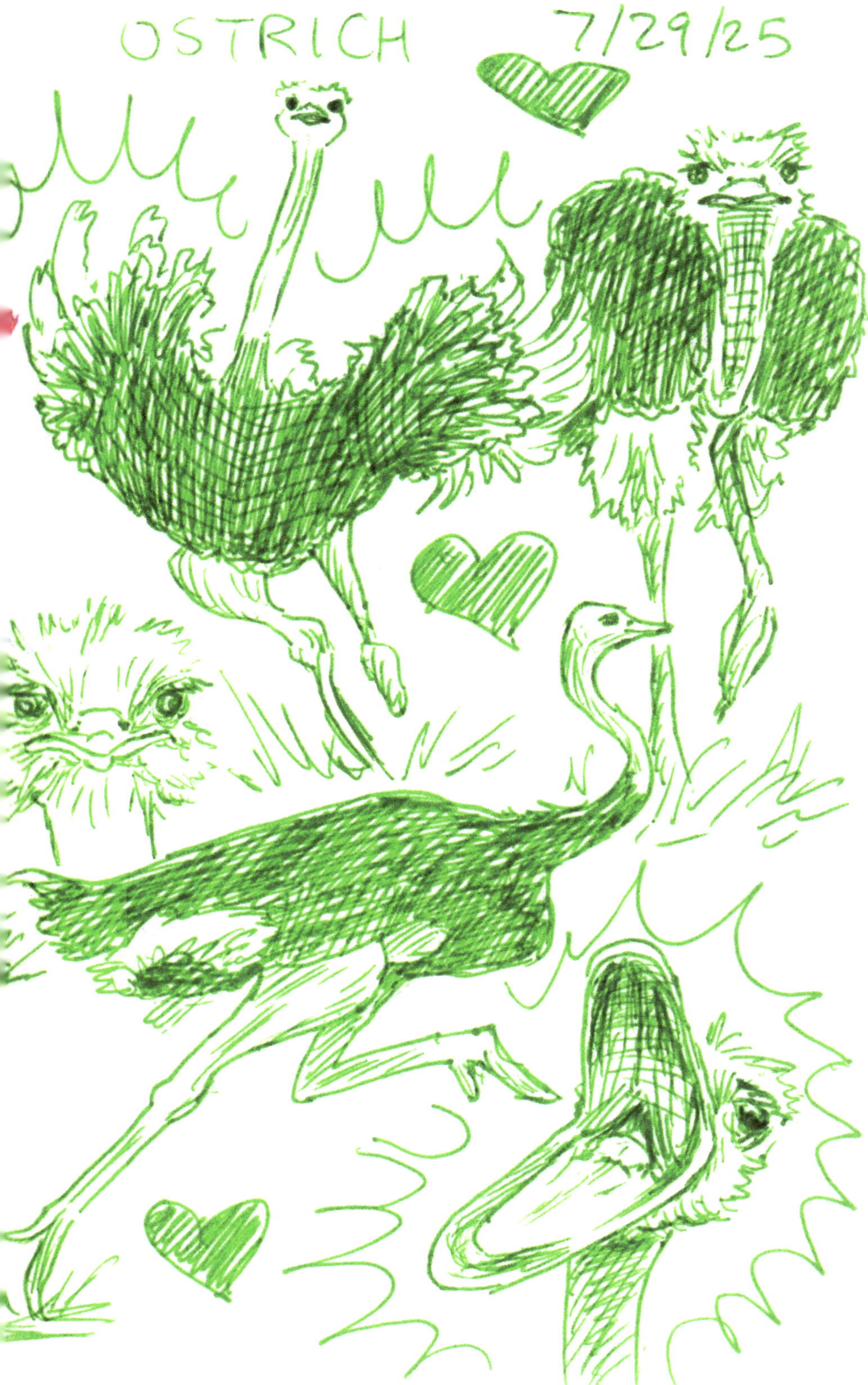
OSTRICH
7/29/25

7/30/25 AARDVARK

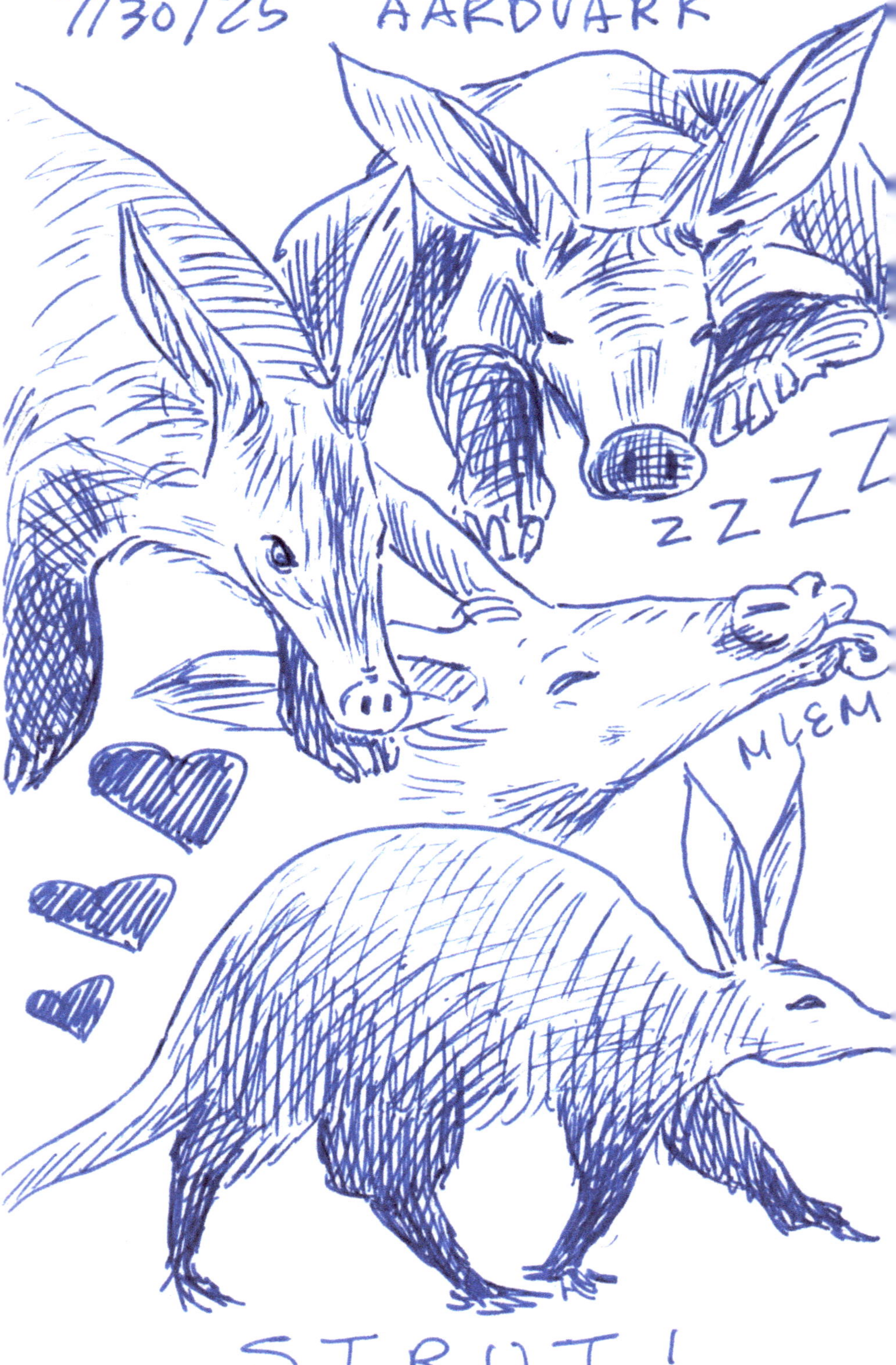

STRUT!

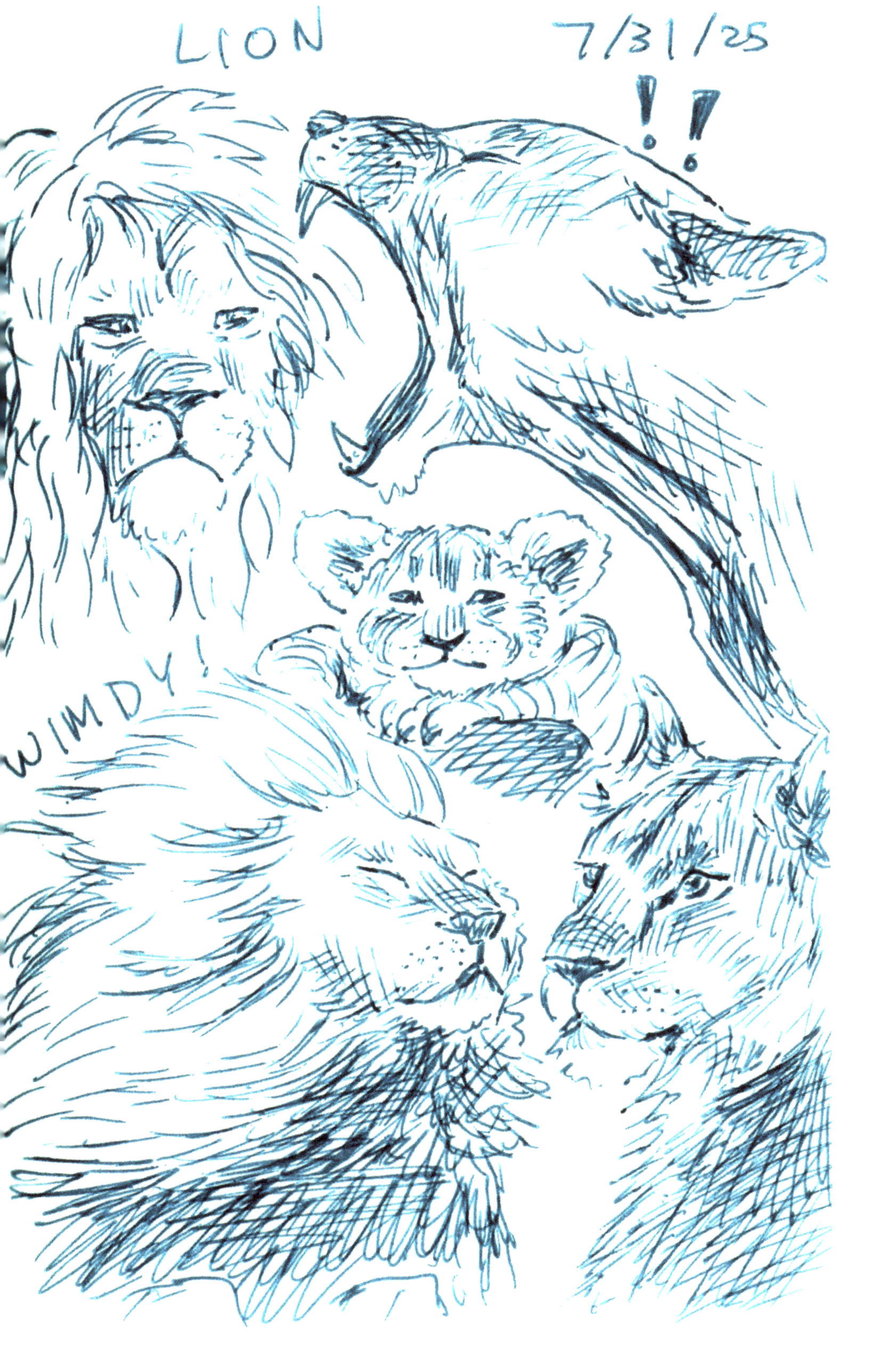
LION
7/31/25
!!
WIMDY!

8/1/25 CAPYBARA

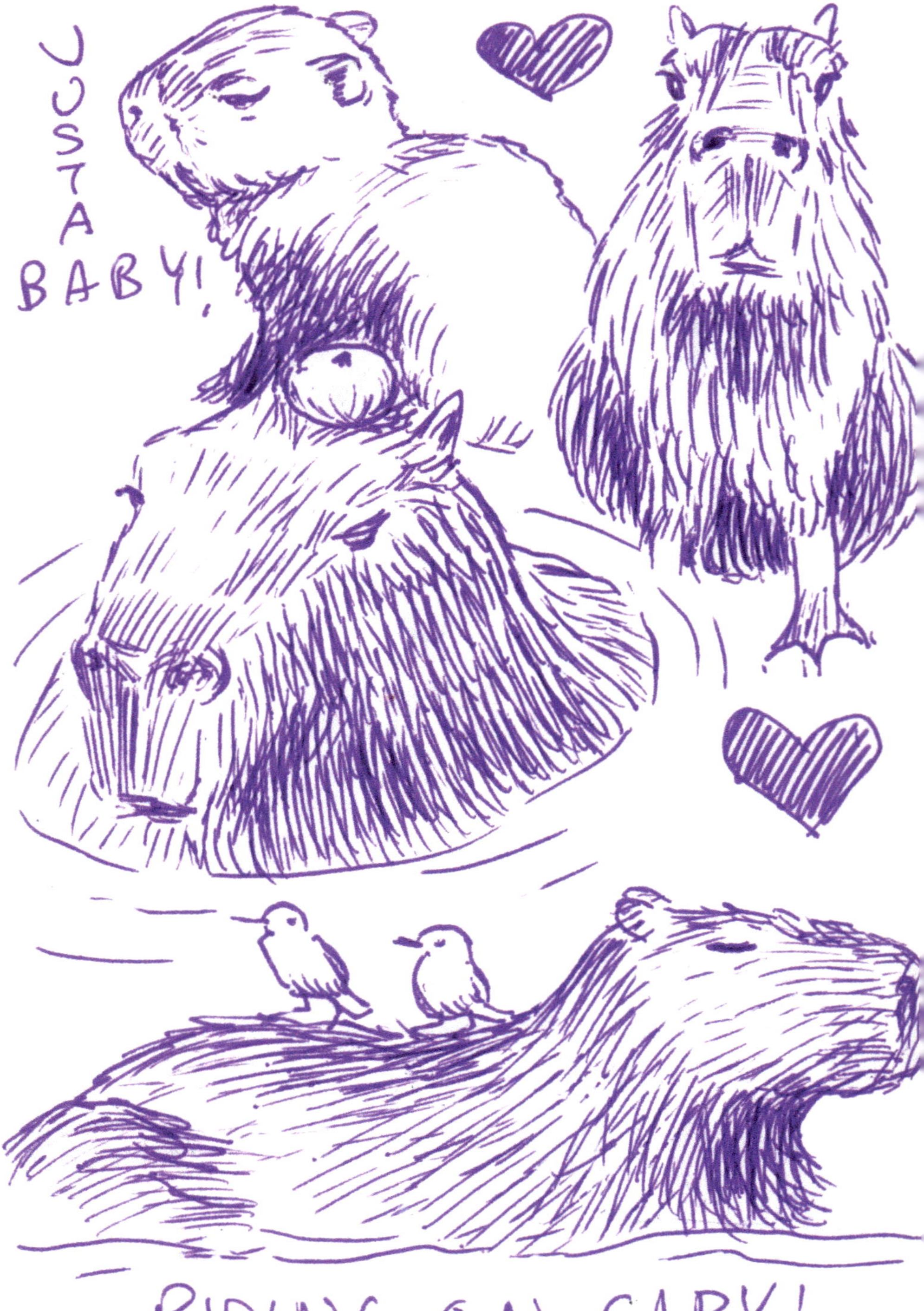

RIDING ON CAPY!

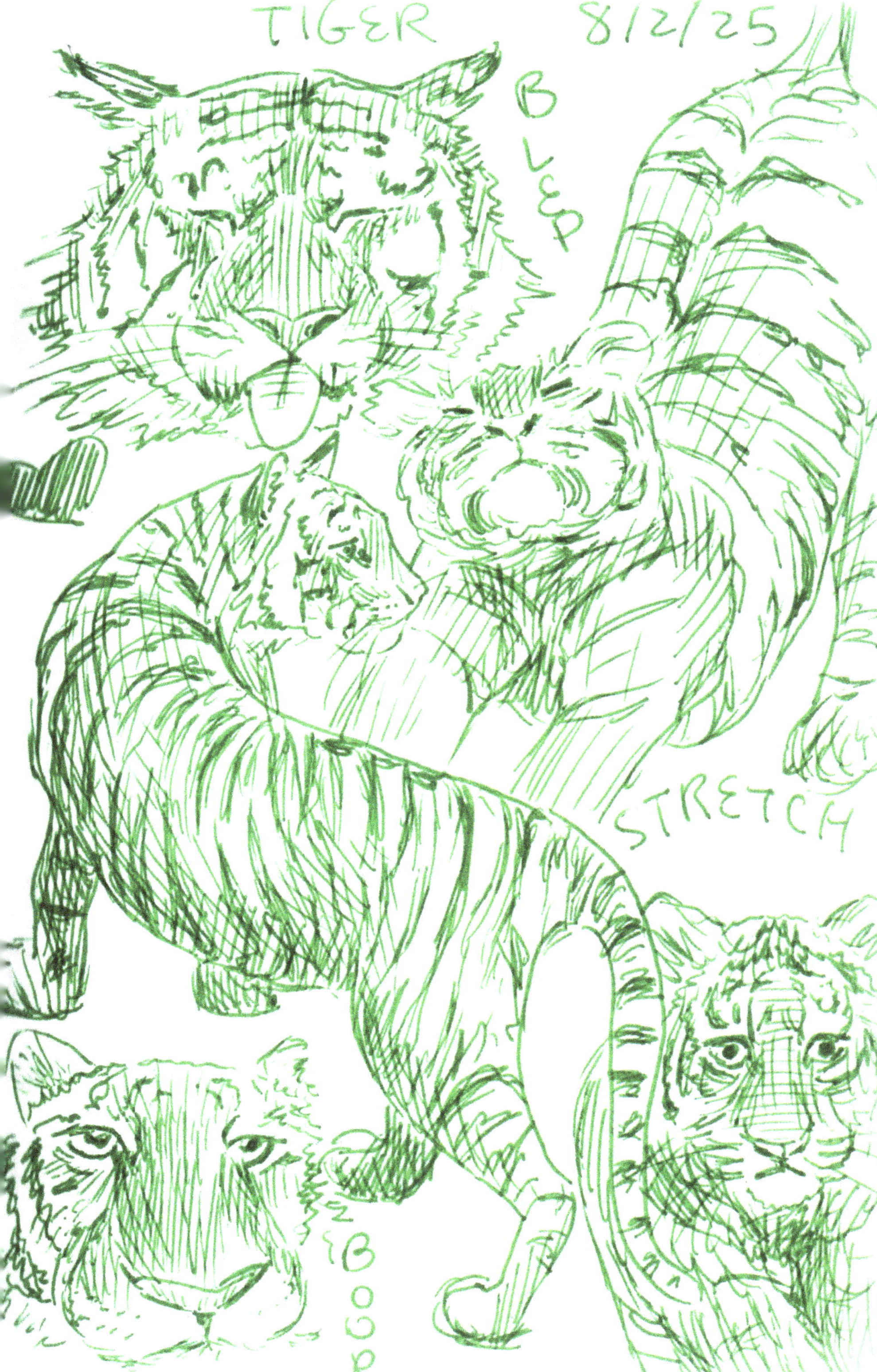
TIGER
8/12/25
BLEP
STRETCH
BOOP

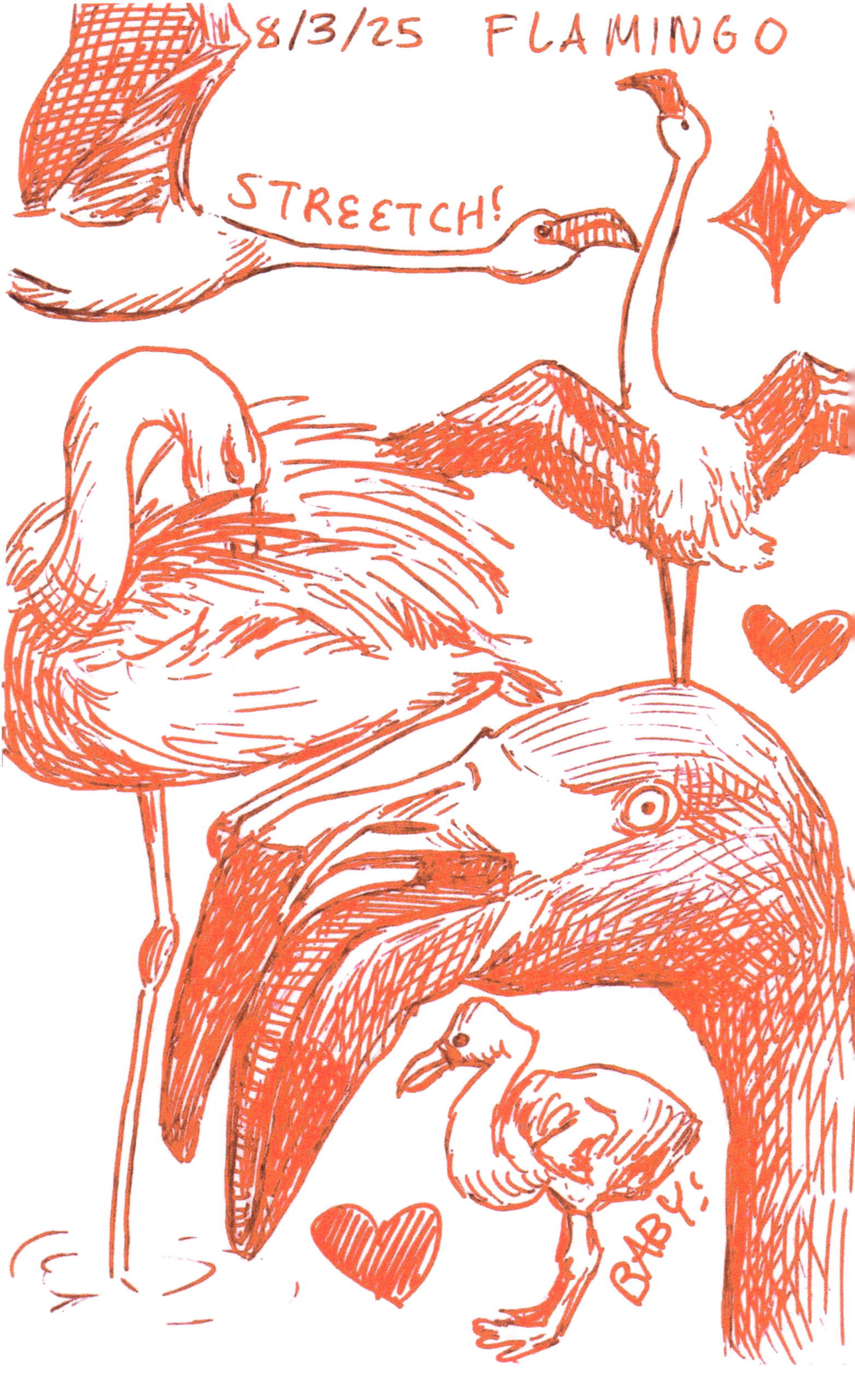
8/3/25 FLAMINGO
STREETCH!
BABY!

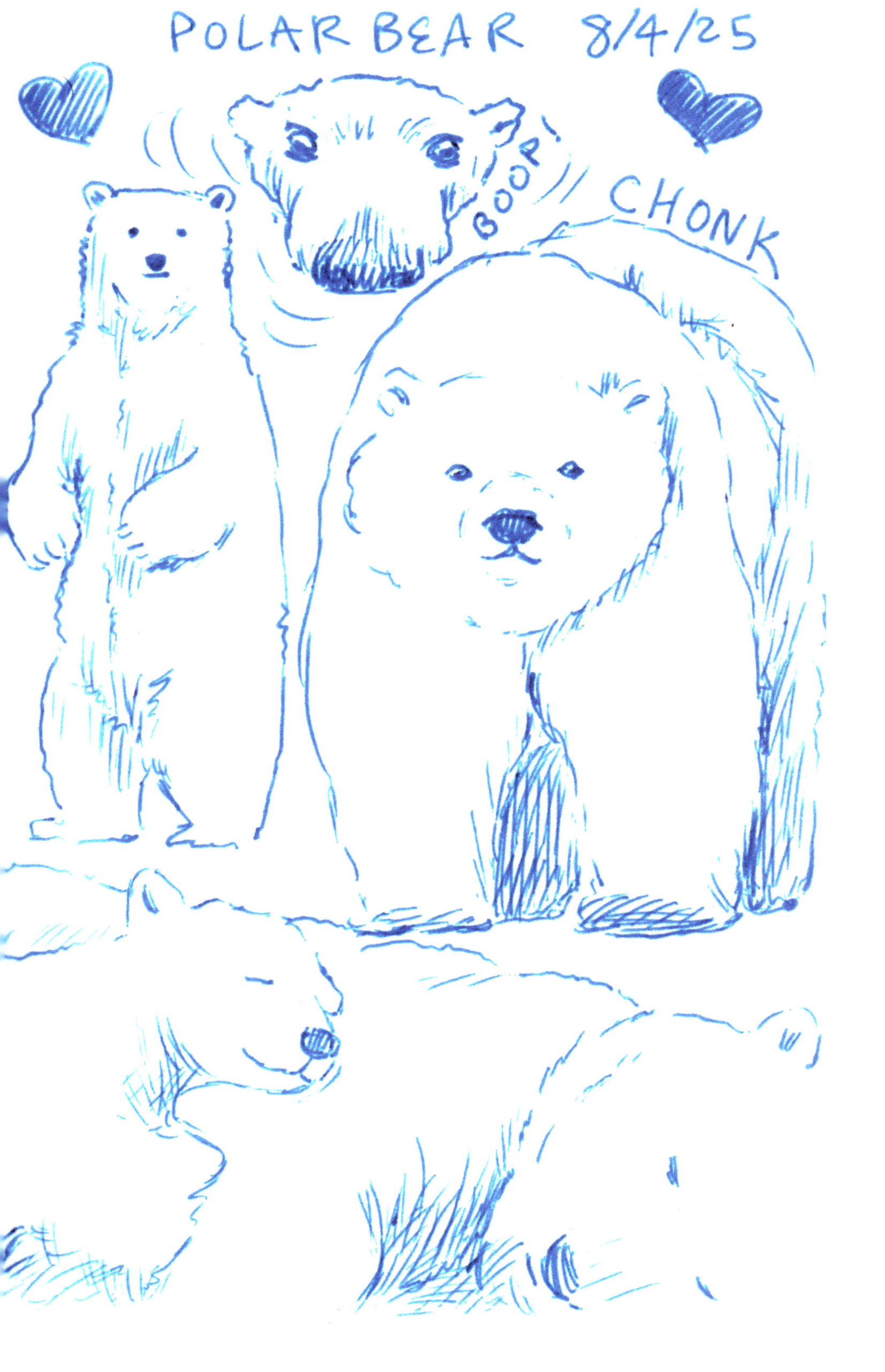
POLAR BEAR 8/4/25
BOOP!
CHONK

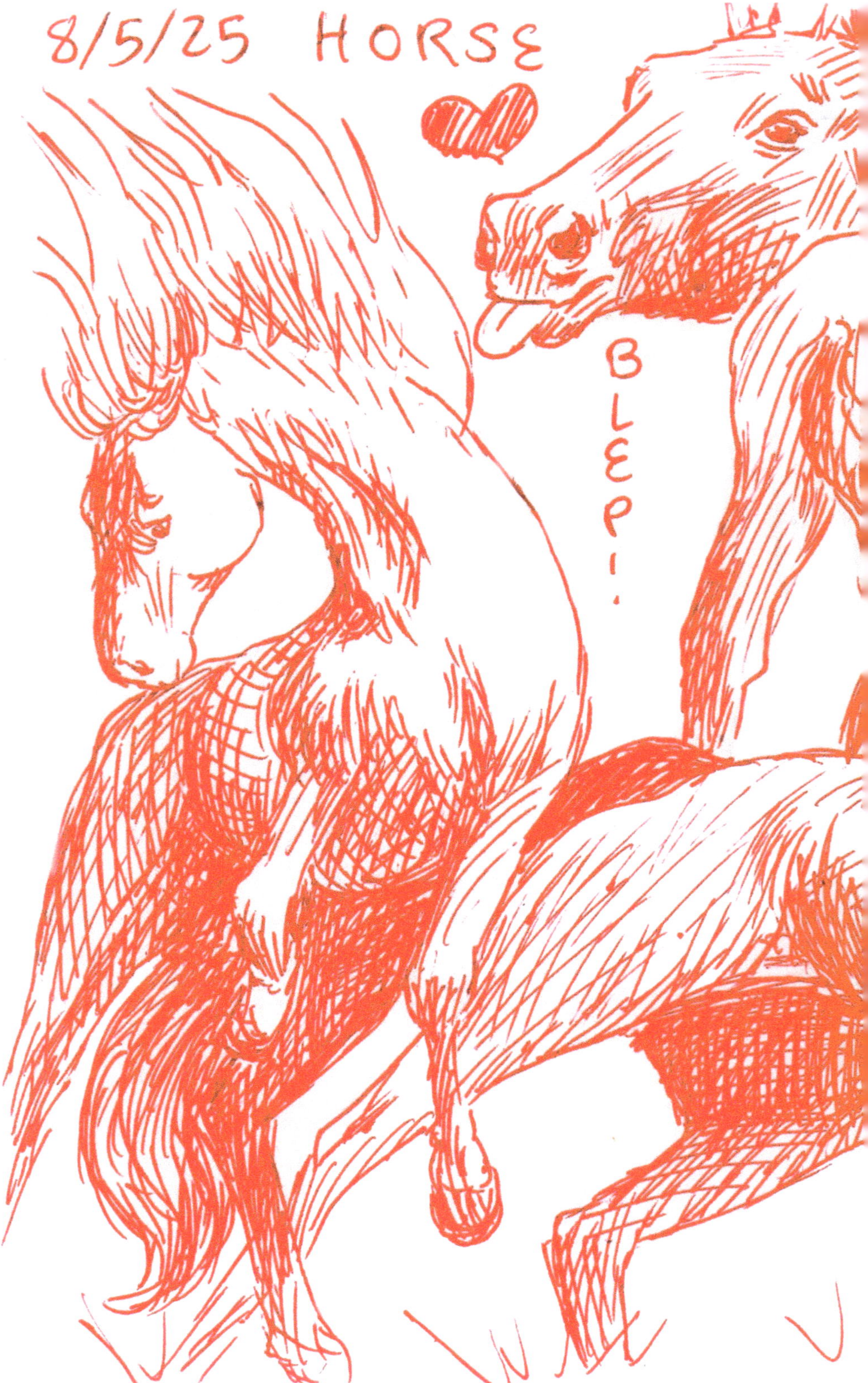
8/5/25 HORSE
BLEP!

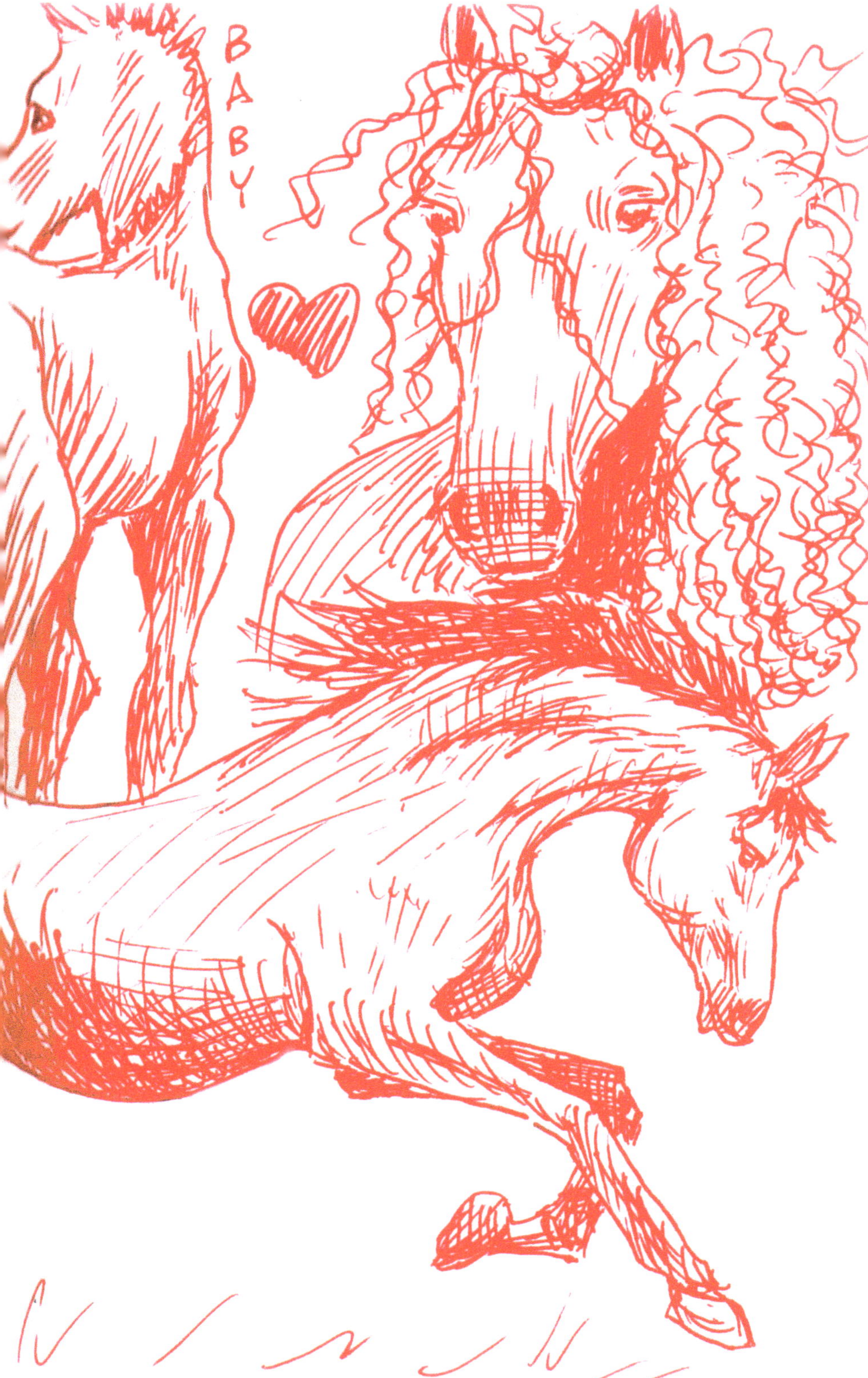
BABY

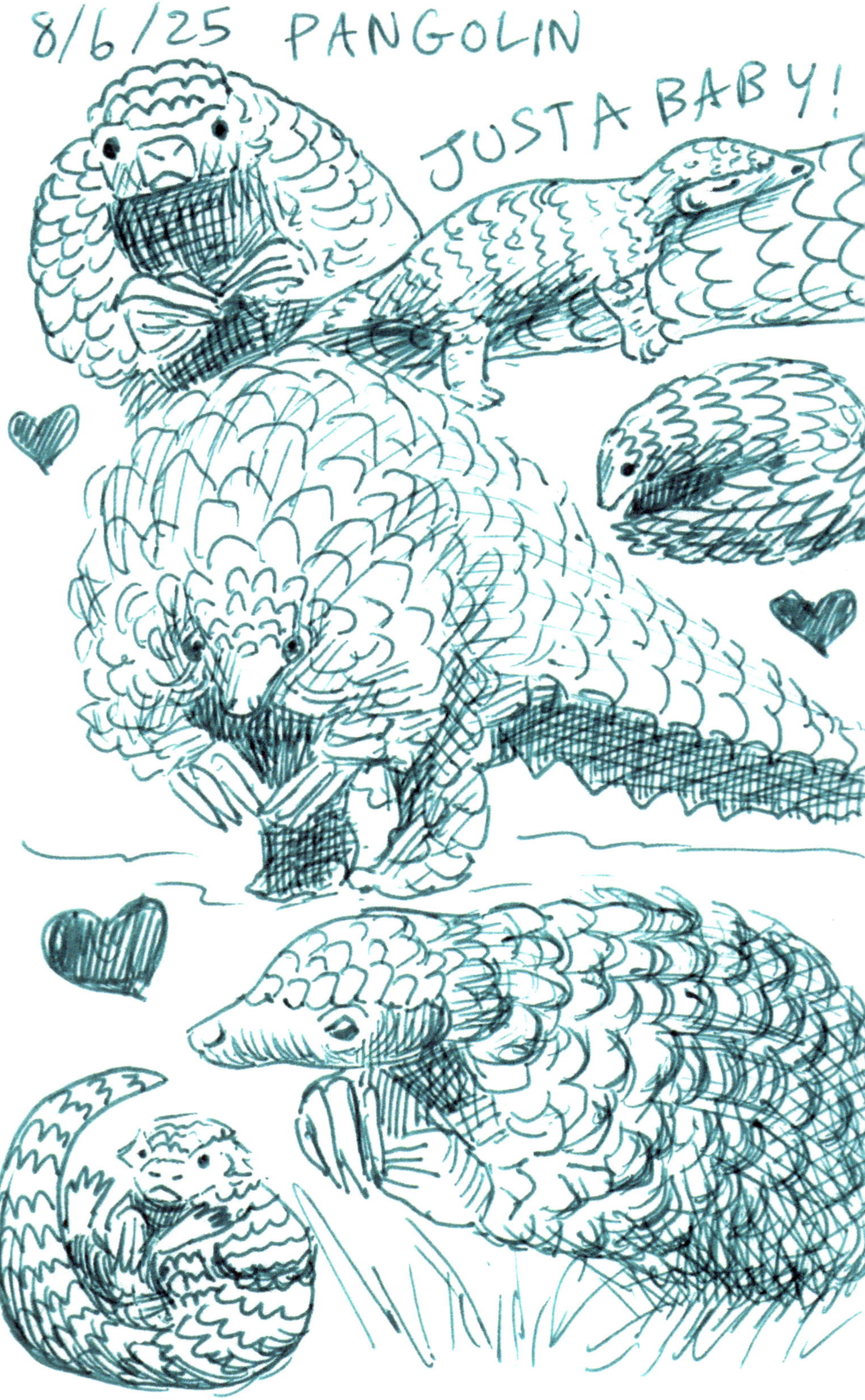
8/6/25 PANGOLIN
JUST A BABY!

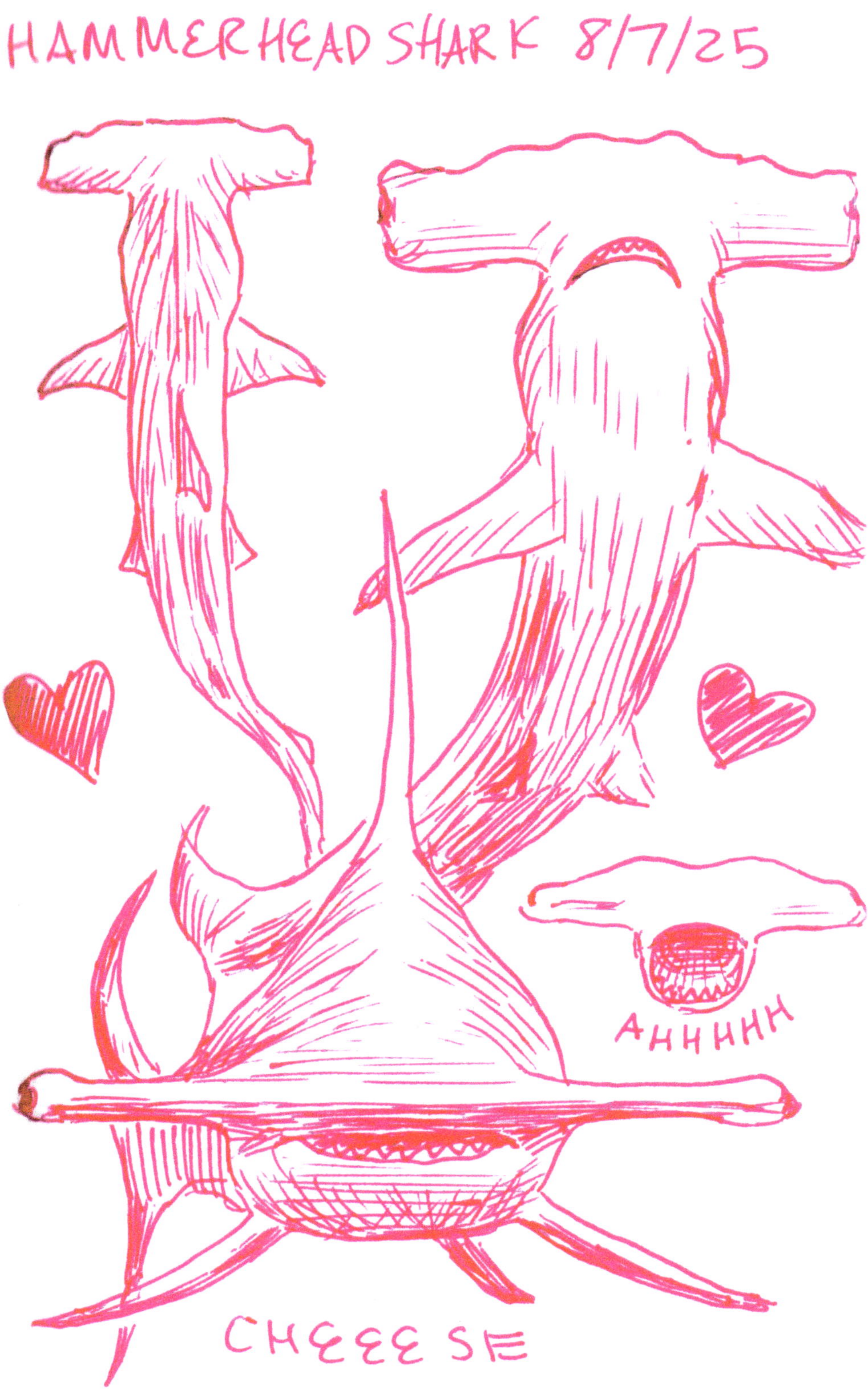
HAMMERHEAD SHARK 8/7/25
AHHHHH
CHEEESE

8/8/25 ORANGUTAN

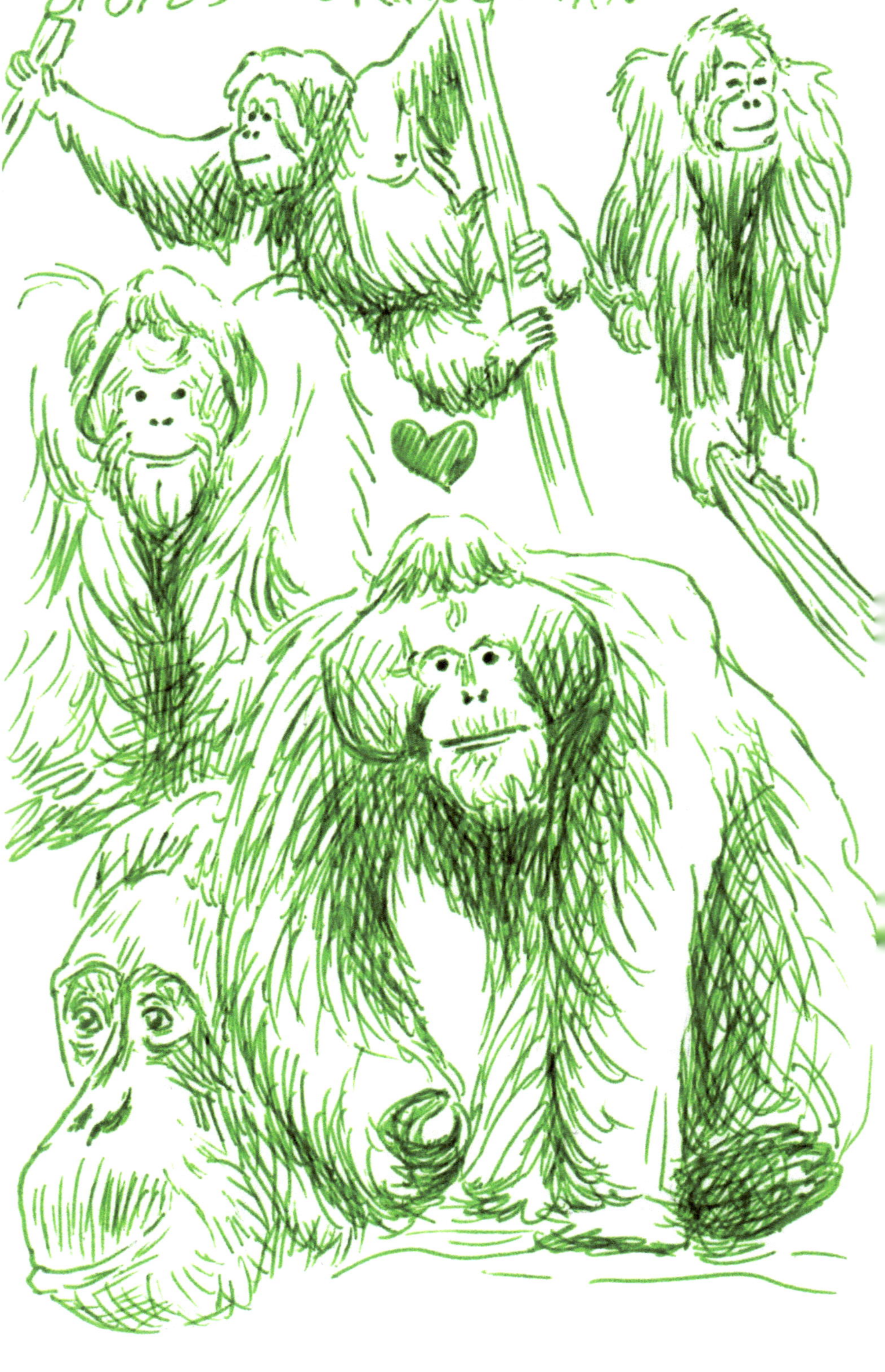

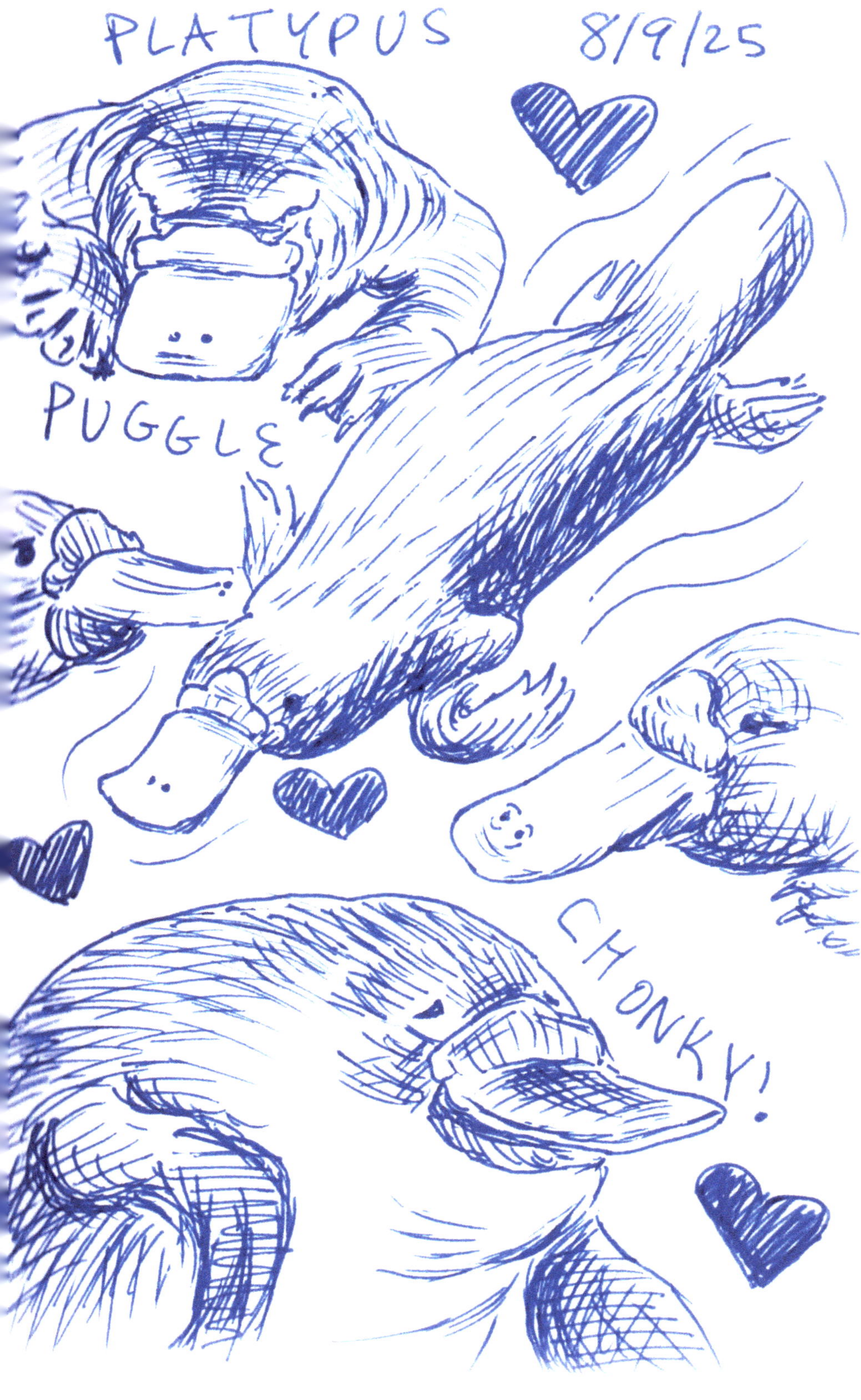
PLATYPUS
8/9/25
PUGGLE
CHONKY!

8/10/25 MOOSE

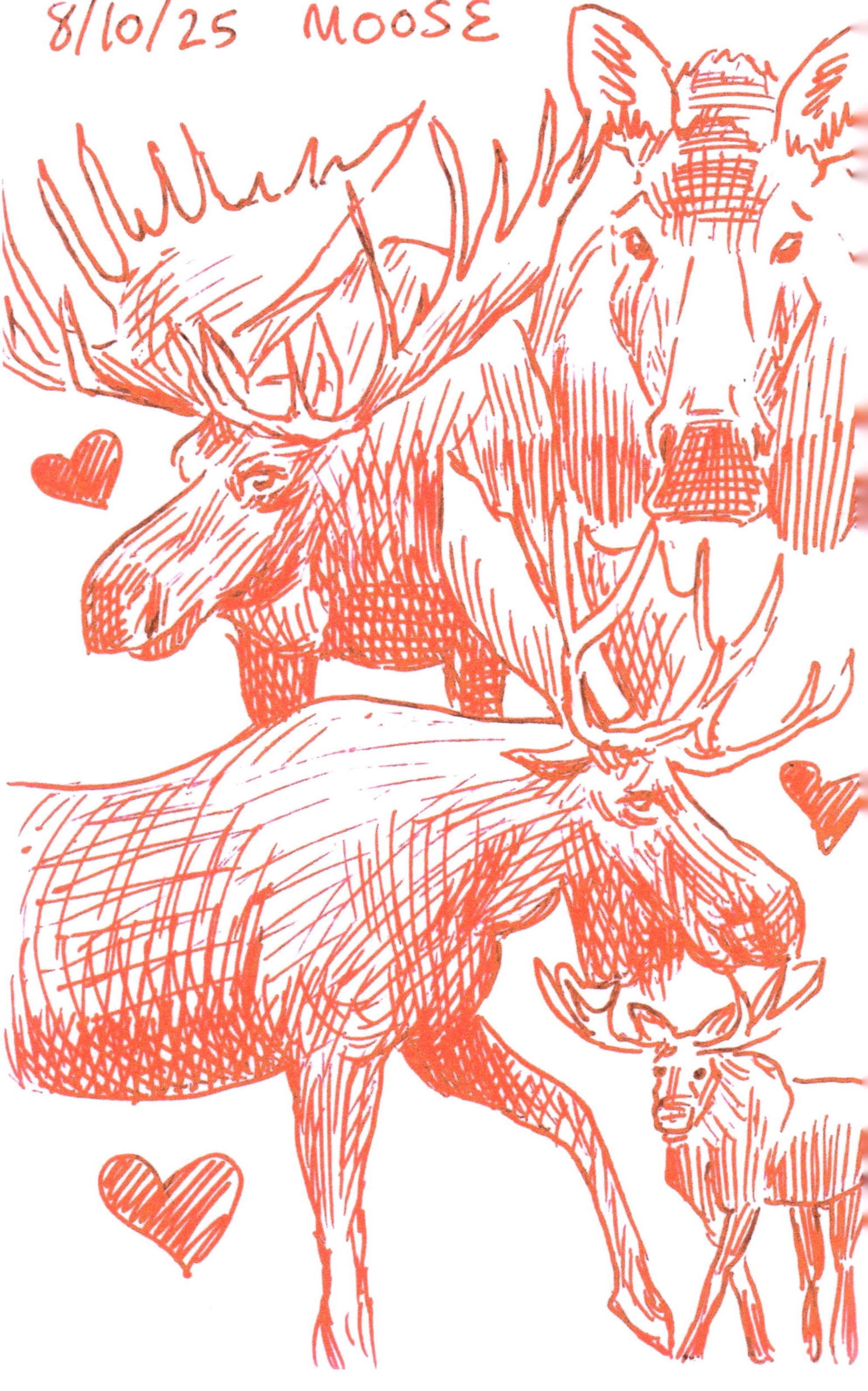

TORTOISE 8/11/25

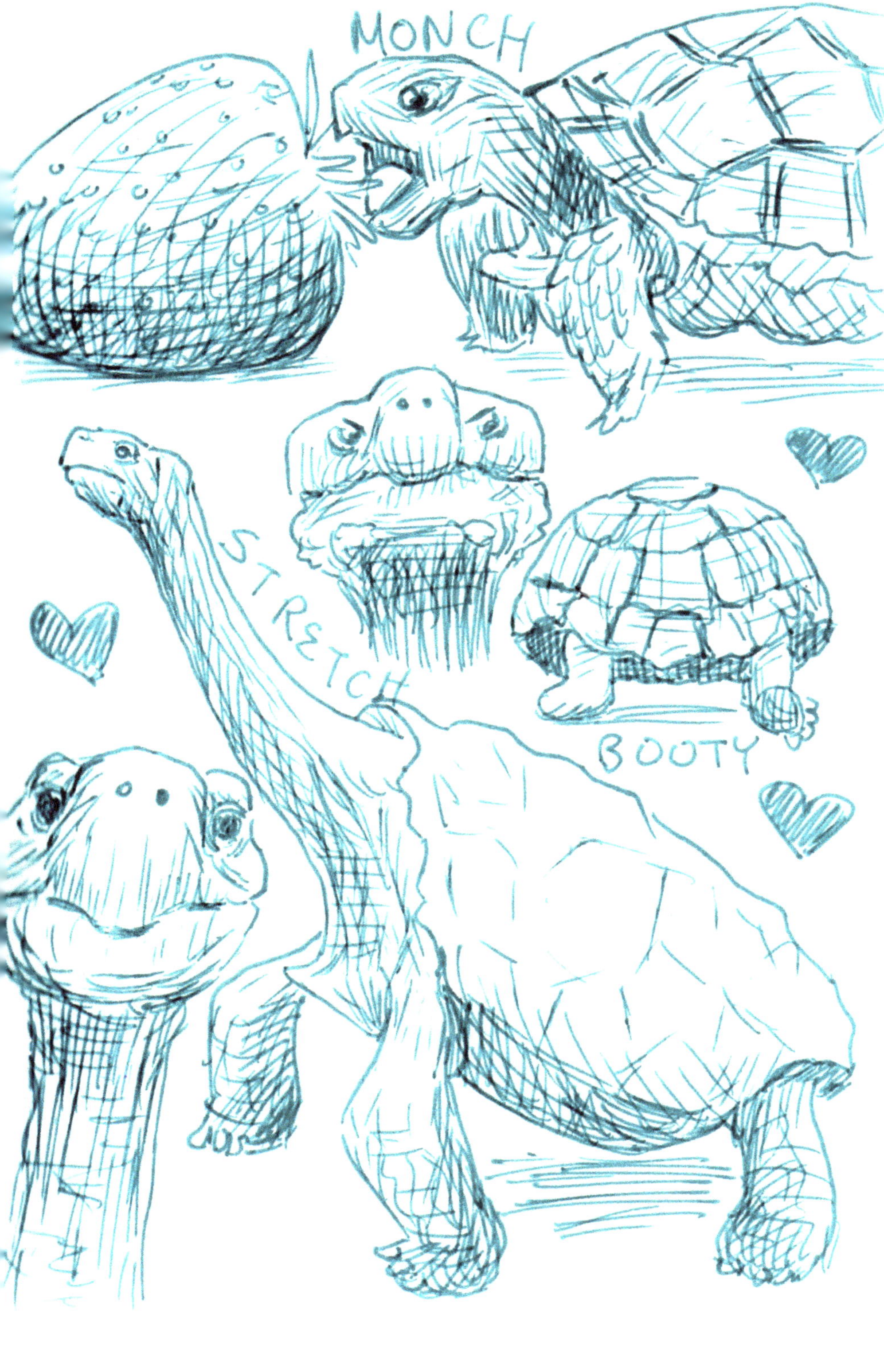

8/12/25 CORVIDS

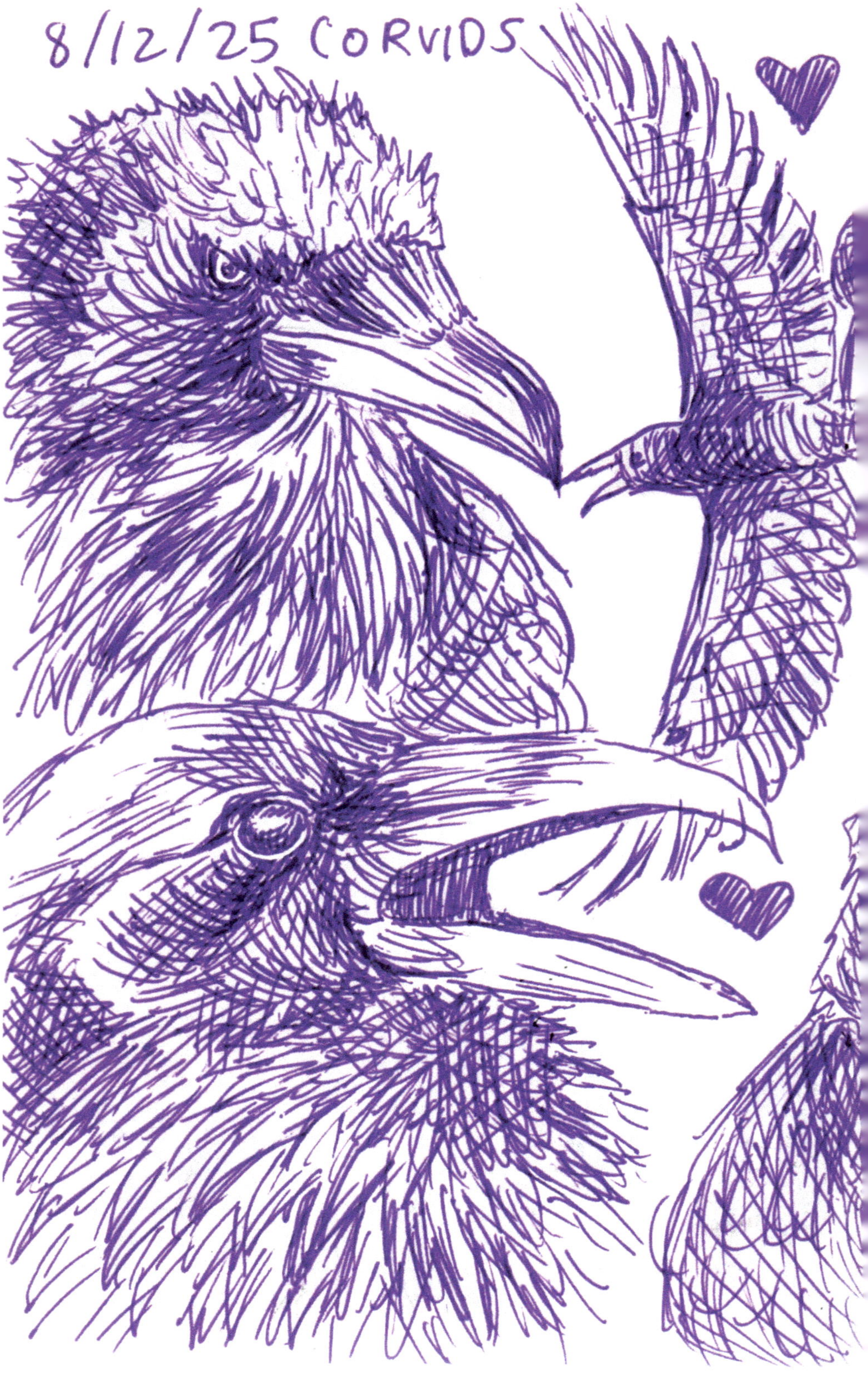

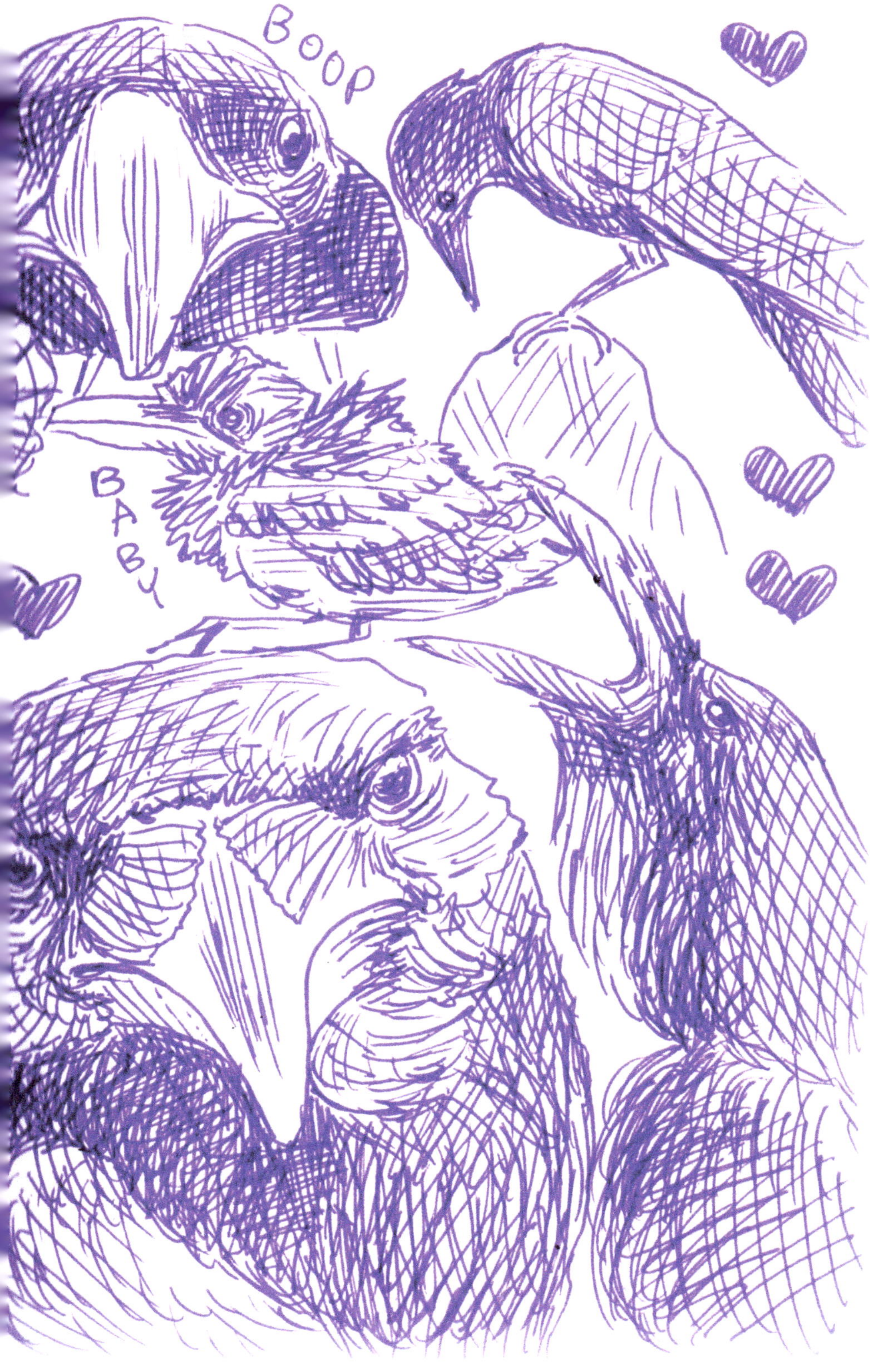

BOOP
BABY

ABOUT THE AUTHOR

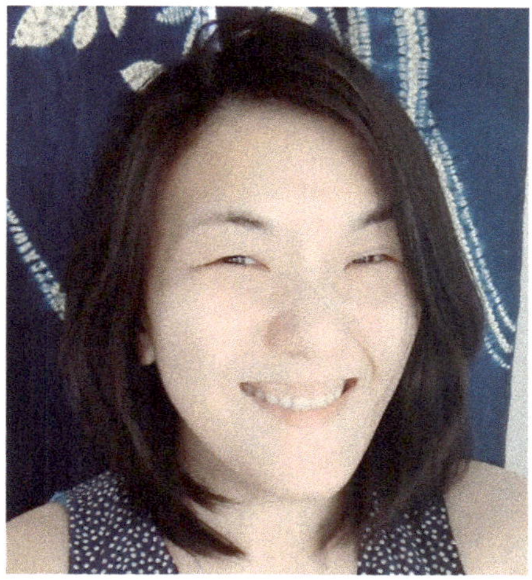

As soon as I could hold a pencil, I was drawing. Inspired by my artist mother, I grew up dreaming of becoming an artist just like her.

Life, as it often does, took me on a detour. I became a lawyer, got married, and raised two wonderful boys. My sketchbook gathered dust as my days filled up, but the creative spark never truly went out. During the peak of the pandemic in my late 30s, I decided it was time to reclaim that part of myself and pursue art seriously.

My career took a wonderful turn in 2021 when I discovered toner foiling, a medium where I apply metallic foil to my drawings for a dimensional effect. Since then, I've also branched out into ink drawing and digital painting. *Detox Doodles* is my first book and it chronicles the 100-day journey back to a regular creative practice.

Creating and publishing it is part of my deeper mission: to spark and spread happiness with my artwork. I hope my art makes you smile, even a little!

www.ingramcontent.com/pod-product-compliance
Lightning Source LLC
LaVergne TN
LVHW050918210926
848482LV00012B/482

* 9 7 9 8 9 9 3 1 2 5 3 0 5 *